The Sky Has Fallen

The Connection Between Abuse in the Home and Societal Dysfunction Throughout the World

Ann Meyer

Morrighan House Publishing
HIGHLAND, NEW YORK

First printing 2008

ISBN 978-0-9792732-2-3
LCCN 2007922425

"Because it is so unbelievable,
the truth often escapes being known."

—Heraclitus, circa 550 B.C.

I dedicate this book to the memory of my beloved parents, who spent the final years of their lives trying to help us through our difficult time, and to my wonderful children, my hope for a better future.

ACKNOWLEDGMENTS

I am grateful for the support of my friends and family, especially Nancy for her role as primary reader; Cheri for helping me come across the best articles; Betty for helping me maintain my D.M. humor; Herb for his helpful suggestions; Ellen for listening and remembering; the other Ellen for not judging; Beth for her enthusiasm, Vicky for her uncritical support; Kate, Sue, Cathy, Deb, Debi, and Del for their masterful assistance; and last but not least, my grandmothers for the use of their combined names for my pseudonym.

TABLE OF CONTENTS

Introduction 1

Part I: A Family Tragedy

Chapter 1: FIRST DISCOVERY 4

Chapter 2: CAT AND MOUSE 14

Chapter 3: GOING FOR HELP 24

Chapter 4: THE LIMITS OF THERAPY 33

Chapter 5: THE BIG CRASH 41

Chapter 6: LESSONS UNLEARNED 48

Part II: Altered States

Chapter 7: LEGAL VERSUS ILLEGAL 60

Chapter 8: A CULTURAL MYTHOLOGY 65

Chapter 9: DEPENDENCY AND ADDICTION 86

Chapter 10: POWER AND CONTROL 97

Chapter 11: HYPOCRISY UNLIMITED 112

Part III: In the Beginning

Chapter 12: CONNECTING THE DOTS 124

Chapter 13: WRITTEN IN STONE 135

Chapter 14: LITERACY RUN AMOK 149

Part IV: Out of the Darkness

Chapter 15: EAST MEETS WEST 170

Chapter 16: POLITICIZING RELIGION 173

Chatper 17: REBALANCING THE PLANET 182

Afterword 194

About the Author 195

Bibliography 195

Index 197

INTRODUCTION

As difficult as it has been for me to write this book—spelling out the details of my family's very personal tragedy—coming up with an introduction is almost more trying. It is tough to explain why I believe what's happened to us stemmed not just from our individual human shortcomings but from our family's unavoidable immersion in an overtly aggressive left-brain civilization, which at this time in history is threatening to destroy all of us everywhere, one way or another. I hope potential readers of my book will at least attempt to put aside notions and assumptions from their past and try to have an open mind concerning the ideas herein. I have attempted to put these ideas together in an arrangement that is different from currently popular explanations for what ails. I have stitched together years of research, concentrating on issues I have come to find particularly relevant to important problems of our age.

Although some people will focus on the marijuana issues I raise and try to use my book as an example of what "drugs" can do to people, it has been my earnest attempt to convince the relatively sane that things are terribly out of whack—and it is not just where this much maligned roadside plant is concerned. New generations of young people do not seem to be giving up the use of this mildly euphoric herb as easily as did their "hippie" parents; many seem convinced it is safer than alcohol. This means that a large portion of our youth—and beyond—must consider themselves criminals even if smoking marijuana is the only illegal thing that they do. It is my belief that legalizing marijuana and treating it like alcohol—with various restrictions (such as age and circumstance) and complete with penalties, fines, and treatment centers when necessary—is much wiser than current policies that serve to alienate and criminalize. More people are incarcerated in the United States today than during the height of the Soviet Gulag system. Too many of our citizens are spending years of their lives languishing in prison cells away from their loved ones, often for having committed nonviolent crimes.

This is much more than a book about marijuana. I have attempted to show a relationship between many of life's ills, as well as to join others in offering hope that change is possible in time to save the world from self-destruction. I am grateful for many of the ideas and much of the research in this book to others who are specialists in their field. Without these scholars and authors, I would never have been able to form my own conclusions (or borrow theirs!) about how and why we humans have found ourselves in such a desperate situation. I would not have been able to come to the understanding that there truly is hope for a better future, and that part of the present worldwide conflagration is simply a backlash against a more humane way of life struggling to regain its force and passion from a dark and distant antiquity.

Part I

A Family Tragedy

CHAPTER 1
First Discovery

Sometimes I wonder if who we are, really, is the sum of our secrets—and if perhaps I am not alone, rising out of bed each morning, reluctantly pushing myself into the mainstream in an effort to charm the world into believing I am really me. Recent events have prompted me to come out of the closet of my relatively inconsequential life and face the fallout from years of capitulation to a certain fear and passivity; the punishment for my lack of courage, action, and failure to prevent fate from delivering its shattering blows will no doubt be meted out in incremental agonies for the duration of my life. Like a good Greek drama, there has been much carnage and few heroes or heroines left standing. I am not sure yet for what reason, but I am going to attempt to put the pieces of my—our—story together. Perhaps when I see all the sentences strung together in order, linking life event to life event, I will be able to fathom just a little bit of what has happened to our small family.

We live in a climate of distrust, where most of us feel the need to continually draw a line separating our superior beliefs from the obviously brainwashed sentiments of whoever is in opposition to us at the moment. Even in times of mortal danger from outside threats, the average person persists in persecuting those nearby who he cannot understand because of relatively minor differences in behavior and/or attitudes. My fear is that if I begin this story by saying my (recently) ex-husband was found guilty of growing five marijuana plants and as a result has lost his zero-drug-tolerance employment of twenty-odd years, I will quickly generate applause from some and incite outrage and sympathy from others, depending on which side of the "marijuana" issue one stands. One must be prepared to give oneself over to the subtleties and complexities of this saga before deciding whether to throw roses, tomatoes, neither, or both at once, at any or all of the protagonists.

This is a true story about a family (mother, father, daughter. and son) and its two-generational relationship with the herb cannabis. Although the people in this family were unique and interesting in their own right before said relationship, they were probably not worthy of an entire tale of woe. As I am both the narrator of and mother in this story, I have decided to use a pseudonym rather than reveal my true identity, not only to prevent personal embarrassment but because I hope it will allow me to be more truthful and forthcoming concerning the many painful details that have transpired. I am also omitting the names of the other characters in my story to protect the innocent and not so innocent. I would love to be able to change my role in this drama to enhance all of my imaginary good qualities, but I'm afraid that however I tell the tale, from this angle or that, I will appear as I am and have been. I have no doubt that while many will fail to understand why I did not act sooner or more forcibly, others will believe I have acted too abruptly and/or harshly. In my ruminating mind, I still oscillate between the two possibilities, desperately wanting the chance to redo fate, but not knowing what choices I would make if I had it all to do over again.

It all started during the summer of our son's fourteenth year. Our little family of four had been living in a new house we had built ourselves. We were all trying to adjust to new lives in a new geographical area. It was summer, and I suggested to his father that he take our son to work with him as his helper on a job building a deck. I believed it would be a good opportunity for him to earn extra money and learn something valuable. One day after father and son returned home from work, I walked down to the garage to greet them and came upon them smoking a joint together. Although this simple act might have horrified some and not others, there was good reason for the possible excess of emotion that occurred at the moment of my discovery.

My son has been an asthmatic from birth, and I had spent many a long night when he was younger carrying him upright so he could breathe during an attack. There had been a number of desperate times when I rushed him to the emergency room in the middle of the night so he could get an adrenaline shot in order to breathe. I used to watch his chest heave in and out with a force so great I thought he was going to burst, and I always worried about being too far from a hospital in case he stopped breathing completely. I remember one particularly awful night when I had to drive my son to a hospital ten miles away in a blizzard; halfway there I honestly didn't know whether I was taking a bigger risk with his life going forward or turning back. My son's entire childhood was colored by this very serious illness, and to make things even scarier, his pediatrician, who was also an asthmatic, died from an asthma attack right in her office while seeing a patient! It was whispered to me later by another doctor in the practice she had been too dependent on her inhalers. I passed the warning on to my son, who was already using a nebulizer (a machine that sprays medicine as mist to breathe) for his asthma attacks.

Over the years, I had put considerable effort into making sure my son was in a smoke-free environment, which was difficult because my husband is a fairly heavy cigarette smoker and he found all sorts of ways to cheat. Smokers always think you can't tell. When my son was two, we took him to an asthma specialist in the big city. My daughter, who was four, was in the room when the doctor told us there should be no smoking allowed around our son. My daughter quietly told the doctor her father smoked in the house sometimes. This was the first time but not the last I would watch my daughter stand up to her father to try and protect the health of her brother. I remember her comment had made my husband angry as he felt this very small child had betrayed him; he behaved compliantly and respectfully in front of the doctor, only to reveal his fury later during the ride home.

Another concern I had in coming upon the father-son pot smoking incident was that my husband comes from a family of alcoholics, and although he avoids alcohol because it wreaks such havoc on his system, he is a regular smoker of cigarettes and marijuana. My husband's tendency toward addiction had always concerned me, and I worried that our son might follow suit. Although I generally feared alcohol and other drugs more than marijuana, I knew that because of his asthma, my son would be more negatively affected than most if he fancied smoking anything. My son was just entering adolescence, which by anyone's standard is a very vulnerable age where much of who we are to eventually become is negotiated. I had felt for a long while my husband's excessive use of pot was infantile or at least adolescent and was tied in with a youthful rebellion of his own that had somehow floundered and left him vulnerable.

As time went on, it became increasingly obvious my husband and son's shared pot smoking was not an occasional thing, and part of the fun seemed to be in hiding it from me. It felt as though another person had come to live in the house, always hiding from plain view, disappearing into thin air whenever I came around the corner. I found enough evidence to know my hunches were correct, but it was hard to establish with certainty that a routine that was threatening not only the health of my son but the stability of our family had developed. I began to feel as though I had three adolescents in the house—daughter, son, and father—but at least my daughter was not involved in this latest insanity, or so I thought at the time. When I tried to discuss what was going on with my husband, he would deny all of my allegations and out-argue me until I finally gave up and left him alone, often keeping my mouth shut just to keep the peace. I had learned that confronting him only made him more secretive, and he seemed to delight in turning things around to make it appear I was overreacting or imagining things.

Sitting around seriously thinking I was crazy became a hobby as the atmosphere in the house slowly but certainly changed. I felt like I was living in a crooked house with funny mirrors. On the rare occasion I could actually get my husband to talk about what was going on, he would say, "Think of all the men who don't go to work or who are out cheating on their wives. What do you want from me?" He continually denied all of the increasingly bizarre images that were coming to my mind, images derived mainly from the copious clues that were left around. His main defense, which usually got me to cease and desist because of my own guilt and internal issues, was to remind me that I also liked to smoke pot upon occasion to unwind and relax. Other than the odd glass of wine or occasional mixed drink, it was the only "substance" I used, and I clearly understood I used it—in moderation—to balance my moods and sustain me in difficult moments. Although I was not in denial that I used cannabis not only for enjoyment but occasionally to self-medicate, I worked hard to make up for whatever harm a small amount might exact on my body by eating healthy foods and exercising. I resented the fact that my very moderate use of this herb should be compared in any way to my husband's out-of-control relationship with marijuana. It was like comparing a person who appreciates a glass of wine with dinner to a raging alcoholic, and insisting that a negative judgment apply equally to both. The bottom line was that my husband, for reasons of his own, was out of control, and he was at this point endangering the wellbeing of our son.

At the time of the first father-son pot smoking discovery, we had only been living in our new house for a short while. I had been carefully designing this house in my mind and on paper for years, and my husband is an ace builder who was ready and willing to build it, with me as glorified gofer. It became an all-consuming project. Before committing to the new house building enterprise I had been forced to deal with one serious drawback: I would have to sell the house I had owned for twelve years before I met my husband in order to do it, and that scared me. I had long considered it one of the few securities I had, and was afraid to give up something that made it easier to flee if need be. My husband's temper, always stopping just sort of physical abuse, had frightened me and my daughter on any number of occasions over the years, and I was reluctant to give up the little bit of extra power having my own house afforded. I decided the only way I would sell my original house and put the money in a house with both of our names on the deed would be if my husband agreed to quit smoking pot, an activity I believed had become a serious hindrance in his life. I didn't like having to make deals, but his smoking had become so out-of-control I would rather divorce him than continue on the way things were, and I told him that in no uncertain terms.

We had many conversations regarding this issue and each time we talked about "it," he wholeheartedly agreed with me he needed and was willing to quit smoking pot; he clearly wanted to build the new house and was at least willing to make promises. Both of our children were about to enter adolescence, and I felt it was the wise thing to do. My husband's attachment to the herb cannabis, as well as his excessive smoking of cigarettes, had become deleterious to his physical and emotional health, and was negatively affecting his functioning as a husband and parent.

I also believed marijuana was safer than alcohol, and my husband would have been in much worse shape had he been an alcoholic. Study after study has shown that an acute knockout state from using marijuana is almost unattainable in humans, and there has never been an overdose death attributed to marijuana use alone. It is an easy substance to abuse because it is essentially mild in comparison with the alternatives; problems a person has with addiction do not reveal themselves as readily as they do with alcohol abuse, for example, and a person who uses pot in moderation could conceivably do so indefinitely without harming themselves in any significant way (and many do just that).

Because of my age and membership in the hippie generation, most of the people I knew had smoked pot at some point in their lives but had given it up for a variety of reasons. Most had no problems admitting to their past marijuana use and even grew melancholy remembering the good old days. Others à la Bill Clinton believed it was safer to lie about activities that were de rigueur for the times. A few people I knew were still cannabis smokers, and had healthy and successful lives, but most of the people I associated with had no relation to the herb anymore—except that their kids were starting to show an interest in it.

Although most of the things I enjoyed in life had nothing to do with marijuana, I still found myself drawn to it upon occasion and did not deny myself its comfort when I needed it. I was careful to limit my consumption, as I do with all things that I put into my body, including food and vitamins. More than once during times of trouble, angst, or ennui, marijuana had saved me from antidepressants or other pharmaceutical alternatives. I was convinced that antidepressants were generally not a good thing after watching many friends and acquaintances tamper with them. They either got off of them very quickly because of the side effects, preferring the feelings of their old life, or got stuck on them for years, switching from one brand to another, unable to withdraw or go forward. I saw them as stuck. They saw themselves as not succumbing. There had to be more to life than not succumbing. It was a time in my life when I really needed to go forward; I viewed building the house and moving as a new opportunity to help propel us toward a better future. I hoped the move would also help my husband get unstuck, yet I knew he needed to get his health together before any positive changes could take place in his life. I was willing to join him in the effort to get healthy and was looking forward to a new life with fresh possibilities for us all.

My husband promised repeatedly that he would quit smoking marijuana, and we began to build our new home. The project would immerse and overwhelm us for a couple of years, during which time I turned a partial blind eye to his smoking marijuana because the pressure was so intense. I would even join him on occasion when I felt the need to unwind, telling myself that as soon as we moved in, things would change. When the house was almost finished, my house of many years sold quite suddenly in the middle of the winter, and we had to move into the new house immediately. With the heat on to finish the house, I did not feel that it was the time to demand that my husband make good on his promise to quit smoking pot; I knew from past experience he would probably respond by stopping work on the house altogether, expert in the passive-aggressive arts that he was.

The move was necessarily swift, and suddenly we found ourselves living in a new area almost an hour away from our previous home with both of our near teens in a new school. The week we moved from our old house to our new house, my husband's brother and best friend died very suddenly from bacterial meningitis. His brother had been deaf from birth; after much consideration, he had decided to undergo an operation to install a cochlear ear implant, a device that would enable him to hear after almost fifty years of silence. Accomplishing this goal had involved many visits to the doctor before and after surgery, and had resulted in the miracle of hearing, for the first time in his life, the voices of his children and the sounds of birds singing, and even the sound of a toilet flushing, which he said had taken him by surprise. My husband accompanied his brother on most of his visits to the doctor and hospital, serving as an interpreter and lending support. Several months after the surgery my brother-in-law began experiencing pain in his ear; at the time we did not know bacterial meningitis could be a complication of cochlear implant surgery. He called my husband and told him about the pain, and my husband, thinking he probably had a flu that was going around, went out and bought him some over-the-counter medications. Within days his brother was in a coma, and almost without warning he was gone.

It was a very difficult time for all of us, especially my husband, who could not even speak of it. It took him over a year and a half to say he should have taken his brother to the hospital when he had called for help, a sentiment that had no doubt been tormenting him since the day his brother went into a coma. If my husband had been willing to talk to a grief counselor, perhaps he could have been able to understand how normal guilt feelings are when someone dies, but he would not acknowledge or talk about the subject of his brother's death to anyone. More than one person has suggested that my husband's subsequent behavior, such as smoking pot with his young son, was related to unresolved difficulties having to do with his brother's death. His brother had chosen *him* to call to tell him of the pain in his ear, not only because of their close relationship but because he had been the one to see him through his surgery and doctor's appointments. Not understanding the nature of what was happening, my husband did not call the doctor who had operated on his brother, and now his brother was gone forever.

My husband's enormous grief and sorrow were mixed with guilt, and the combination was overwhelming. Instead of giving up smoking marijuana as he had promised, he began smoking more to dull his pain—much more. I did not have the right or the power to try to make him live up to his promise at that moment in time, and I was definitely of the persuasion it was better pot than alcohol, which would have destroyed him quickly in the shape he was in. I could only imagine his pain, and let him deal with it in whatever way he found necessary. Fortunately or unfortunately, depending on how you look at it, this meant a gradual but pervasive distancing between us. Slowly I began to feel my husband was turning into a stranger, and it frightened me that I had given up the security of my old home.

Coming upon my husband and our son smoking pot down by the garage reminded me of the many times my husband and his brother had hung out together smoking. As I watched them, I stood stunned and speechless, sensing with a chill the displeasure my arrival had engendered. When confronted, they both angrily stood up for their right to smoke a joint together. I pleaded with them to consider the boy's asthma, pointing out he shouldn't be smoking anything at all. I had birthed and nursed and cared for this child for fourteen years, and now I was fearful he could easily slip into my husband's world of addiction and the weird isolation and secrecy that sustains it—and possibly even die because of it. I believed the loss of his brother had left an empty hole in my husband's life, and he was attempting to fill that void by creating a new relationship with our son, a relationship that would by necessity alienate me as I became increasingly the watchdog and naysayer.

For the next year I watched helplessly as my son became another person. One of the first things he did was to drop his two best friends from his old school, who now lived an hour away from us. They were wonderful friends who my son had cherished for years, spending most of his weekends with them in carefree play. Although when we first moved he had been very anxious to get together with these old friends on weekends, now he avoided them. He stopped talking about them and somehow never managed to fit them into his new life. Any queries about this new situation were met with barks and grumbles. Perhaps he had changed so much he didn't know how to reveal his new identity to these boys who knew him so well. It seemed he was feeling inauthentic, and he certainly was beginning to act it. He was charming to those in authority (like teachers and parents) and to those he considered allies or friends, but was quick to anger with anyone who challenged or irritated him. This was not the easygoing, accepting son I had known for a decade and a half. He became more critical of people, especially his sister and me, and others who disapproved of his new self; it was as though he felt we didn't measure up to his new standards.

One incident particularly caught my attention because his behavior so did not resemble his former personality. A friend of his sister's, who had always slightly annoyed him because of her exhibits of "superficiality," began behaving promiscuously after a bad breakup with her boyfriend. My son took it upon himself to harass her about her behavior at a party; I heard later what I had already suspected—he had been drunk. I had just become aware of the fact that more than marijuana smoking was going on; alcohol was also a problem. When I heard about this incident, I believed it was more likely alcohol fueled rather than pot inspired, just from my observations in life concerning the effects these two substances have on people. The report of my son's insulting behavior to this girl stunned me; he had never acted hurtfully to anyone publicly like that before, although privately I was becoming more familiar with this new persona. I was watching my wonderful, gentle, loving son turn into an alcoholic/addict.

It wasn't long before I realized my son had started drinking alcohol regularly. He began retiring to his room earlier in the evening than usual, saying he was tired and wanted to sleep. I discovered later that he would put a rolled-up towel under the door to make his room look dark so I would think he was really sleeping. But I would occasionally run into him late at night as he came down for food, and when I tried to talk to him, he could not look me in the eye and his words were slurred, and I could smell the alcohol. He took great pains to avoid me during these times, which in itself was painful because of our former closeness. He would grow defensive and angry the minute I started talking to him, vehemently refusing to answer questions about what was going on.

At first I could not figure out where he was getting the alcohol. I knew kids sometimes got it from each other, remembering back to my high school days when some teenagers carried fake driver's licenses. It never occurred to me his father would be the procurer because my husband rarely drinks—and I could not fathom why a parent would do such a thing to his child, especially if he didn't do it himself because he had witnessed the devastation alcohol had caused in his own family. If I tried to talk to my son about what was happening, he got angry and stalked away. If I tried to talk to my husband about what was happening, he got angry and stalked away. My son started locking his door, and if I knocked, he would open the door and stand with his six-foot frame clearly meant to block the doorway so I could not come in. It was hard to believe this was all happening; I felt powerless to stop it and found myself suffering terrible anguish and pain on almost a daily basis. There are many ways one can lose a child, and I knew I was facing a difficult, uphill battle to save my son from slipping into the darkness of addiction.

CHAPTER 2

Cat and Mouse

A woman spoke to me recently about her brother, a former addict; she told me that although he had been clean for years, he still behaved like an addict. When I asked her what she meant, she said the main thing was that he was a habitual liar, even when there was no apparent reason for it. One of the saddest and most difficult things for me to deal with concerning my son's new persona had been his recent proclivity for untruthfulness. I had never considered him to be a dishonest child, and don't remember any specific incident when he had ever lied to me, although I'm not so naïve as to think it never occurred. But now I felt surrounded by deceit, and it was becoming harder to tell the difference between truth and fabrication.

I became aware of a strange new feeling when I entered the house after being out for a while; it felt as though something was artificial but I just couldn't put my finger on what it was. When I would try and initiate a conversation with my husband or son about issues concerning pot and alcohol, they would earnestly tell me they were doing nothing—and I was imagining things. Although they often didn't look or smell like I was imagining things, they were clearly making a concerted effort to keep certain activities outside on porches, used breath mints, and so on—and I often felt fooled and frustrated. I was certain the behavior of some of the occupants in the house was different when I was absent, but I just couldn't prove it because they could always hear me coming up the driveway. We have a long, gravel driveway, which enables occupants in the house to hear a car coming for quite some time—long enough to permit a person to move from one part of the house to another.

I spent a year playing a ridiculous cat-and-mouse game with a father and son who together could outwit me every time. I knew what I was looking at when I saw it—I just couldn't prove how it got that way. I decided to look for a therapist for my son. I asked around and found a male therapist who took our insurance; I made an appointment to talk about what was going on in our family with the idea that my son would then become the patient. The therapist acted rather cavalicrly when I told him about my son's substance abuse with and without his father; I told him all about the smoking, the drinking, the asthma, the anger, and the lying. He told me most people outgrow substance abuse problems on their own when they're in their mid-twenties. (What about my husband?) He believed that given time, the problem would most likely resolve itself. I had already noticed that my son's breathing, particularly when he was sleeping or exercising, was labored, and I wondered how much time it would take for permanent damage to occur in already weak lungs. I had heard many horror stories about asthma and sudden death, and I didn't feel at all consoled by the idea that years hence the problem might resolve itself.

The therapist could see I was upset about all that was going on in my family, so he suggested I continue to see him rather than my son. Because of my son's obvious resistance, the therapist felt he couldn't help him anyway. I had specifically chosen him for my son because he was a man—I would never have opted to see a male therapist myself, but considering I was already there, I agreed to see him. I found unloading all the painful details, which I had shared with only a few close friends, was cathartic. Talking about it openly created a rush of emotions and I cried for the first full session. Thus began several months of treatment where I basically cried a lot, and wondered how the human body was capable of producing the vast quantities of tears and snot that would erupt from my body for one hour each week. I was mourning the loss of my son.

Feeling discouraged and defeated when the therapy produced no tangible results after what I considered a respectable try, I stopped going and started planning a different course of action. To my dismay, I found that going to the therapist had actually produced negative results, because of the fact that *nothing happened*. Look, the boys in the family probably determined, she goes to therapy and tells the guy all about what's going on, and nothing changes—nothing happens. The fact that I had reached out for help, and none had arrived, had actually empowered my husband and son, and they became bolder. They now practically laughed at my attempts to achieve some sense of order in the house. When I had previously threatened to seek counseling about his addict behavior, my husband had always told me I wouldn't dare because it would threaten his job. He was right, but that was before my son was involved; before I had always backed off, afraid of repercussions and not wanting to tamper with the status quo. My husband had relied on my fears to perpetuate an intolerable existence, at least for me, but I knew I could no longer afford to be weak now that my son's life and future were hanging in the balance.

With the advice and encouragement of some friends, I decided to enroll in graduate school so I would be prepared financially to divorce my husband, as it was clear to me the relationship was no longer viable. I thought that maybe in helping myself I could help my son. I had been a mother, housewife, and artist for almost twenty years, and realized my financial dependency had to end if my life was to move forward. A friend who knew about my problems at home told me about a graduate program nearby she believed would be well suited to my needs and temperament; I proceeded to apply and was accepted. I knew the next couple of years were going to be rocky and would require hard work and perseverance if I were to survive.

One of the first signs of my son's growing relationship with both marijuana and alcohol was his diminished interest in school. Ten years of regular school attendance with time out only for real illness was replaced with attendance that was so spotty, it became a rare week he attended the full five days. He also began having a harder time getting to school on time on the days that he did attend, complaining regularly of lost sleep and exhaustion, although it seemed at times as though his sleep was interminable. Although he would not admit it, it was fairly obvious he was suffering from hangovers regularly. As I became increasingly concerned, I also became increasingly the bad guy. I had gone from the loving mother always there for him to an annoying nag looking for evidence. He had developed ingenious methods of barking that cut me off at the pass, and I was left with continual feelings of frustration and impotence. It didn't help that my husband was aiding and abetting the wayward teenager, teaching him the tricks of the addict's trade: hide, hide, and hide some more.

Although my husband had been thrilled when our second child was a son, he left the real work of raising him almost entirely to me, just as he had done with our daughter. Because he was not supposed to smoke in the rooms inhabited not only by his asthmatic son but by other family members as well, my husband spent most of his time secreted away in one or two smoking areas. He would make brief appearances into our family life, usually on his way to get another cup of coffee to accompany his cigarettes and joints. When his brother died, my husband's need to insulate himself from the outside world increased. I often sensed my husband felt abandoned, not only by his brother but by me; he really missed having someone to sit around and smoke with him, and he was always trying to entice me. I was busy with a house to run and things to do, and was growing increasingly intolerant of my husband's excessive smoking, especially as our children were growing older and there was more at stake. Our new house was not as big and spread out as the old house, and it was almost impossible to completely hide the odor of burning cannabis. I felt like one of my new responsibilities was as "smoke monitor," a duty that helped place me at increasing odds with my husband.

My husband started showing more interest in our son as he approached manhood; it seemed as though he was attempting to stake his claim on his son's newly forming psyche. A new *male*volent streak entered my husband's conversations—like dropping negative comments about women drivers or spewing missives about general female ineptitude; missed hits with a hammer were now often punctuated with hissings that included pejorative words for the female sex. It felt eerily like preparation for some sort of male initiation ceremony was taking place in our house, and increasingly the conversation would stop when I entered the secret world of father and son. They suddenly started spending lots of time together on the computer. I often got the feeling they quickly changed sites when I came around, but I could never quite prove it, and I didn't want to appear nosy or invasive. After all, it was a parent-child relationship, and I should have been able to trust that my husband was being the parent, even though I was inwardly nervous and concerned this was not the case. It began to feel more and more like aliens from another planet had come to live in our house. The change in my son's personality was disturbing; toxicity and secrecy do not become him. I had already discovered how debilitating that combination can be in a relationship, and had grown over the years to rely largely on relationships and activities outside of my marriage to survive emotionally.

Among the most important of those relationships had been the ones I had with my children, and until my daughter entered into adolescence, I had always felt good about the level of intimacy I had with both of them. Part of my daughter's youthful rebellion had involved a negative reaction in the extreme toward her father. Years later she confided in me that one day she was at the mall and saw a father and daughter walking and laughing together, and the image so upset her she had felt like crying. She knew girls were supposed to be close to their fathers, and she wasn't. For a couple of years, my daughter rebelled almost continuously—against her father, a couple of teachers, and finally against me. She was old enough now to understand what she had missed, and she felt a lot of anger as well as sorrow.

At that time, before the problems with my son emerged, I was not only dealing with the move to a new house and a rebellious adolescent daughter, but the first signs of real distress were emerging from aging parents far away. They were talking about moving closer to me so I could help care for them. At the time, I was the offspring best suited for the job because I did not work outside of the home; within months they sold their house of fifty-one years and moved across the country to be nearer to my little family. I picked them up at an almost-empty airport two weeks after September 11, 2001, and helped them move into their new apartment. It seemed like they had both grown very old all of a sudden and were in need of a lot of assistance—medical and otherwise. It seemed as if the whole world was coming apart, and even grandma and grandpa no longer represented stability.

My son's first year in his new school had been difficult socially for him because until our house was ready and our old house sold, we remained an hour away from his school. By his second year we had moved into our new home closer to the school, and he was able to make friends with a large group of very nice kids—mostly boys. The following couple of years were filled with activities and friends, and my son was clearly happy and doing pretty well in school. He wasn't the most serious student, and always seemed to be lagging in one subject or another, but he was intelligent, had a great curiosity, and was always learning in his own way and at his own pace.

I had always felt joy in his presence and had no reason to think something might happen to change things or to undermine our relationship. My belief in the purity and intensity of the mother-child bond blinded me to a certain extent when it came to identifying and recognizing early on what was going on in my house. But even when it was clearly apparent something was happening, I usually couldn't figure out exactly what it was or to what extent it was happening, and I was uncertain as to how to approach the matter. The reaction of the few people I confided in was so mixed I felt like some of them were living on separate planets. It was hard to imagine another subject or another substance that could elicit such mixed reactions. Sentiments ranged from abject horror to "Oh well. What else is new?" Still, nobody had any good advice as to what to do about it.

I was finally feeling a bit of relief once I had made the decision to return to school, but then my daughter, who is two years older than my son, began showing acute signs of distress. She suddenly told me that she wanted to see a therapist right away. My daughter refused to talk to me about what was troubling her, but she was obviously very upset about something. I stepped up my efforts, quickly found her a female therapist, and made an appointment. When my daughter returned home from her first session, she told me she didn't want to go back to see this woman. After her insistence that I find her someone pronto, I was surprised she wanted to quit before she even started, and I became really concerned. I told her if she just didn't like the particular therapist I'd found for her, I would continue looking until we found someone else. She replied it wasn't necessary for me to do that, and she just didn't want to go to therapy anymore.

My daughter left a phone message for the therapist saying she was not going to keep her second appointment, and I was surprised when the therapist called back the very next day to ask her if everything was all right. I could only hear my daughter's end of the conversation, but the woman seemed anxious to find out why she did not want to see her again. I wasn't sure if the woman was concerned about losing a client or if she really was concerned about her. My daughter wasn't talking and was trying to act like whatever it was that was bothering her before was now resolved, although she didn't seem to be crediting the therapist. In fact, she complained that the therapist had used phrases such as "when you go out drugging with your friends" when she mentioned some casual alcohol and pot use among her peers. It was the only clue she gave me as to what was discussed in their onetime session. Further prodding on my part went nowhere, and the subject of therapy was closed.

The one thing I truly never suspected was that my daughter had become part of a new triumvirate in our household. As my daughter and her father had experienced difficulties communicating with each other for years, I misread subtle clues I had recently observed, such as my husband's offer to help our daughter clean her room, which was almost always a mess. Who wouldn't want to read the fact that he offered and she had accepted as a positive note between two family members who were in emotional arrears? My husband had been married once before and had two daughters from that relationship, and he had somehow given my daughter the impression she didn't matter much. My daughter had often felt she was the third-born daughter of a guy who'd always wanted a son, and then finally got one.

I had been so involved with trying to figure out what to do with the problems I knew about that I completely missed the newest complication: My daughter had been included in the secret smoking club. It took a long time for my daughter to tell me the whole story of her involvement, but her revelations began when she could no longer stand silently by and bear witness to the damage she felt was being inflicted on her brother at the hands of someone who was supposed to be protecting him—their father. She could see her brother was taking full advantage of what was offered him with seemingly no concerns about how it was affecting his health, his life, and his relationships.

My daughter, now spilling the beans in their entirety, told me she was especially worried about her brother's alcohol consumption, as she felt this seemed to be harming him the most, but she was also concerned about his excessive marijuana use. Having to lie or answer evasively to me to protect her new club members had been taking its toll on my daughter's emotional equilibrium. She had hoped finding a therapist to talk to would help, but discovered that once in the therapist's office, she couldn't possibly tell the woman everything that was happening in our house; it was just too bizarre. She certainly wasn't going to have the only person who knew her secret be someone who used phrases like "out drugging with your friends," especially as her friends were all really great kids. She had wanted to talk with someone who was aware of what was going on out there in the world in general before she shared what was going on in her very specific life in her very specific house. She had made an attempt to reach out for help but could not follow through. Now I understood why the therapist had called her; she had gotten just enough information to be rightfully concerned.

My daughter's finally letting me in on what was happening, confirming what I had already suspected but could not prove, was incredibly brave—just as she had been incredibly brave when she spoke up for her two-year-old brother in the asthma specialist's office more than a dozen years earlier. She knew at the time what she was risking—her relationship with her father and her brother—and to date, this is exactly the price she has had to pay for sounding the alarm.

My daughter told me that the first time she ever smoked pot with her father was on the night his brother died. She was alone with him in his vehicle driving up to the hospital on that blizzarding night in January when we got the call his brother was fading fast, after several days in a coma, and her father offered her a joint to share during what must have been an agonizing ride for him. Their relationship had been strained for a long time, and she must have had mixed feelings about accepting that joint. She may have seen it almost as a peace offering. She was fifteen years old, and the only way her father knew to communicate with her about the impending loss of his brother was to smoke pot with her—a ritual he had often shared with his brother. She accepted his offer, and I, trying to negotiate the snowy roads in another car with my son, never suspected a thing.

But now my daughter was talking, and what I was hearing was especially upsetting as all of the information she was telling me was stuff that I, specifically, was not supposed to know about. There were four people living in the house, and three of them were engaged in behavior that involved purposeful lying and keeping secrets from the fourth, and the show was being run by my husband. My daughter told me that almost every time I left the house, the three of them would gather together to smoke, drink, and party. When they heard me coming up the driveway, they would all run back to their respective places in the house, and I would reenter my home to find my son lying on the couch watching TV, my daughter on the phone in her room, and my husband upstairs in his smoking room—which in the summer was a screened-in porch and in the winter was a bathroom with an exhaust fan. No wonder my daughter was having a hard time telling all this to a therapist. It wasn't as though I was so stupid or naïve I didn't notice things were different, but my children were entering their teen years and everyone I knew was talking about their adolescents and how secretive and grumpy they had become.

All three were brilliant actors. Everyone did his or her part to act like everything was normal when I was around, which made me think I must be going crazy, as things certainly didn't feel normal. Three-quarters of the household clearly wanted me to believe in a reality that no longer existed, and since

I wanted to believe in that old reality, I participated in the game by choosing to believe that my children's strange behavior was because of adolescence. My kids used to fuss and complain whenever I went out for the evening to a school meeting or to meet a friend for a movie, scolding me if I went out more than one night a week. Now they asked me about my comings and goings in a different way, leaving me with the odd feeling they wanted me to go out. Putting two and two together wasn't hard in my son's case. I knew what he was up to with his father, but I never guessed my daughter was involved with this new family subgroup. I was grateful to finally discover the truth. In retrospect, it seemed her relationship with her father had improved, but because the purpose of everything I was allowed to see was to prevent me from discovering what was going on, great care was taken to make sure nothing was obvious.

My daughter told me there had been many, many lies. She had been warned by her father that if she told me about everything that was going on while I was out of the house, *she* would be the one responsible for the divorce he knew would ensue. I had brought up the D word way too many times in the past during difficulties for him not to know that this behavior would be the last straw. So although she had been concerned for some time about how this new lifestyle was affecting her brother, she knew that to reveal what was going on in an attempt to stop it would possibly result in a divorce, with her to blame—or so she thought. The bravest she could be at that point in time was to request therapy. That having failed her for whatever reason, she was now doing what she knew she had to do—confide in me.

Suddenly all of those little things I had observed that made no sense made sense. Realizing that I was not crazy and not imagining things and something sinister really was taking place under my roof would have been somewhat comforting had it not been for the full realization of what I was now facing: a divorce from a crazy person—with our children in the middle. Confronting my husband was almost anticlimactic, as my new information wasn't really new; it was just confirmed. But now that the truth was out, it became a legitimate topic of conversation, unlike before when I was routinely chased away from the truth as though I were a crazy lady fabricating mischievous stories.

My husband immediately began blaming my daughter for all that was transpiring, as she knew he would. He seemed to feel no shame in laying the cause of our potential divorce, now very close to a reality in the making, at her feet. He often pointed to the spot in the living room where she was standing when she was finally able to speak the truth aloud, as she did one day in front of the three of us. More than once he carried on with great passion about her "betrayal." He had no trouble attracting our son to his side, who joined his father in believing that his sister had acted out of anger or spite rather than out of genuine concern for his health and safety. As a mother who had so far survived my daughter's adolescence, I was well aware of her vitriol, having on more than one occasion been the recipient; but there was no doubt in my mind she had risked destroying her relationship with both her father and her brother to save her brother. For the first time in a while, I felt like I had someone on the same team in the house. I had given up long ago trying to change my husband, but I was not about to let him destroy my children—at least not without a fight.

CHAPTER 3

Going for Help

Before I found out about my daughter's involvement in the smoking triad, I had tried lecturing and making deals with both my husband and my son about smoking and drinking but had gotten nowhere. Almost every time I left the house, I would approach father and son and plead with them to abstain. There would be a lot of, "Yeah. Yeah. I know...don't worry..." or "We're not..." but there was little indication anything was changing based on the rate of accidental discoveries, usually made by my daughter, who they were less careful around. I listened to my son's breathing when he fell asleep on the couch, and it was clearly labored. I wanted so badly to help him.

At about the same time I was informed of the events taking place behind my back, I came across a bunch of marijuana plants growing in the basement. As discussed earlier, my views concerning marijuana are liberal. I spent the early part of my college days in California where I fully participated in listening to rock music, going to love-ins, and smoking my share of pot. After graduating from college with an almost worthless degree in art, I dropped out of graduate school a couple of times to devote myself to my own work, and generally lived the life of a struggling artist in a rural setting a couple of hours from a big city. It was not uncommon in those days to smoke marijuana while communing with other artists. It was a very casual affair often accompanied by tossing a few seeds into the ground to avoid the paraquat and insecticide contamination possible with commercial varieties.

The pot smokers I knew were not wild and crazy maniacs, desperate for a hit. In general they were conscientious and moderate people who for the most part took better care of their health than the general population, usually eschewing alcohol and cigarettes and all other drugs, legal and illegal. They were often the first people to show concern about the pesticides added to our food supply, participated in new age schools that attempted to make learning pleasurable, and focused attention on environmental problems and the need for alternative energy sources. As the years went by, pot smoking became less frequent and less visible among most of these people, but some still secretly preferred the mild high of marijuana to the heavy toxicity of alcohol. My own experiences with marijuana compelled me to believe that our society would be better off removing the harsh penalties it imposes on those in possession of this relatively mild herb, and come up with ways to integrate and incorporate its moderate usage into our culture—with restrictions of course.

Yet for all my liberal sentiments, at this particular juncture in time I did not want to be dealing with any pot plants, and my husband knew it. When I discovered the plants growing in the basement, I told him in no uncertain terms I wanted him to get rid of the plants—*Immediately!*—which he did, angrily. On that fateful night at three o'clock in the morning, he woke me out of a sound sleep, swearing at me, threatening me, and complaining loudly about the fact that I had forced him to pull out his marijuana plants. I got chills as I listened to him hiss that he was going to get me, just "wait and see." His rage was palpable. The bed heaved up and down as he bellowed and carried on. This was the first time in our twenty-year relationship I had ever been physically afraid of my husband, although I'd always considered him a scary guy because of his quick-trigger temper. My heart was pounding with fear. I wasn't sure if I should let him know I was awake, or pretend I was sleeping. Finally, I got up and left the room; it was a frightening and sleepless night.

It was apparent I could no longer deal with our problems on my own; I had to try once again to get professional help for our family, and this time I was determined to find someone who took the situation more seriously than the first therapist. The very next morning, exhausted after a sleepless night, I got on the phone and called around trying to find information on therapists who specialized in substance abuse. Finally, I spoke to someone in the city who told me there was a drug treatment facility right in my own small town. Although I considered our problems to be much more than just substance abuse and was fearful of calling attention to this illegality at a place specializing in drugs because of my husband's job, my desperation propelled me to call and make an appointment for myself and my children. I knew my husband would not agree to go, which at that point was fine because I did not want his intimidating presence at the first session as we all needed to be able to talk freely. I also knew my son would be representing my husband, and I was curious to see whether or not he would admit to what was taking place in our lives. There was some comfort in finally knowing, thanks to my daughter, what was going on in my own home; it gave me the strength to do what I knew I had to do.

The new therapist took our situation very seriously. He zoned in quickly on the fact that my daughter and I were feeling terrorized. Although my son did not in general deny the goings-on in our house, he did not understand the element of fear my daughter and I were experiencing. My husband was treating him like a long-lost prince—it was as though they were reenacting some male initiation ritual from ancient times, and my daughter and I were expected to wait back in the hut for the new young warrior to emerge. Any complaints or attempts to influence the young man with our values were seen as heretical, and we were viewed as witches. Now that my daughter and I were talking about things previously hidden from open conversation, we found we had both felt the ambience in the home shift over the past couple of years. We agreed that the newly patriarchal slant emanating from the two males in the house had made life pretty miserable for its female occupants. It had all crept up so slowly it was hard to notice or pinpoint the almost imperceptible, incremental changes that had altered the power balance to such an extent that it now required our full attention.

Quite simply, I felt like I had lost my power as a mother. I could no longer ask my son to do anything and expect that it get done, or get done in a reasonable manner or timeframe. His schoolwork was also suffering. He was continually telling me he was too ill to go to school, and although there was no specific physical thing wrong with him, other than his asthma, he often looked sick. Although my son did not dispute his sister's version of various happenings around the house, he was furious we felt it should be anyone's business outside of our family. He essentially believed his behavior and that of his father were acceptable. Watching him express himself to the therapist with such vehement anger and justification, I felt like I was watching my husband.

The drug counselor took all of this in and managed to convince my son to come to therapy on a regular basis. As this was obviously a family affair, he also set up sessions that sometimes included his sister and me. My daughter and I also began to see him privately on alternate weeks. I felt a huge sense of relief we had finally found someone to help us deal with our mess. From the beginning the therapist tried to encourage my husband to come in, but it never happened. My son would always arrive at therapy sessions with the news that his father was too busy and couldn't take time off; he bristled every time he saw the therapist and viewed him as Public Enemy No. 1. At home, he could be seen conferring with his father before and after every session. The therapist might as well have been named Lucifer, the way his name was hissed when mentioned by either of them.

My son particularly disliked the idea of group therapy, and after the first group meeting refused to go back, believing the other members were much more severely afflicted and addicted—thus he couldn't relate or get anything out of therapy with them. He said one woman's mother had died from an overdose of heroin—certainly not his level of problem. He continued to go to private sessions, making no effort to hide his contempt for the whole process and especially for the people involved in getting him there. When the drug counselor told my son his father's smoking pot and drinking with him was child abuse, my son laughed and said that was a ridiculous thing for him to say. My son felt nothing was happening to threaten his safety, and he spent most of his time pissed off at anyone who felt otherwise.

Several months slowly and excruciatingly passed, and very little changed except for the anger quotient—which rose in almost imperceptible increments. By now it had been well over a year since things started to go significantly downhill in our family, and signs were not promising that anything was going to get better now that we had found another therapist to help us. Once again, it seemed things had gotten worse by going to therapy; the pot was being stirred. Talking, objecting, arguing—all seemed to be aimed, on the part of my husband and son, to deceive and perpetuate a certain madness they used to cloak their deceptive activities. Had my daughter not decided to open up to me because she feared for her brother's health and safety, I don't know if I would know today most of what was going on. One thing now was for certain: Both my husband and I were fighting for the right to influence our children, and my husband was now showing overt hostility on a daily basis, clearly in hopes of winning through intimidation. I think in his mind, the meaner and madder he got, the quicker we'd run; after all, it had worked many times before.

My husband was from a large Irish Catholic family, and he prided himself in having helped his younger sisters defend themselves against a male sibling predator. Even though he had always claimed to be against the physical abuse of women, I had long understood the anger that had erupted from this abusive brother was also firmly implanted inside of my husband. He had always been a human volcano of sorts, staying reasonably calm for periods of time, then erupting with a vengeance when something irritated him.

My daughter and I still occasionally find ourselves talking about the holes he used to punch in the walls sometimes when he got angry. He would not fix them for months to remind us on a daily basis of the potential of his wrath. Once he put his fist through a wooden kitchen cupboard; he didn't need to go any further. The problem was that the time between his outbursts had become shorter, and the outbursts themselves scarier as he tried to establish control over his son and create a miniature patriarchy within the microcosm of our family. It was not long before both my daughter and I were routinely treated with contempt by both of the males in the house, having tampered with something sacred and precious: a father's relationship with his son.

The subject of divorce came up right away during my first private session with our new therapist. I told him I had wanted a divorce for some years, but my husband had always argued me out of it, twisting and turning things to try to make it appear like I was a weak person who always saw divorce as the only answer when surely the wiser thing to do was to work things out. It was always amazing how quickly my husband could become a saint when he realized I had one foot out the door.

Another impediment to divorce was that I worried about what would happen to my children if we were to divorce—giving them up on weekends to his care was something that really concerned me, even before recent events. I simply did not trust his judgment. I decided it was best to stay in the relationship at least until my children were on their own. I had not anticipated how much worse things were going to get, or how quickly they would get that way. Previously, both of my children had been good kids and had led active lives involving friends and activities, with no huge problems; now that difficult issues were emerging, I felt overwhelmed and really didn't know what steps to take next to ensure their safety.

I began thinking that possibly my husband was seriously ill with a brain tumor because I had heard lung cancer often metastasizes to the brain, and he was, after all, a heavy smoker. I insisted he get checked out by a doctor, who found nothing wrong other than a little arthritis and early-stage pulmonary disease, which was to be expected. I was so convinced there had to be a physical explanation for my husband's behavior, I made an appointment with another doctor and even went with him just to make sure I was hearing the truth. Once again he checked out okay.

My daughter, meanwhile, was feeling threatened as there was a lot of anger floating around the house, and she had experienced sudden, quick attacks from my husband a couple of times in the past when she had displeased or disobeyed him in some way. I knew she was capable of talking back when angered, and I feared she might say something to push him over the edge. Once he threw her clear across the room because she called him a name that was disrespectful. I noticed I was planning my days around her and her father's schedule, trying to make sure they did not end up alone in the house together. I couldn't believe I was thinking and behaving that way—but I was. Much later, when my daughter and I spoke of this time, she told me she was afraid her father would lose his temper and completely lose control and accidentally kill her (or me). I realized that was what I was afraid of as well. Although he had never physically abused me, my husband had used his temper throughout our relationship to control me and protect himself from the possibility of change. It was disheartening to see him now try to control his daughter this way, and I realized how brave she had been to challenge his behavior.

I wish I were a poet so I could accurately describe the mood and pervading ambience of those days. There was so much darkness and intimidation. My husband's method of trying to stop what I had already started (my commitment to getting professional help for our family) was to act furious at all times when in the company of my daughter and me, as if to say, "This is the me you will get if you don't let me do 'my thing' without objections and interruptions, and this time, 'my thing' includes our son."

By now it was de rigueur to come across issues of *High Times* in the house, a magazine that celebrates the smoking and cultivation of cannabis, a magazine of youthful rebellion I remembered from long ago. I felt uncomfortable with it lying around my home, especially as there were often young people around—my adolescent children as well as their friends. By this time there was so much secrecy and so many lies, my objections resulted in the magazines simply being left out less frequently.

At one point, I found a stack of pages from the Internet with all sorts of cannabis information, a lot of it about growing; I remembered all of those times I had walked in on them at the computer and had felt like an intruder. The more I discovered and the more I complained about what I had discovered, the more I was relegated to the role of "nag" and "bitch."

At one point when I was away from home, my daughter and my husband got into some sort of altercation; she claimed her father had become physical after she threatened to tell me certain things. According to her story, he became infuriated and lunged at her, ripping the wires out of the computer she was using to write an essay for school—losing hours of hard work. When this incident was discussed at the therapist's office during a session with my son, my daughter, and me, my son protested loudly that my daughter had kicked their father first. As she tried to describe how her father had gotten in her face, with his face full of rage, pointing his finger at her menacingly and threateningly, I recognized the stance she was imitating immediately. In many of our arguments, he would get me to back off by becoming angry and menacing just up to the point where I didn't dare see if he was going to go any further. My daughter had tried to kick him away from her, and he exploded. The problem is, nothing ever gets settled that way; there's never any sense of catharsis or agreement or compromise. You back off because you can't stand the heat. I knew because I'd done it any number of times. The therapist tried to help my son understand how intimidating this kind of behavior can be, but he had already changed so much that even though he used to be critical of his father on the rare occasions when he had acted violently toward his sister, he now seemed to believe his father's anger, not his sister's fear, was justified.

The therapist told my daughter and me he feared for our safety and advised us to have our bags packed and to arrange for a place to go at a moment's notice, which we did. He realized things were heating up because of the fact that we were seeking help, and my husband was threatened with this change in our behavior. Since we had always backed down before, it was unknown how he was going to react if we just kept going. There were times over the next few months when things got so bad the therapist told us we should go to the police; he believed there should be a record of things that were happening in case we needed it at some future point. Although we felt thoroughly intimidated, since we weren't actually being beaten up I couldn't bring myself to follow his advice. Meanwhile, as more time passed, the sense that once again nothing was going to happen settled in, and my husband continued behaving as he pleased, largely ignoring events going on around him of which he did not approve, and expecting that my daughter and I do the same.

I had called the second (drug) therapist after my husband woke me out of a sound sleep and physically threatened me for making him pull out the marijuana plants he was growing in the basement. Not one to be easily intimidated, it soon became apparent that my husband, after telling me he had thrown the pot plants out, had actually transplanted some of them; I discovered almost a dozen plants one day when I was out walking. We have a few acres of land, and it hadn't occurred to me he might put the plants out back away from the house. It took me a while to discover the plants as he had carefully camouflaged the area with some flowers. The fact that he cared for these flowers endlessly and the hose was always with them when I needed it for my garden eventually led me to discover his plants.

As mentioned previously, I have liberal attitudes about marijuana. People aren't lying in the hospital with their livers rotting away from cannabis use. I believe marijuana should be decriminalized and monitored in a reasonable manner, preferably not by hypocritical politicians. People should be able to learn about its health benefits as an herb, and at the same time learn that misuse or overuse can be injurious to health and spirit. People should be able to buy marijuana in the same way they buy coffee or alcohol, and that part of the taxes the government collects from the sale of it should go to education and substance abuse awareness programs and toward the support of the concept of "harm reduction." Harm reduction, where a responsible relationship is sought with a given substance and not necessarily total abstinence, could work better with marijuana than most other substances that are currently considered harmful and addictive—legal or illegal. Marijuana has often been used to soften the difficulties that accompany sincere attempts by people to discontinue the use of more harmful substances such as alcohol, cocaine, or heroin. People should be allowed to take out a license to grow a few cannabis plants in the same way they get a license to go fishing or hunting. I live in an area where it is common for elderly Italian guys to grow their own grapes from which they make their own wine; they don't bother anyone, and no one makes a big deal about it. I imagine that what they are doing is legal, but I honestly don't know if it is and have never heard anyone talk about it. And just because these guys grow their own grapes and make their own wine does not make them drunks.

My husband knew that generally speaking, I had those feelings, but he also knew that at this point I absolutely did not want him to grow those plants. When the therapist learned what was going on, he was amazed my husband didn't seem to care that his behavior was being monitored; his attitude was basically telling us to bugger off and screw the consequences. At that point, after discussing the situation with his colleagues, the therapist decided he had to report my husband's "abuse" of his underage son to CPS, the local child protection agency. My daughter was now just over eighteen, and no longer considered a child in need of protection. Our therapist and his colleagues agreed he was obligated by law to make the report, considering my husband had had plenty of opportunities to come in and talk, and continued to refuse.

I was partly horrified and partly hopeful; maybe now someone could actually do something! I'd always heard awful stories about child protection agencies—they always seemed to either be not looking when help was needed, and children died, or to insist on persecuting innocent people when nothing was happening. The therapist didn't have the power to exercise any authority over the situation, and I had obviously failed in my attempts, so perhaps this would be a good thing. Not.

According to one of the many rules that encumber social welfare agencies, once notified of a potential abuse situation, the CPS worker has to make contact with the parties involved within a couple of days. The fact that the worker assigned to our case would be leaving on an extended vacation within days of the initial contact, unable to follow through on what she was about to begin, was apparently not considered to be dangerous by CPS standards. An arrangement was made through our therapist for the CPS worker to speak to my children and me, each individually, and then a letter was prepared for *me* to give to my husband, telling him that he was under investigation for child abuse. I was told I had to give the letter to my husband that very day, even though the worker would not be contacting him until she got back from her vacation a couple of weeks later. Nice. No consideration at all was given to what might happen to my daughter and I back at the ranch, with both of the bulls rushing around as though the picadors from the bull ring were chasing them. Upon hearing the news that CPS had become involved, both my husband and son were soon snorting, kicking, and furious.

CHAPTER 4

The Limits of Therapy

It was early summer when the therapist notified CPS, two years after I had first discovered my husband smoking a joint with our son. Despite all of my efforts during that time, things had only gotten worse—much worse. Each attempt on my part to halt or moderate objectionable activities had been met by triumph from the opposing camp. My son was slipping further and further away. He seemed to consider his father's acceptance and complicity in his pot and alcohol activity to be a recognition of his manhood, while my objections to his overuse and abuse were an attempt to regulate his life, a motherly overprotectiveness that needed to be discarded. I could accept his adolescent rebelling as normal. What was not normal was that his father was providing the ideas and stimulants with which to rebel and using them with him, to the point where the kid was having problems meeting his responsibilities, at school, at home, and even with friends.

One of the saddest things for me to witness was the disintegration of my son's relationships not only with his sister and me, but with other people in his life as well. He spent little time with his grandparents, who adored him, and also spent less time with other friends who had once been important in his life. He rarely went to movies anymore—or anywhere else for that matter. While he and his sister used to hang out together, sharing friends, the line between their two rooms gradually became more demarcated. A couple of his closest friends shared his new life with him, hanging out together, not going out much. More than once I was happy to see some of his other friends show up like old times at the beginning of an evening, only to leave a few minutes later.

I didn't want to think what I was thinking—it was so preposterous. My daughter unfortunately confirmed my fears when she much-after-the-fact told me her father had given her an ounce of pot to take to a party of her peers to try and sell; she had been too embarrassed to ask anyone, and instead brought the pot home and told her father nobody wanted any. Her father also told her he was growing pot, and when she went away to college, she could sell it for him. Even though most of her friends were at the age where they were not strangers to wine and weed and they had to go somewhere to buy it, my daughter knew she did not want to be involved in what her father wanted her to do. I am grateful for this.

I had to face my dark suspicions that the purpose of the *High Times* magazines and the pages of information off the Internet and possibly even the short visits from my son's friends were all related to marijuana being supplied by my husband. I also believed my husband's plans had not yet fully gotten off the ground—and my vigilance and my daughter's concerns had tripped him up enough to prevent things from going too far. But I was now very clear about my husband's intentions and felt a real panic as I contemplated the possibilities and various outcomes if he were to be successful in what he wanted to accomplish. I felt physically ill when I realized the extent of the secrecy and lies, and I began to truly wonder about the sanity of my husband. There had been many clues, but I hadn't wanted to believe all I was now forced to accept with great pain.

Meanwhile, one of my husband's sisters who lived a couple of hours away had commiserated with her poor brother for having been forced to pull his pot plants from the basement, and she had agreed to grow some plants for him. More secrecy invaded our lives as communications arrived about the plants and plans for splitting them, each apparently to take half. When I questioned my husband, he told me without skipping a beat that because he knew how much I liked peonies, he was having his sister grow some for me. Needless to say, I never saw any peonies. My son and daughter had been told about their aunt's pot crop, I discovered later, and the mother of one of my son's friends told me she had heard about my husband's sister's plants from her son. I couldn't fathom what my husband was thinking to be doing this and trusting sixteen–year-olds to keep quiet about it. I told everything to my therapist, but he was in a powerless position, and at that point the CPS worker was still on vacation. My husband's outbursts became more frequent, and my daughter and I hunkered down, waiting for help that never arrived.

The house was clearly divided between two camps, and neither side was budging. I was amazed at my husband's stubborn willingness to risk everything for his right to do exactly as he pleased. The fact that our drug counselor was sitting around with his colleagues discussing his outrageous resistance, and that CPS had been notified as a result, did not faze him. His actions became even more combative and menacing, as if increased punishment would force my daughter and I to cease and desist. His past experiences with my requests for change in our relationship had convinced him I would only go so far in trying to challenge him before I gave up and went back to living my life unaltered. But he had to be noticing now that our son and daughter had entered into the equation my battle tactics had changed, and I was no longer avoiding therapy and thus the risk of exposure just to save his job.

His behavior with my son had become more blatant rather than less so. Now when I arrived at home from an outing, my husband and son would be together in the garage or in the basement doing "man stuff." When they returned to the house with red eyes and smelling of beer, they brushed past me in hurried attempts to disappear into their rooms uninterrupted. This was the result of two years of attempts to address the situation and find solutions we could live with as a family.

It's not that the therapist was doing nothing—at least my daughter and I had an outlet to express what to us had become almost unspeakable. I was surprised to find out later how little my daughter had revealed about her home situation to her friends, because when I was her age I told my friends everything. She later told me she was simply too embarrassed. She watched the fathers of her friends dote on them, always showing interest in their lives and feelings. She believed these girls could not possibly understand what she was going through. I have been fortunate throughout this mess to have had some good friends in whom I could confide, but they also felt completely powerless to actually do anything. My mother tried to speak to my husband, so upset was she at what was happening to her beloved grandchildren; but he defended his position and insisted that smoking pot was the one and only thing he did wrong and he wanted to continue and would continue, whether other people liked it or not. Although I had some support, most people knew nothing about what was going on. Living the lie was hard and as time went on I became more inept and unenthusiastic about maintaining a false identity. I felt more and more like just fading into the woodwork when I was out, adhering to an "if you don't ask, I won't tell" policy of social interaction with those I was not willing to confide in—which was most people.

The therapist continued working with my son during regular weekly visits (they were originally supposed to be biweekly, but my son kept slipping out of appointments), trying all the while to convince him to do rehab—treatment that would essentially involve renouncing marijuana and alcohol completely and attending twelve-step meetings. This could begin on an in-patient or out-patient basis, would involve urine screens, and needed the cooperation of my son. He was not court mandated and I wasn't willing to force him, believing it would backfire and make things worse. He was, after all, very close to the age of consent and I did not want to alienate him completely and have him walk out on treatment altogether.

At one point the therapist called an in-patient clinic to see if they had a bed, and they did, but my son would not agree to treatment. My son was very clever and spent the whole summer leading the therapist and me on, explaining he didn't want to quit for the summer, because, you know, *summer.* He told us he would be happy to give the total abstinence thing a chance in the fall. The therapist said he'd never done it that way before, continuing to see someone while he or she was gradually getting ready to quit, but he agreed to wait as he had nothing else up his sleeve. I had turned down his suggestion of putting my son on PINS (a program for young people who are misbehaving that would have involved a probation officer and urine testing) because of my very real fear something this drastic would chase my son away. I had serious doubts about the efficacy of any plan at this point and was happy to pass the responsibility off to the therapist, hoping along with him that the agreement for the fall plan would hold.

When fall came, my son announced his decision not to give up using alcohol and marijuana completely. My son said he'd only promised to *think* about giving up pot (and alcohol? I don't even remember), and he had decided he didn't want to quit after all. I couldn't force him because he was at the age where he could, after all, just walk out the door. I was afraid that if I forced anything on him, he would go off with my husband into never-never land for lost boys.

Communication between my husband and me had reached a total impasse. I was looking forward to beginning school, to beginning a new life, but with great trepidation. At this juncture, I believed my husband was crazy, and I was buckling under the strain of trying to protect my children and myself from harm. I even managed to tear cartilage in my knee that summer before graduate school started and spent months limping around; I was, in general, feeling pretty much like a wounded animal. A divorce between so-called normal parents is difficult enough for most kids. I knew the upcoming year or so would be overwhelmingly difficult to bear for all of us, and I could see my making the impaired decision to avoid this pain too many times in the past had led us to this agonizing situation. I could not back down now.

I had contacted the second therapist in early spring and by the middle of summer nothing much had happened except an acceleration of anger coming from my husband and son, who both felt unfairly scrutinized. After all, complained my son, it was not as if his sister and her friends have never used alcohol or smoked pot. It's not as if his mother, he added, who came of age during the hippie generation in California, has never done these things. What was the difference? The difference was the excess.

Because it is illegal, marijuana comes with the extra burden of having to defend one's right to smoke it at all; it is also necessary to keep the smoking of pot secret, which is hard. One of the reasons marijuana has remained such a popular device for youthful rebellion is that when used in moderation it does not produce the more obvious effects of alcohol intoxication on the mind or body. Many people who have smoked pot even for long periods have been able to give it up or modify their use of it without suffering serious consequences—if they have used it moderately. One can get totally involved—be a complete stoner even—and then come up for air and join the establishment with little or no harm done. By the time many people realize the damage alcohol, heroin, cocaine, or amphetamines have inflicted on their bodies, it is often too late, and multiple organs have been diminished or destroyed. It is no wonder there are cultures that eschew alcohol in favor of the cannabis plant for relaxation and other medicinal purposes. It has been decades now since the youth in this country began challenging laws governing cannabis.

As each generation matures, there are more people who choose not to renounce all youthful rebellion and continue to engage in the careful but casual use of marijuana. There are also people who become excessively involved with the use of this plant. It is not surprising issues arise when a person who has shown a tendency toward dependency or addiction engages in the excessive smoking of marijuana, if that is their mood-altering substance of choice. The fact that pot is illegal creates a lot of difficulties for the addict, including maintaining a supply and paying for it. There is no doubt in my mind that my husband's sharing of his supply with his children had created a need for more marijuana than he was able to pay for; many of the awful things that were happening in our home were a result of his desperation to find solutions to this problem so he could continue along his chosen path.

Certain problems exist because we live in a culture of total hypocrisy concerning the use of drugs—legal and illegal. There is to date no real cultural agreement as to which drugs are harmful and not harmful, and which should be illegal or legal. Many people believe alcohol and cigarettes are among our most dangerous drugs, and recent studies have shown prescription drugs to be a leading cause of death, right after heart attacks, strokes, and cancer. Most people do not have a problem listing heroin, cocaine, amphetamines, and ecstasy, among others, as dangerous drugs, but many have taken exception to prevailing attitudes about marijuana use, believing it to be the lesser of many evils, if it is to be considered an evil at all.

Many believe wholeheartedly in the efficacy of what they believe to be a wondrous plant bestowed upon us by Mother Nature, and attribute all sorts of health remedies to its bounty of leaves, flowers, roots, and seeds. Indeed, the red eyes characteristic of marijuana use are because of blood vessels dilating, reducing pressure on the eye. This reduction of pressure is credited with saving eyesight and preventing the ravages of glaucoma, which now causes 15 percent of blindness in our country. The Narcotics Act of 1914, which did not go so far as to prohibit narcotics but instead imposed a stamp tax, excluded marijuana because it was so commonly used as a medicine, especially for glaucoma and migraine sufferers. Many antidrug reformers have conceded that marijuana is not as significant a problem as opiates or cocaine (especially considering that there has never been an overdose death attributed to marijuana use alone) and some even allow that cannabis contains medicinal properties. Statements from cancer patients concerning marijuana use claim that the difference between using cannabis and not using it is the difference between living with cancer and dying from cancer; a recent poll showed that three-quarters of older Americans support the legalization of marijuana for medical use, but the government that is supposed to represent us still says "no."

With all the research my son had done on his now favorite subject, it would have been impossible to convince him that smoking pot was a terrible or especially harmful thing to do, except, in his case, for potential damage to his lungs. He lived in an age when many of the songs he listened to and movies he watched glorified the use and even the cultivation of marijuana. I had always realized it was likely both of my kids would experiment with drugs, and I hoped it would go no further than alcohol or marijuana. What my son didn't understand was the fact that we objected to the excessiveness of his behavior. Yes, his peers were experimenting too—but most of them had it enough under control to keep up with their studies and go to school regularly. I was tired of speaking to parents who didn't have a clue as to what was going on in their children's teen world, as if by pretending that it wasn't happening, it wasn't. I also knew that the vast majority if not all of the kids my son hung out with had both parents trying to steer them through the minefield of adolescence, and even if they were divorced, they worked together on goals for their children. How many kids wouldn't sign up for the parent who gives them beer and pot even on school nights, and then helps them lie to their mother to hide it? Perhaps many would be like my daughter, who at first enjoyed her invitational status, but finally broke away because she knew what she was doing was harmful for everyone involved.

An old friend from my high school, the son of two school teachers, is currently spending the rest of his life in jail because he was caught using and dealing amphetamines. His fate was decided, I was told, by the "three strikes, you're out" law. His crimes weren't violent or heinous, but the need for an addict to get his drug often leads to dealing, and dealing is a big no-no in our culture, even though if one believes what one reads our own government has knowingly benefited from international drug smuggling. At any rate, a person becomes a dealer the first time they turn to a friend and suggest they buy an ounce of weed together and split it, maybe selling a third share to another friend to help pay for it, with that other friend perhaps paying five dollars more for not having to go through the hassle of procuring the illegal substance.

I can think of few things sadder than the fate of this old friend, especially as he was one of the kindest, nicest people I'd ever known. It just doesn't seem right that he must spend his entire life behind bars—a life essentially wasted. I am sure his parents (his father was once my history teacher) are brokenhearted. It is painful enough to deal with trying to save a child from addiction, but the thought of my son ending up in jail for dealing was more than I could bear. I realized I had reached the point of no turning back with my husband, and I was determined to fight him in whatever way was necessary to try and save our children. At the time, I had no idea what that would come to mean, no clue of the destruction that would come to pass.

My friends and family had varying opinions on whether or not I should force my son into rehab against his will. Some felt I should send him to rehab immediately; others maintained I should kick him out of the house. And there were those who felt I should give him lots of love and do nothing. None of these appealed to me. What I wanted was moderation.

Adolescents in all families rebel and experiment; parents hope they have taught their children to love themselves enough to make the right judgments when the time comes. For me it has been and still is the most difficult stage of parenting so far—letting my children make their own decisions. As a parent familiar with the effects of both alcohol and marijuana, I have always feared alcohol more, and have considered marijuana to be the least harmful substance with which teenagers could experiment. They are much less likely to be mangled in an auto accident if they have ingested cannabis and not alcohol. The amount of damage they could cause to their bodies in a few short years of alcohol addiction is much greater than with cannabis used in moderation, with self-love and careful judgment. Unfortunately, moderate usage was not what I was dealing with, and the fact that my son was asthmatic was making the situation far worse. I couldn't understand why my husband was not concerned about this issue. Wasn't he worried about losing his son forever? I sure was.

Faced with what appeared to be an overwhelming fascination with and dependency on alcohol and pot on the part of my son, initiated and fueled by my husband's interventions, I found I had no other choice but to continue working with the drug counselor, even though my son's attendance in therapy had become spotty. My daughter also saw the counselor less frequently, partly because she was busy but also because talking about "it" upset her. She had lost a lot by coming clean with me, and even though she was still firmly committed to getting help for her brother, she often found the entire subject too painful. She was still an adolescent herself and wanted her old life back with all the normal teenage problems that had once seemed so difficult. The only ones who didn't seem to want change were my husband and son.

CHAPTER 5

The Big Crash

The summer was long, muggy, and tense. I continued seeing the therapist—someone had to go!—and for that I was punished by both husband and son in myriad ways. They felt that all of our problems had started after I contacted someone who was willing to take our situation seriously, unlike the first therapist, whose effect on the situation was more like sprinkling sugar on yeast. "Normal" communication ceased to exist as each side geared for its own imaginary battles. The fear quotient in the house was high, and neither my daughter nor I felt secure. Decisions had to be made about divorce, rehab, custody, and so forth, and the acrimony that often invades these subjects was enveloping our lives. CPS looming in the background upped the ante by quite a lot, and as is my husband's nature and style, he did not want to talk about it. He didn't feel his behavior was unreasonable; he certainly had no intention of changing.

It began like any other antihalcyon day, hazy and morose with the promise of a lot of heat. I went for a walk with a friend and gave the usual report of daily occurrences in a house divided, as she reported on tidings in her life. As usual, it was difficult to accept advice from a well-meaning friend, as each person had a different twist and moral interpretation on events that all agreed were horrid. This particular friend thought I should tell my husband and son to leave, but I could not abandon my son. Even those few friends I knew who smoked pot were aghast at my husband's behavior, feeling betrayed. They wanted to live in a world where the use of cannabis was accepted as the choice of responsible people; they didn't want someone like my husband on their team, screwing up their chances of being accepted as *normal.*

Among my responsibilities in our house had always been the handling of all the money issues that came into our lives, individually or as a family:

monthly bills, school and town taxes, insurance, school payments, mortgage, the IRS, allowances—everything. If it arrived at our house in an envelope, I dealt with it. I was the bank—paying bills and doling out money to family members on a regular basis. Building a new house had increased financial tension, requiring vigilance and resourcefulness to keep bills paid. The combined tragedy of my husband's brother's death and our move to a new house, with new lives and responsibilities, had taken its toll on all of us. New financial planning on a more humble level was required while we caught up, and it became increasingly difficult for me to dole out money to each and every family member and cause without creating a deficit. We live in an area where school and property taxes are hefty. In August, anticipating the six-thousand-dollar school tax bill that would be arriving in September, I decided to check the account the money was resting in, awaiting its liberation. Much to my horror, I discovered the money was gone. It had been removed over the past three months by my husband.

I had smelled expensive pot as of late on the porch, my husband's favorite summer hangout, and I now knew where he had gotten the money for such an extravagance. I was continually giving him money from another account to use for his daily needs, but it was not enough to keep him in expensive marijuana. Discussing the situation later with some friends, they couldn't believe he could spend six thousand dollars on pot in three months. They said he must be on something else. But I told them to do the math. Anyone smoking a couple ounces or more a week of good weed among friends (or their own children!) can easily run up a six-thousand-dollar bill in three months. I never questioned that it was anything but pot, and my husband did not deny it; he had nothing else to show for the money. He had removed money from accounts in the past to finance his excessive pot smoking, but it had been a while since anything like that had happened, as he knew this particular activity had come very close to destroying our relationship. My husband's financial problems predated our relationship and had often been a bone of contention, but I thought we had reached a truce in that area.

I had to wait all day to confront my husband about the six thousand dollars, and it was not a wait that alleviated stress. When he arrived home, I demanded to know what had happened to the money that had been saved for school taxes, and he could not deny he had spent it on marijuana. I understood him too well for him to be able to lie his way out of this one. He started bellowing and ranting and raving, and claimed he had a right to spend the money on anything he wanted. As usual, he tried to make something he had done my fault, leaving me to figure out how I was going to pay the school tax bill, which would arrive in less than a month. At some point the anger spilled over into a space that made both my daughter and me very uncomfortable, and we ended up fleeing the house, without time to grab our packed bags. Not knowing what to do, we headed toward our therapist's office, which was not much more than a mile away. Unfortunately, he had left for the day, but we were given a number by the office to call, which we did.

When he heard the story of what had taken place, and how physically threatened we had felt by my husband's bellicose behavior, he once again told us to go to the police. He did not see things getting any better until we got some real support and encouraged us to take this action, for documentation purposes at least. We were very upset, and although it went against the grain of everything I believed in or wanted to happen, going to the police seemed the only option left. The police station was less than a block away from the therapist's office, and we walked over. The police officer in charge asked a lot of questions, and when they heard we were told to come over by someone at the drug counseling place, it opened up a whole new line of questioning. At first we were very careful about what we said, still busy protecting the status quo; but they were very clever and promised that nothing would be used against us, and after a while, we began to trust them and believe they really wanted to help us as a family. They could see we were upset and were desperate for some help.

At some point, after some skillful questioning by the police officer, again offering immunity, I made mention of the plants. They knew I was concerned about my husband's job and had reassured me before I revealed this information they didn't want him to lose his job either. I reasoned and hoped that since there were only five female plants left in the ground (the males had been pulled to help create sinsemilla), the charge would be a misdemeanor slap on the wrist and would finally bring needed help to our beleaguered family—such as mandated treatment for my husband, at least. I pleaded with them to not let this impact my husband's employment—the man needed help, not the punishment of job loss. But my husband needed to be forced to stop, as he was truly destroying our son and our family.

My revealing this secret was a last-ditch effort to bring things under control. The policeman in charge assured us once again he did not want my husband to lose his job either—that he understood my fear and that I had done the only thing possible under the circumstances. I felt that finally help was near. When we left the station, my daughter expressed surprise I had told them about the plants, but I was still feeling it had been a positive thing to do and would in the long run prevent more misery, possibly even saving my son (and husband) from prison or other ruination.

A couple of days later, my daughter was driven home by her friend's mother, who is also a good friend of mine. When they arrived at our driveway, a police car was waiting at the bottom, and followed them up. The officers had already gone up into the property and removed the plants. They told my daughter to have me call them when I arrived home. Later my daughter told me that having the police on the property had made her feel safe for the first time in a long time, and how strange that had felt. I felt sad, realizing that was how I felt, too.

When I contacted the police, they told me they had bad news, which turned out to be *really* bad news. The plants had just begun to show their tiny white female hairs, which would eventually turn into buds, the smokable part of the plant. All the rest—leaves, stems, roots—were good for rope and clothes, perhaps, but worthless as anything smokable, as only the buds contain a sufficient amount of the active ingredient THC. As all five plants had just begun to bud, nothing had yet developed on them to smoke. The resin that comes later was not yet present; there was no THC. It would take another couple of months for buds to form that would be ready to smoke and have enough THC content to make people want to smoke them. The police weighed the entire five plants—leaves, stems, roots, and wet dirt—and said the weight came out to be eleven pounds, and anything over ten pounds was by law a *felony*. They were going to charge my husband—and did—with not one but two felonies (one for growing, one for possession), when there wasn't enough smokable pot for even one joint on all of the plants combined. My heart sank. I felt totally betrayed. What had happened? How could this be?

Hunter Thompson, always interested in the law, began his book *Songs of the Doomed* with a quote warning that he who goes to the law "holds a wolf by the ears." The Kafkaesque nightmare that had been my life for the past couple of years had just gotten worse—a lot worse. To the suffering I had already endured was now added the overwhelming burden of guilt and even more fear. Waves of panic and nausea consumed me. When someone reads in the paper that someone was caught with eleven pounds of marijuana, they picture kilos or bags of marijuana buds ready to sell. Five marijuana plants would produce nowhere near that amount of marijuana to smoke, even if they had been mature. First of all, when the freshly picked plants dry, they will weigh considerably less, as anyone who has ever dried a flower for a keepsake knows. Nobody in law enforcement, from the police to lawyers, paid any attention to my protests about the dishonesty of the charges. The lawyer I eventually hired for advice said that if my husband's case went to court it would eventually come out that it was only five plants, but it usually was not a good idea to go that far. It was better to settle out of court, he said, so you would not run the risk that something really awful might happen, like jail time. That's a real Catch-22, and it's one of the nightmares of our legal system: If you admit guilt and plea-bargain you're better off than if you fight for your innocence. A man who is growing only five fairly measly plants has to shut up and confess to growing eleven pounds of mature marijuana buds if he does not want to risk the possibility of an excessively harsh punishment. I felt like we were being welcomed into the poor man's justice system.

The few people who knew the truth—I was too ashamed to tell most friends the exact details of what had happened—kept reassuring me I had done the right thing. I will never know whether or not I prevented something worse from happening by doing what I did, or whether things could have been worked out without this tragedy; I do know that I had reached the limit of abuse I was willing to take, and a feeling of action just took over, almost without asking my permission. I had a new understanding of abused women and their often criticized position of silence (why don't they just leave?) when they or their children are being victimized; the alternative to silence is just another form of pain. To have believed I could get help for my family without paying a severe penalty within this present day social/criminal justice system was truly naïve on my part. My husband had understood that making me fear the consequences of the law would force me to acquiesce and tolerate his unacceptable behavior; he just hadn't understood the concept of "enough is enough." He was trusting that I would never crack under the strain, and by overestimating my ability to absorb and bury massive amounts of pain and anger, he put us all in danger.

To add to the general grief factor that my husband might lose his job, health insurance, and pension was the fear—no, *terror*—my husband would find out who turned him in. Of course both my husband and son heavily suspected my daughter and me because of the timing of the incident, right after the fight about the missing six thousand dollars. We felt safer denying any part in it. I felt totally betrayed by the police. They knew the difference between five plants and eleven pounds of marijuana—probably about ten pounds, once the plants were completely matured, harvested, and dried. A couple of months later my daughter ran into one of the arresting officers at the local diner, and he asked her how we were all doing. He mentioned to her that he had grown up in a family where his father was abusive, and he didn't like to see it happen to anyone. He also asked her how her brother was doing. I understood his concerns, but did he have any concept of the impact his decision to put a thumb on the scale, or whatever, was going to have on our lives? Did he really care if we lost our income and health insurance? As victims, we now felt invisible as the system geared to squash our abuser, partially destroying each one of us in the process.

The police had promised help and leniency and then betrayed us. It probably looked good for them to have made the "haul," totally handed over to them by a naïve mother wanting to save her family from potentially devastating troubles ahead. After the double felony arrest, I went down to the police station and begged them for mercy, reminding the sergeant of what he had said a few days before, which had encouraged me to reveal the plants. He basically said, "Tough!" The safe feeling my daughter and I had momentarily felt once the police got involved was gone—it had all been an illusion. It was back to them against us—although I wasn't quite sure who "them" or "us" was anymore. At some point I got the courage to ask the sergeant if there was anything he could do to prevent this from going into the newspapers. He said there was nothing he could do. Within a few days all three local newspapers, covering an area of a couple hundred square miles, carried the story of my husband's double felony arrest for growing eleven pounds of marijuana. No mention was made that there were only five plants, and that the weight mentioned was that of immature, wet, completely unsmokable cannabis plants.

A year of a new kind of hell was about to start, one with the focus on lawyers and court dates and trying to save my husband's zero-drug-tolerance job of twenty-two years. The only good part was that the situation finally led to my husband's moving out of the house. Although that made my son very unhappy, the decline in overt tension around the house was palpable. During the following year my son's behavior slowly improved. He was still very angry at all that had happened and placed no blame on his father for anything. He found his sister and me culpable for any ill wind that blew.

A new problem that resulted from the chaos was my son's refusal to return to therapy. My son despised his therapist and blamed him for his father's arrest and all of the problems our family was now having because of it. He didn't know the details of what had taken place, but he blamed him anyway. I told my son I knew it wasn't the therapist who turned his father in, but in truth, had we not gone down to his office that fateful day I doubt very much we would have ended up at the police station. In fact, I know we wouldn't even have considered it, and I would have accepted the argument and missing property tax money as one more bitter pill to swallow, as I'd done many times before.

I have often wondered whether I would have been better off ignoring the therapist's suggestion that day to go to the police, as I had several times in the past. I also shudder to think of what could have happened if I hadn't gone. To be sure, going to the therapist stirred up a lot of anger, but that anger was already stirred up, and had already made my daughter and I feel physically threatened as well as emotionally blackmailed. This wasn't simply a situation of a father and a son sharing an occasional beer and a joint. All that had happened and was happening was just too unbelievable. If I had mentioned this absurd scenario to my husband when we first met, I am sure he would have been as outraged as I am now at the thought of a father doing such a thing to his family. He had clearly snapped. Whatever it was that had made him change so drastically, he was as usual more than willing to blame everything on me; he claimed it was my fault because I had "rejected him," causing him to go off the deep end, so to speak. As there was some truth in what he was saying, despite the obvious what-came-first-the-chicken-or-the-egg scenario, it made me feel even more shame and guilt for all that had transpired. Isn't it always mother's fault?

CHAPTER 6

Lessons Unlearned

My husband's double felony arrests had paved the way for our relationship to come to a head and for him to move out of the house. He was worried about his job and urine testing, and as he coincidentally had two weeks of vacation starting the very next day, he made plans to go upstate and hide out. My daughter and I, terrified he would lose his job, were busy buying detox formulas for him from various health food stores. These products have become a major business with the advent of urine testing at places of employment. Unfortunately, they didn't work for my husband; he had too much THC in his system.

The CPS caseworker investigating my husband was back from her vacation but had still not managed to connect with him. Our therapist called the CPS worker on the day my husband's arrest appeared in the papers to apprise her of this new development. The CPS worker quickly called my husband and hurriedly made arrangements to come by the house, where she found my husband with a suitcase all packed and ready to go. The CPS worker interviewed my husband at the kitchen table. Sitting in another room, I listened while my husband told the CPS worker he had only smoked pot with his son once, and it had been the biggest mistake of his life—and he would never do it again. It was unbelievable after all we had gone through he was able to minimize it to that extent, even in a purposeful lie.

My husband told her he was going to move out of the house that very day, and his packed bag sat in the room to prove it. He also told her he was going to relocate upstate permanently. "Okay," the CPS worker said. "If you're moving upstate, I'm going to close your case." Sort of as an afterthought, she added, "You're not taking your son, are you?" My husband replied in the negative. His case was closed and he was essentially given carte blanche to continue behaving as he pleased. I learned that he reported to my son within minutes of the CPS worker's one and only visit with him that they were off the hook—case closed.

My husband returned from upstate two weeks later and resumed living in the house without explanation or discussion. I was too frightened and full of guilt to protest. He had detoxed enough while he was upstate to pass a urine test at his place of employment and resumed smoking pot with my son. He awaited the decision of the courts as to his fate and the fate of his job. We were all on pins and needles.

I began sleeping on the back porch; there was an early cold snap that year and some nights were freezing, but I simply would not move back into the bedroom. For me, we were very clearly separated. The extreme nature of his indulgences and my inability to cope, which some would call enabling, had resulted in our arrival at this particular juncture, and I felt he should leave the house. My son was still attending high school and needed the stability of a parent who wasn't getting him stoned and drunk. My daughter needed to be not afraid of the man living in the house. I needed that, too. His role as parent and husband seemed a shadowy illusion from the past.

To complicate matters, I was just starting my first year of graduate school, and I knew I was not going to be home a lot of the time. I knew it would be disastrous if my husband continued to live in the house with us. After much cajoling and arguing, I finally told him that if CPS knew he was back in the house, our son, who was under eighteen, could be taken from us, which was true. He finally agreed to leave. My son was angry and upset, and although my daughter and I both felt enormous relief, it was a relief mixed with sadness. We were no longer a family. Or we were going to have to learn how to be a family all over again—a family after divorce.

The police had assured me on that fateful day that my husband would never find out who had turned him in. But after they slapped him with two felony charges for five plants, they informed me there was a possibility the district attorney would have to reveal this information after all. I couldn't believe they hadn't told me about this earlier, and I found myself once again pleading with the head cop for the mercy that had earlier been promised us.

I had spent the last two years with therapists who had no power to do anything real, and this lack of threatening activity coming from the outside had actually increased my husband's resolve to undermine my efforts, making him overly self-confident. I learned much later he had even planned and encouraged my son to look into his grandparents' medicine cabinet for my father's painkillers—OxyContin, which they both knew to be a highly controversial drug-of-the-moment. My daughter became alarmed when she found out he had stolen some of the pills and warned her brother in front of their father not to drink any alcohol with the painkillers. She told me later her father interjected, "You can have some alcohol with them, just not too much!" Knowing that my husband was teaching my son to lie and steal and sneak around was almost as painful as watching him turn our son into an addict. *What was he thinking?*

It had been many months since I had first insisted my husband go to the doctor to check out certain symptoms he had been having, such as back and stomach pain, which I knew could be signs of cancer from friends who had succumbed to the disease. It would have been a relief to find some organic cause for his behavior, such as a brain tumor. What other explanation was there—I was married to a sociopath?

With my husband finally out of the house—he moved in with his daughter from a previous marriage who lived about a half-hour away—things slowly began to calm down. My son's angry outbursts continued to be less frequent, although powerful and devastating when they did occur. He now had as part of his arsenal angry demands for facts about who had turned his father in.

It was, and still is, difficult to face this issue. I can go around and around on it, but I will never know what might have happened to my son if he had become the dealer his father was training him to be. I know my son will never admit to what was going on, but I have no doubt my fears were founded. There was so much evidence, and my daughter's testimony was all I needed to be sure.

At one point I had to drive to the city and speak to my husband's lawyer. He had called me several times and insisted I come in and tell him step-by-step what happened. He said if I really wanted to help my husband keep his job, it was essential I speak to him in person. I asked him if he was allowed to keep something I revealed to him from his client, and he said he was not. He said not to tell him anything I did not want my husband to hear, although at the same time he indicated the truth would eventually come out. He knew. I know he knew, and he knew I knew he knew, but nothing was said at that meeting about who went to the police. He asked me why I had not just pulled the plants. I told the lawyer I was too afraid of my husband at that point and had already tried dealing with him on a rational basis for a prolonged period of time. I knew my husband's ability to act charming and innocent would prevent the lawyer from seeing what kind of man he was really dealing with, and I decided not to waste much time trying to defend my actions to him.

I could have told him that I thought, under normal circumstances, people should be allowed to grow enough marijuana on their property for their own personal use, but I didn't. People get lost in the subtleties. They think something is either always good or always bad where so-called "drugs" are concerned. Trying to explain my belief system to people was often confusing. A person could have a serious problem with alcohol, a far more dangerous drug than marijuana, yet the idea of substituting marijuana for alcohol to assist in alcohol withdrawal and abstinence would be considered blasphemy under current social conditions. The reefer madness mentality from decades past still influences because people are afraid to admit knowing anything about an illegal or disapproved of "drug" for fear of retribution—legal, social, and/or economic. It is hard to fight this mentality because people do not want to expose themselves in a culture that has been overly punitive and arbitrary about "drug" issues.

I left the lawyer's office feeling worse than ever. At this point my husband had been suspended from his job because of his felony arrests, and I had held out hope this lawyer would be able to fight the charges based on the fact there were only five plants and they had not yet matured into buds with sufficient THC content to render them smokable. How naïve! There should not have been any felony arrests, but now that there had been two, a sort of madness set in. Suddenly I was faced with the reality of the situation: Income, health insurance, pension—*everything*—was seriously threatened. It was unbelievable. First, you can't get anybody to pay attention or help, and then all at once the attention and punishment is overwhelming—and for growing five plants of a species that grows wild alongside roads and fields in many parts of the country. It wasn't fair, and we still as a family were not getting any help. We were just being punished—all of us. And to think many of my fellow citizens would call it justice.

I decided to hire my own lawyer; I needed to start the divorce proceedings anyway. I paid him to call the district attorney handling the case and try to plead my husband's case to him—to let him know how harmful it would be to all family members if my husband lost his job. Fortunately, we were given the opportunity for a short period of time to pay for a reduced health insurance policy until his case was decided. I found out that if my husband was found guilty of any felony, he would absolutely lose his job and most of his benefits—apparently those were the rules at his place of employment.

For weeks after leaving the office of my husband's lawyer, I could barely eat or sleep. I would awaken after only a couple hours of sleep from terrible nightmares. I could not forgive myself. My lawyer told me I had done the right thing—that sometimes you have to amputate a limb to save the body. Fortunately, the few people who knew the *whole* truth all believed I had done not only the right thing but the only thing that could have been done under the circumstances. That helped a lot, but I still suffered terribly knowing I was responsible for having taken this action against my husband, which ironically prevented any of us from getting the help we needed as soon as we lost our health insurance for good.

Although my husband had moved out, he still spent a lot of time at the house, coming over during the day when I was at my fieldwork and nights when I was in class; sometimes he even came over when I was at home. He and my son would hang out in the garage together, occasionally glancing surreptitiously up at the house to see if I was watching. I was lied to about my husband's visits when I was out of the house, but the clues were everywhere, and my son was usually sound asleep and smelling like pot and alcohol by the time I arrived home from class around ten at night. More confrontations and more denials ensued.

One day in October, a couple months after my husband's arrest, I happened to notice my son go down to an unused van on our property, which had once belonged to his deaf uncle, and I watched as he took something out of it. Later, I walked down to the van to investigate and found it full of pot plants, just harvested and in need of drying. An electric fan was set up, run off an extension cord from the garage, to help in the process. The buds on some of the plants had been removed and were drying on trays. I realized immediately these plants must be my husband's share of the crop his sister was growing for him upstate.

The next morning while driving my son to school, I broached the subject of the pot in the van and was met with the usual outrage. He said he wished I would stop making such a big deal about everything. I asked him if he thought perhaps his father was taking some awfully big risks, considering what was going on in his life. I told him I wanted the pot plants out of the van and off the property immediately. When my daughter came home from school that day with a friend, they found my son cleaning out the van, putting the pot in bags for his father to pick up. My daughter asked her brother if this was their aunt's pot, and he replied in the affirmative.

As outrageous as it was that my husband would dare to bring his sister's marijuana onto our property when he wasn't even living there anymore, this was not to be the end of the insanity. Several weeks passed, and one day I returned home to find that the electricity had been temporarily shut off because of an auto accident nearby—someone had hit a pole. I commented to my son that because there was no water coming out of the faucets, the pressure pump in the basement must have shut down when the electricity went off and would have to be reprimed. I could tell immediately something was going on by the way he tensed up. We have a relatively small basement that houses not much more than the furnace and water shutoff. There is no reason for me to go down there on a regular basis, especially as the only entrance is from an outside door. I went down the basement to reset the pump, and decided to check out the spot where my husband had previously been growing his pot plants.

I could not believe what I found. He had totally perfected the walled-off space, so not even a sliver of light escaped into the surrounding darkness. As I jimmied open the door, carefully closed and concealed, I was met with a blast of light and the vision of a new crop of marijuana plants. If I had any doubts that my daughter's and my trip to the police at the urging of our therapist was necessary, finding two new marijuana crops in a matter of weeks—one harvested and one still growing—helped to dispel those thoughts. I couldn't believe my husband was behaving in such a manner when his job was at stake. It was also upsetting that my son took it all in stride, willing at a moment's notice to defend any and all of his father's actions. I confronted my husband when he came to pick up our son, and once again had to force him to get pot plants out of the basement.

Months later, the oil company called and asked if I wanted a routine cleaning done on my furnace. Without thinking, I told them yes, that would be fine. I was so busy it never even occurred to me to think about the basement and what clues might be left from my husband's endeavors. One truck and then two arrived to do this usually simple job, and after a while one of the guys came up and told me they had come across the "weirdest thing." While cleaning the chimney to the furnace, they found several lights that appeared to have been used to thaw frozen pipes, but the strange thing was they couldn't find any water pipes in the area. He just couldn't figure out why all those lights were there; he looked truly perplexed, or was he just letting me know I should take care of it? In a small town like ours, it was possible he knew our story. My husband knew I always took care of filling the oil tank and having the furnace cleaned. What was he thinking by putting me in that situation? The oil guys could have discovered the pot plants growing down there if I hadn't first, and then what would have happened?

My husband had never sought nor received therapeutic help from anyone after his brother's death. His unwillingness or inability to talk about the unexpected tragedy must have made dealing with his grief extremely difficult. In fact, research in the field of grieving says that not dealing with death or loss makes it difficult or impossible to resolve—that the grief will fester and disturb rather than heal and integrate. My husband had helped his brother achieve his goal of hearing, and he felt invested in and probably somewhat responsible for the final outcome. One day, more than a year after his brother's death, my husband spoke one sentence: "I should have taken him to the hospital when he called." That was all he could bear to say. I knew that this thought, now a sentence, must have been in his mind all along, during his months of silence. I not only felt empathy for my husband, but I missed his brother as well. He was truly a unique and special person, who died because of his enormous lust for life. His dying, just weeks after we moved into our new house, left us all saddened and brittle. I believe it made my husband feel insecure and lost. The mirror that had most reflected his maleness was that brother, and my husband was not emotionally able to resist plucking his son out of late childhood/early adolescence to try and replace him. I'm not sure he expected such a strong resistance from me, as he seemed to think it was his right as a man and a father to suddenly take over the raising of our son.

Looking back, I can think of many things I could have done differently; but for anything to have succeeded it would have required the cooperation of my husband, and that was clearly not happening. My daughter and I could not go on the way things were—feeling threatened and trapped—and the reality is that life—not plans—suddenly took over. We had been pushed over the edge and suddenly snapped back—it was a law-of-physics thing and happens all the time. It had just never happened to us—not anything with this intensity anyway.

My now ex-husband's double felony arrest for growing five marijuana plants happened more than two years ago. The outcome was not good. My husband lost his job and half of his pension, which he is keeping in full (I was entitled by law to half), in exchange for me keeping the house and the mortgage. My ex-husband does not pay support payments of any kind, believing that since everything was my fault, he shouldn't have to help support me and his children. He does come over and fix things occasionally when they break, which is a huge help as I am not in a position to hire anyone at this time. He went through a period of being angry, but things seem to have settled down a bit. I suspect he does understand that his behavior was largely responsible for how things turned out, although he would never admit it. The pressure all of this has put on me to reinvent myself has been enormous, to say nothing of what it must be doing to our children, who are at important developmental stages in their lives. There is no question the unfortunate outcome of all that transpired has made life more difficult for the entire family.

Many likely do not understand why, in spite of everything that has happened in the past few years, I am still pro-legalization of marijuana. I truly believe it is a safer substance than the other options available, and used moderately (definitely the key) it could help supplant the much more dangerous culture of alcoholism. Marijuana is already used by so many millions of people in this country it seems a shame that instead of regulating and taxing it, we use it to criminalize otherwise law-abiding citizens. People who use marijuana should be able to get the help that alcoholics receive, if a dependency should arise, without the threat of losing their jobs or ruining their reputations. Penalties should apply to those who are not willing to follow basic regulations and restrictions, such as pertain to age and circumstance.

To insist that marijuana is a dangerous drug, when millions of people have discovered otherwise, creates mistrust. Young people often see the law as unreliable and inauthentic for the first time when they are exposed to antimarijuana campaigns showing evil outcomes for pot smokers when they can see that for the vast majority of users, this will never be the case. Those who choose to use marijuana despite its illegality usually enter the criminal world for the first time in their lives from the moment they share their first joint; this forever changes the way they view themselves in relation to the law. Since decades of nonstop antimarijuana warfare has not halted the activity, and millions of young people choose to enter the criminal world every year via their decision to smoke pot, wouldn't it be wiser to legalize it, monitor it, and tax it?

Had a sane system been in place to help my family rather than punish us when our troubles first became apparent, all four of us would be much better off today. The system we found when we went for help crushed and crippled our spirits and destroyed us economically, making it more difficult (actually impossible) to obtain the assistance we needed for change. The tragedy experienced by my family could have been avoided if secrecy had not been such a priority, and if asking for assistance had not been an invitation for the legal system to violate and punish. In order to reduce addiction and other harmful and self-destructive behaviors, we must be able to see each person as an individual responding to the circumstances in their lives, and provide the resources to help them rather than to continue endorsing systems that punish and destroy those who do not have the clout or resources to resist annihilation.

"Going to the police" became more than just another significant line of demarcation in my life. Many of the others had been celebratory: graduating from college, having a baby, and so forth; but crossing this new line cast the die in a way I had not anticipated. Everything that was happening felt utterly alien as I watched our bitter tragedy unfold. I just couldn't understand how things had gotten so horribly out of control; just a few short years ago we were a family building a house, looking forward to a future. Wanting to understand more about what had happened to my family and why, I began to do a lot of research. This ultimately pushed and pulled me in many different directions. Graduate school offered many opportunities for me to delve into my specific areas of interest: I studied substance abuse, domestic violence, mental illness, family stress, nutrition, history, among other subjects.

After a while it became clear to me that my husband's problems were part of a much broader picture; it was as if he were a cog in a machine, doing his part to uphold an antiquated system of domination and submission that was loudly and with exaggeration going through its last death throes. Unfortunately, my daughter and I were supposed to play the submissive parts, and we were not acting out our roles properly. With all that I'd already been through in my life, I was not willing to go backward. My daughter had been born into a time that had at least given lip service to equality between the sexes, and she was definitely more accustomed to willfulness than obedience. My husband was an individual responding to the many influences not only in his life but in the larger world surrounding him; his particular tragedy happened at a time when things seemed to be once again rearranging themselves between men and women.

After his brother's sudden and unexpected death, my husband went a little crazy and started behaving in ways that were destructive not only to himself but to everyone around him. His behavior became overtly defensive and aggressive as he tried to come to terms with his loss. It didn't help that the society he existed in was also going through a defensive and aggressive period as it dealt with a resurgence of feminine values and a perceived loss of masculine influence. My husband joined his energies with others who were attempting to return to a past that no longer existed. It is not unusual in this kind of situation for a person to start abusing a substance they may have previously used recreationally without incident. Excessive amounts used to deal with pain can easily push someone over the edge—no matter what the substance. My husband had already been responding to the stressors in his life by smoking too much—cigarettes and pot—and the death of his brother pushed him right over the edge into full-fledged, out-of-control addiction. If he had chosen to abuse alcohol, cocaine, heroin, or methamphetamines, there is no doubt in my mind he would be dead by now.

Part II

Altered States

CHAPTER 7

Legal Versus Illegal

Before I met my husband, I hadn't thought much about issues of substance abuse and how they had or had not affected my life. I had witnessed from afar the ravages of this kind of abuse on various people, but they were not family members or people who had direct or frequent dealings with me or mine. Or so I thought. When I looked closer, I could see that many people I knew were dealing with a relative or close friend who was a substance abuser of some kind, even if that substance was "only" food. When I was growing up, the closest I ever got to witnessing substance abuse was dealing with the occasional obnoxious drunk at parties; sometimes one of those drunks was my date or a friend going through a hard time. Years went by before I heard through the grapevine that certain old friends or acquaintances were having problems in their lives because of excessive drinking or drug use.

The sixties and seventies introduced other drugs for users to potentially abuse besides the ubiquitous alcohol, including and especially marijuana. Later on, a few people I knew became addicted to painkillers and other prescription drugs, often after originally using them for a legitimate physical ailment. I also knew some people who got intensely involved with the cocaine mania of the seventies and eighties, to the detriment of some but not others (who were natural survivors, I guess). Antidepressants became many people's drug of choice in the nineties, and so far seem to be holding their own in the new millennium. Actually, if one can gauge what's going on by the running commentary of the media and rudimentary gossip, the new craze in drugged-out states seems to be pills for erectile dysfunction for men and antidepressants for women.

And then there's heroin. A few years ago good friends of mine lost their thirty-year-old son to an overdose of this dangerous drug. As a young man he was an altar boy, played Christian Youth Organization basketball, and sang in the youth choir. He also played Little League baseball, was on a soccer team, and was a Boy Scout. In high school he played baseball, football, and golf, and was a member of the ski club. Somewhere along the line this young man lost his way. He had not used heroin in a number of years but had an unfortunate relapse after a series of disappointments in life. "Tough love" was suggested to his family by professionals and friends alike, and they decided to try this often-heralded "cure" when they discovered their son was using again. They told him he would have to leave their home, where he had sought temporary refuge, and live elsewhere, which he did for a number of weeks, rooming with sympathetic friends. When it was obvious tough love wasn't working, knowing their son was in very real danger, my friends contacted an in-patient drug rehab in the area and reserved a bed for their son; they began searching for him but did not find him in time. He had already died of an overdose. The newspapers wrote an article about bad heroin in the area; as it turned out a few other users had also succumbed. These friends tell me: *Don't ever try tough love.*

Recently, I spoke to another longtime friend with whom I had been out of touch for a while because of busy schedules. She informed me her daughter had just graduated magna cum laude from a prestigious East Coast university, and her son was currently serving a two-year sentence in prison for relapsing on heroin. He had apparently fallen asleep behind the wheel of his car, which crashed; fortunately, it was a single-car accident and nobody was hurt.

These recent happenings brought back painful memories of my youth. While attending college on the West Coast, I had experienced the pain of losing someone to heroin. A beautiful and creative young man with whom I had become acquainted returned to New York City—where he had attended art school—for a visit. A short time later, he was dead from an overdose of heroin. He was at a disadvantage in the newly experimental drug world, I was told, because he'd had a kidney removed as a child.

Later, when circumstances found me attending college in another time zone, I met a talented, smart, attractive woman with whom I became close friends. I'm not even sure at what point in our friendship she started using heroin. I first noticed her newest friends kept going into the bathroom a lot when I visited her, coming out with a glazed look in their eyes. Ultimately, the drug and lifestyle consumed her. Years later, long after I had decided I could no longer maintain our friendship, I heard she had died of AIDS. I was saddened but not surprised; I was also haunted by my rejection of her because of my own fears and wondered if there was anything I could have done to help prevent circumstances from unfolding so tragically.

Last but not least on my personal list of drug tragedies is the old friend from my high school I already mentioned, who is serving a life sentence in prison for using and selling amphetamines. He asked a loyal friend who wrote him letters not to bother anymore because it was too depressing to hear news from the outside world. The boy I remember was a kind soul, as undeserving of such harsh punishment as anyone I knew. To serve life in prison you should have to be a monster of a person who will kill if set free. This young man's crime was that he was an addict.

Because of the environment in which I had lived for most of my life, the people I knew who had problems with addiction were generally white and usually educated; most hailed from privilege of one sort or another. The majority of people with whom I came in contact during my fieldwork in graduate school were poor and underprivileged. Most had experienced brutalities relating to their socioeconomic situation; some had experienced the incarceration and even murder of family members. It was clear that staying afloat financially created enormous anxiety for these families, as did fears for the safety of their loved ones in crime-ridden neighborhoods. Use of legal and illegal substances to alter consciousness is often part and parcel of lives replete with uncertainty and worry; it is not surprising people who are disadvantaged might reach out for something to soothe their rattled spirits. It is also not surprising people from ancient cultures (e.g., those from Africa, India, or Latin America) are attracted to the mysterious plants their ancestors used to ease their sorrows in life—especially cannabis.

During the time I was still working on keeping my family together, I was grateful my husband wasn't abusing alcohol, cocaine, or heroine. But I knew his smoking problem with both pot and cigarettes was serious, and it was not only affecting his health but the health of our entire family. I understood my husband was self-medicating—obsessively so because of his massive sense of loss and guilt resulting from his brother's death.

As I looked around me, I saw that many other people were doing the same thing, albeit with different substances and for different reasons. Alcohol abuse seemed to be causing the most damage as far as I could see. Its toll on individuals and society was clearly enormous, but there appeared to be a popular assumption that since alcohol is legal, it is less harmful than all illegal substances, including marijuana. Most people seemed to subscribe to this notion and spent very little time questioning the status quo where mind-altering substances were concerned. There were, however, growing pockets of dissenters from more than one generation who were questioning the order and wisdom of things, sometimes loudly.

My life experience had shown me that certain drugs could indeed be dangerous, and alcohol and cigarettes—both legal—were killing far more people than all of the rest of the drugs combined. What became apparent while researching and trying to understand substance abuse was that there are hordes of people attempting to alter their state of being and to relieve the anxiety of life. The legality issue was pushing most of them in the direction of alcohol and cigarettes without regard to the comparative lethality or danger of these two substances. And the so-called "drug" that appears to be the least harmful to humans, with no known fatalities and testimonials going back thousands of years—cannabis—remains today cloaked in secrecy, hypocrisy, and fear. The alcohol, cigarette, and pharmaceutical industries have the most to fear as they have much to lose if people became aware that you don't have to destroy your liver, get fat and stupid, and lose your sex drive to lift yourself out of the doldrums now and again.

The profits of pharmaceutical companies would suffer much if cannabis were made legal, as more people would learn of this simple herb's capacity to help relieve temporary depression and anxiety. Undoubtedly, many would prefer this mild stimulant and forego the use of pharmaceutical creations replete with disagreeable side effects. Although antidepressants have been widely prescribed to ease everything from major depression to commonplace maladies of the spirit, they have in recent years come under attack for causing a number of users to commit acts of violence—even suicide and murder. But where are the "antidepressant madness" movies? According to an article in *Mother Jones* magazine, some drug manufacturers have produced a "prosecutor's manual" for their lawyers to use in courts to counteract the ever-increasing claims that defendants' use of antidepressants has caused them or a family member to commit acts of violence. The pharmaceutical companies that advertise drugs meant to "help" people certainly do not want anyone believing the antidepressants they are touting as beneficial are possibly responsible for the commitment of murderous acts of rage.

In 2001 one of the world's largest pharmaceutical companies, Pfizer, successfully argued that this special prosecutor's manual ought to be resealed and kept out of the public record after a woman whose husband shot and killed himself after six days on Zoloft managed to have the document introduced into her lawsuit against the company. In another case involving a fifteen-year-old boy who shot and killed his grandparents after taking Zoloft for just three weeks, Pfizer refused to release the sealed documents, and the boy's defense attorneys were currently battling for the right to see them, last I heard. Another woman who was taking Zoloft and then Paxil killed her four-year-old twin boys, and in yet another story a sixty-year-old man who just hours before had taken two sample tablets of Paxil killed his wife, daughter, and granddaughter, and then committed suicide. Billions of dollars worth of annual sales are at stake, as well as countless lost lives. Advertisements on TV for drug litigation lawyers these days rival those for the drugs themselves, and yet the federal government seems to care more about hunting down and incarcerating people who defiantly choose to relieve their anxiety or depression (or just give themselves a lift) by using a mild herb that has been tried and tested by humanity for thousands of years.

Although it might appear that the wise thing to do would be to abstain from ever ingesting or absorbing anything "unhealthy," clearly this is never going to happen. It's hard enough to get people to eat the right foods, which should give a clue as to the odds of totally eliminating other substances. Is it such a preposterous idea that maybe some of these substances are here on earth for us to use carefully and holistically, as was done by our ancestors? It is difficult to foster an atmosphere of careful and holistic use of marijuana when there is so much hype involved, including the secrecy, lying, and bonding that often seem to take place with hidden use.

CHAPTER 8
A Cultural Mythology

At any rate, mind-altering substances are part and parcel of the history of being human, and it is highly unlikely that the need for them and the supply of them would ever or could ever be eliminated. Also, it has always been difficult and controversial to determine exactly which substances we humans ingest are healthy and which are unhealthy, as there are benefits and detriments involved in the use of all substances, including water. Our cultural mythology is we have eliminated the harmful substances by making them illegal, and people who keep trying to get to those substances are inferior (even evil) beings who must be stopped at any cost. The U.S. has 5 percent of the world's population and 25 percent of its prison population, and a substantial portion of inmates in this country are in prison for the commission of nonviolent crimes related to drugs. We need to spend more time studying the relationship between incarceration and drugs. Who benefits? Who suffers?

An increasing number of people believe our society has not chosen the least harmful of mind-altering substances to represent the culturally normative way to unwind and/or socialize. Alcohol is currently the most socially acceptable form of relaxation and/or celebration in this country. There are few major social occasions—weddings, funerals, graduations, and so forth—that do not involve the use and oftentimes abuse of alcohol, and its consumption in private homes on even a daily basis has been given the stamp of approval, generally speaking. There are also many homes in recovery whose inhabitants are still consumed by one or more members' alcohol addiction or recovery; many people consider that their lives will forever be tainted and even ruined by past or present lives in alcoholic homes.

Since the repeal of Prohibition there has been little protest over the almost ubiquitous use of alcohol, despite overwhelming evidence of the harm caused by this substance. We have agreed as a nation to accept responsibility for our intake of alcohol on an individual basis and to be accountable for our behavior under the influence, or accept the consequences—this despite the fact that research shows chronic use of alcohol damages every system in the body, especially the liver. The liver of a regular user of alcohol is increasingly unable to cleanse the blood efficiently or perform other tasks vital to health and life; water and sodium retention increase as toxins build up in the alcoholic's blood, and the enlarged liver squeezes the blood vessels passing through it, putting extra strain on the heart.

Vitamin malabsorption syndrome also frequently results from alcohol use, as the body's ability to absorb or utilize certain vitamins (such as zinc, sodium, calcium, phosphorus, magnesium, vitamin A, vitamin D, vitamin B-6, and folic acid) is seriously diminished, causing further health difficulties. Chronic drinking of alcohol can also result in blood sugar abnormalities and interfere with the way the body metabolizes fats. If a person obtains 10 percent of his calories from alcohol (and many do), his or her body will slow down and expend less energy, storing unused fat in the "beer belly" often seen in drinkers of alcohol. Alcohol is also cardiotoxic in excessive amounts, causing damage to the heart muscle itself; chronic alcohol use seems to damage not only heart muscle but all striated muscle tissue. Alcohol is also a neurotoxin and has been shown to cause brain damage and memory problems. Research suggests that possibly 75 percent of alcoholics have cognitive impairment from alcohol consumption even following detoxification, and that perhaps one-third of all nursing home residents are there because of permanent, alcohol-induced damage to the brain.

Certain cultures in the world have a long history of eschewing alcohol in favor of cannabis because they believe cannabis to be the milder substance and far less damaging to the body. There are any number of books that have come out recently filled with research on the time-honored use of cannabis for a variety of medical ills; some list conditions that can be helped by using cannabis in one form or another: eye problems, anxiety, inflammation, fever, digestive disorders—even "overachiever's complex" is mentioned as a condition warranting cannabis!

Not only has there never been an overdose death attributed to cannabis use, but throughout history this relatively mild herb has been used in certain societies to increase health and longevity when used purposefully and in moderation. I think that it's important at this stage of the game—since so many people are involved with its use—to make sure we are not ignorant on the subject. Martin Booth has written the most detailed and intriguing book (*Cannabis*) that I have read on the long history of this popular plant, and I recommend it to anyone who would like to know more about the subject than I am about to divulge. There are many other good books regarding cannabis and its use, but none seems to be as comprehensive.

Cannabis has a record of use dating back almost ten thousand years, according to pottery shards dating back to that time, which reveal the use of impressed pieces of hemp cord. It appears that the hemp crop was of major economic significance in a number of ancient cultures, grown for its cloth, paper, and grain as well as used for medicinal purposes. Ancient Chinese medicine was among the most sophisticated in the world, and there is evidence they mixed cannabis with wine to use as an analgesic. Around 2000 B.C. some cannabis-using tribes migrated from central Asia, and spread the use of the herb. It is believed that some of these nomadic Aryans moved into the Indian continent and brought with them the name bhang or bhanga for cannabis. According to early Hindu-Sanskrit (about 1100 B.C.) texts, bhanga was brought down from the Himalayas as a gift from God for people to enjoy. The Vedas, holy Hindu books of faith, considered bhang to be a sacred plant and believed that through its use, mankind was cleansed of sin.

At any rate, cannabis was widely known to provide temporary relief from the ills of existence; the Assyrians in 900 B.C. called cannabis the "drug for sadness." As the Israelites were in constant trade and contact with cannabis-using cultures, some researchers believe that certain references in the Bible refer to its use, and that the holy oil that the Hebrews used to put them in a religious trance was quite possibly extracted from cannabis plants. The word Messiah means "the anointed one," and some scholars believe that Jesus used cannabis oil for at least the treatment of eye and skin problems. The ancient Egyptians also used cannabis medicinally for ailments that ranged from calming the spirit to preventing glaucoma-generated blindness. The Greek historian Herodotus wrote in the fifth century B.C. that the Scythians who had settled in Macedonia from Siberia threw cannabis leaves on red-hot stones during funerals, the fumes of which would transport them and elicit shouts of grief and joy. Galen, an early Greek doctor who treated the horrific wounds of gladiators, also wrote about cannabis, declaring that hemp (cannabis) cakes eaten in moderation produced a feeling of wellbeing but if taken in excess produced "intoxication, dehydration, and impotence." The Buddhists used cannabis to calm the nerves of soldiers going into battle, to fight off fatigue, as a treatment for dysentery, insomnia, fever, and to help create a sense of union in body and spirit. Legend has it that Prince Siddhartha existed for six years eating nothing but one hemp seed a day.

Cannabis seeds can be found in Neolithic grave sites all across Europe. It is not entirely clear whether they were used to grow hemp for cloth and rope or as a spiritual aid during shamanistic rites—or both. When the Romans invaded Europe they brought hemp (cannabis) seeds with them and reintroduced cannabis to the Europeans, who were at that time more sophisticated farmers than the Romans. They were so impressed with the plant that from that time on they included hemp as one of the main crops in their successful three-crop rotation system. The Arabs' knowledge of Chinese hemp paper was brought with them when they occupied Spain, and eventually this papermaking knowledge spread throughout Europe.

When Johann Gutenberg first printed his Bible in 1456, it was printed on hemp paper using the same process the Chinese had been using for thousands of years. The European Renaissance brought with it the building of many ships that needed lots of rope, and the hemp industry thrived, using windmills to assist in the labor-intensive fiber extraction process.

The importance of hemp was recognized by King Henry VIII in 1533 when he made it legal to fine any farmer who refused to plant hemp on a portion of his land. When England became the leading maritime power after the defeat of the Spanish Armada in 1588, the need for hemp rope increased. To compete with Russia, the leading exporter of hemp, Britain turned to its colonies to grow the hemp. Even though the colonists preferred to plant food crops, it was demanded of them that they grow hemp. King James I ordered flax and hemp to be grown in the English colonies in 1611. Colonists in Virginia preferred to grow the more lucrative tobacco, but the Virginia Company ordered each colonist in 1682 to grow one hundred hemp plants, with the governor agreeing to raise five thousand himself.

Hemp was actually made legal tender and used by farmers to pay off their debts. By the 1730s hemp was accepted in Massachusetts as tender with which to pay taxes (at a rate of four shillings per pound), and legislators in Connecticut and Massachusetts ordered each family to plant a teaspoon of hemp seed for the good of all. An early rebellion of the colonists against the English involved the settlers making their own cloth from hemp and wool, rather than buying ready-made clothes from England with raw materials that they had exported to them, as was required by law. Thus the American textile industry was born and with it the further commercialization of the hemp industry.

Because of fears about the actual value of a U.S. silver dollar, hemp became a currency in itself in some parts of the country because of its permanent demand and consistent quality. Both George Washington and Thomas Jefferson grew hemp, and there is some indication that Washington, at least, used his cannabis for more things than rope and cloth, as he commented in his diary about forgetting to separate the males from the females (which increases the amount of THC in the female flower) and because he ordered hemp seed from India, where the cannabis was known for its psychoactive properties. It is also rumored that presidents Madison, Monroe, Jackson, Taylor, and Pierce enjoyed the use of cannabis. Washington is said to have preferred hemp to alcohol, and James Madison reportedly used hemp to inspire thoughts about democracy. Hemp required lots of manpower but with the help of slavery became the second most important crop in the South after cotton—for a time.

Black slaves enjoyed the use of cannabis, as they knew about its properties from their African heritage. They used it to ease the pain of slavery, although many continued to smoke it long after they were emancipated. After slavery became illegal, some of the Caribbean islanders who no longer had the free labor of slaves imported indentured laborers from India to work their plantations; these new foreign inhabitants brought their bhanga (now called ganga) with them. The Indian influence was powerful, and even today cannabis (ganga) is popular medicinally and is used for pleasure and relaxation in the Caribbean, especially Jamaica.

The end of slavery in the United States resulted in opportunities for many Mexicans to come across the border and work for low wages. Cannabis began to be called "marijuana" during these peasant migrations north across the Rio Grande. Marijuana was the name the Mexicans had for the cannabis flowers and leaves they smoked to help deal with the difficulties of life and to add a little pleasure to their burden. Marijuana imported from Mexico could be found in stores on either side of the border. Pancho Villa and his men, busy raiding border towns to steal supplies for their army of insurgents, were immortalized in the song, "La Cucaracha" ("The Cockroach"), which basically says that the cockroach doesn't want to walk anymore because he doesn't have any marijuana to smoke. The slang term for "roach" comes from this song. Like many who came before them, these Mexican soldiers probably used cannabis to relax and to prepare themselves for battle.

American soldiers also smoked marijuana in the little towns along the border between the United States and Mexico, and later smoked in the Panama Canal Zone as well, picking up the habit from the blacks and Mexicans working on the canal. In Panama, a military tribunal run by a colonel in the U.S. Army Medical Corps was set up to study the situation. In the trial, four military doctors, two military policemen, and a number of soldiers all smoked marijuana. The results of the trial concluded marijuana was not addictive and it had no significant "deleterious" effect on the user. The military banned the smoking of marijuana anyway.

Mexican immigrants were not popular to begin with in the United States, but animosity grew when farmers and businesses alike began to hire them because they were cheap labor, putting local citizens out of work. The smoking of marijuana was now viewed as suspect and alien—more because the Mexicans did it than from any serious problems resulting from it. The fact that cannabis had been used in U.S. patent medicines for decades was roundly ignored by those who wanted to vilify Mexicans. In 1906, marijuana was listed as a dangerous substance along with opium, morphine, and cocaine, even though it was not in the same league as any of those drugs. In 1914 the Harrison Narcotics Act demanded that a stamp tax be paid on drug transactions—an effort by the government to regulate and control, but not eliminate, certain "drugs." Marijuana was originally included in this group, but was later excluded as federal lawyers agreed that because it was a commonly used medicine, especially for glaucoma and migraine sufferers, its use should not be restricted. The unfortunate part of this 1914 legislation was that because of the bureaucracy involved, prices rose on other drugs and an illegal market for them arose. Many who needed drugs for whatever reason turned to the illegal market that developed in response to this need; some people even turned to street crime to be able to afford the newly pricey drugs.

Marijuana still didn't figure much into the new rules and regulations and was legal in most states, at least for medicinal purposes. If a state voted to make marijuana illegal to use, it was usually because of its fear of the minority populations who used it, namely blacks and Mexicans—not because it had caused significant problems or was even a very visible commodity.

In 1911 a couple thousand "Hindoos" arrived in California from India to work and aroused the antipathy of those who considered themselves culturally and morally superior. These mostly indentured laborers were hated upon arrival in San Francisco for their strange culture and food, and especially for their use of cannabis. Although they worked hard, used no alcohol, and used ganga moderately, they were considered the next "yellow peril" after the Chinese, who had earlier been vilified for their smoking of opium. The Chinese had also been accused of taking the jobs of Europeans as they too were hardworking and responsible immigrants. Some Chinese, especially men, had enjoyed smoking opium to relax after a long day, just as they had done for centuries back in their homeland. When new legislation no longer allowed them to smoke opium legally, it drove trade underground, where it was quickly determined that the adulterated version of opium—heroin—was more powerful, lucrative, and less bulky to conceal as a smaller amount was needed to cause the desired effect. The smuggling of heroin quickly replaced the opium trade, and a problem was born, a far more serious problem than the smoking of opium. When the Americans acquired the Philippines after the Spanish American War, one of the first things they did was wipe out their time-honored opium dens, once again paving the way for the international use and abuse of heroin.

Cannabis is a far milder intoxicant than opium, or even alcohol, so it should not be surprising that many people and whole cultures have chosen to use it instead of its more dangerous alternatives. Even so, most people in the developing stages of our largely northern European–immigrant country were probably unaware of its psychoactive properties, and knew of it only as a medicinal ingredient or as raw material for making rope. Smoking marijuana was appealing to many of the newly emancipated African Americans after the Civil War because they believed smoking marijuana not only helped them relax and unwind but also enhanced their creativity. Some of them were to go on and use this relaxed creativity to invent the new melodies of blues and jazz.

African-American musicians also liked marijuana because it kept them alert and prevented exhaustion, unlike alcohol and opiates, which they felt not only fatigued them but dulled their senses. They believed cannabis helped lighten their load and created a feeling of belonging in an increasingly industrialized and impersonal world. The majority culture's fear of blacks and jazz and the sex and liberty implied by their music was enough to set the stage for the entrance of the man who almost single-handedly made marijuana illegal in this country.

Harry Anslinger began his career in law enforcement investigating pearl smuggling but soon enough he acquired an obsession with European rum-running, resulting in his appointment to a leading post in the Prohibition movement. Once alcohol was no longer against the law, Anslinger turned his attention to cannabis and soon developed a fixation on all it represented. He used his new obsession with cannabis as a springboard to become the most important player in domestic and international drug policy history *ever*. By 1930 Harry Anslinger—who was known to many for his disregard for the truth when facts proved contrary to his chosen argument—had been appointed the first commissioner of the Federal Bureau of Narcotics (FBN), a position he was to hold for more than thirty-two years.

The federal government did not discourage him from unlawful activities in his antidrug zeal, and when a personal headline-grabbing rivalry with FBI chief J. Edgar Hoover (whose enemies were "commies" and "spies") required an even greater villain, Marijuana Smoking Blacks and Mexicans were there for the pillorying. It helped that it was the time of the Great Depression and jobs were scarce. Anti-Mexican attitudes were not only growing due to these immigrants' willingness to work hard at low paying jobs (putting "real" Americans out of work), but because it was rumored that Mexicans were spreading marijuana use across the country. This was a fallacy, but many were arrested and deported on these grounds. Publisher William Randolph Hearst was a supreme racist who popularized anti-Mexican sentiments through his newspapers; the use of sensationalized and unprincipled news coverage was coined "yellow journalism" in honor of his efforts. Hearst introduced the word "marihuana" to the popular media, linking the word in people's mind with degeneracy and the dissolution of American culture.

When tax revenues fell because of the Depression and funds for his agency were threatened, FBN chief Anslinger realized he would have to make it appear there was a serious menace to society to maintain and even increase funding for his agency. Anslinger's campaign to vilify the herb cannabis, now known as marijuana, went so far as to depict smokers of this roadside plant as murderous rapists who committed atrocities with bestial lustfulness after inhaling the smoke of this "evil" weed.

Prohibition of alcohol early in the twentieth century created a criminal element that worked to supply illicit booze to the many who were willing to risk violating the Eighteenth Amendment for a little pleasure and relaxation. Because of the mob-related violence spawned by alcohol prohibition, it was not hard to invoke public fear concerning possible crime scenarios involving marijuana, even though cannabis had been used peacefully since the country's inception. Once alcohol prohibition ended, because of its unpopularity and impossibility to enforce, legal distributors of liquor began to fear marijuana would take away some of their business, as marijuana use had increased during Prohibition because of the scarcity of alcohol. Harry Anslinger almost lost his pivotal position in the antimarijuana melee when he referred to a black cannabis user as a "ginger-colored nigger," but his articles on Mexicans and Negroes raping and murdering while under the influence of cannabis apparently made him indispensable to a growing racist population, so he was allowed to keep his post despite protests against his outspoken bigotry.

He became even more popular when he started making antimarijuana movies, such as one that depicted students who smoked marijuana ending up in insane asylums with shattered lives. Some of these movies were financed by distilleries that had a lot to lose if people discovered that smoking marijuana was relaxing and enjoyable and caused less violence, turmoil, and bodily harm than did alcohol consumption. One of Anslinger's favorite stories was about a young man who murdered his parents, his two brothers, and a sister with an ax after smoking marijuana. Anslinger failed to mention any facts concerning the man's past psychiatric history, which was extensive and included hallucinations and homicidal impulses, nor did he mention that the police had tried unsuccessfully to have the ax murderer committed to an insane asylum before the murders took place. The man was finally ruled criminally insane, and although there was no mention of marijuana in his hospital records, Anslinger still used his tragic story as proof of marijuana's evil influence.

Other tactics to fuel the fear of marijuana involved tales of wild sexual orgies under the influence of marijuana. Yet something even more sinister was needed to almost completely arrest cannabis use in the United States, and that something was pure unadulterated greed. Although hemp was an important crop for the country's economy, it was difficult to work with and required a lot of manpower to ready the plant for use. It had been the complaints of Thomas Jefferson's slaves that had first inspired the future president to work on a threshing machine that would make hemp less labor-intensive, but it was not until 1919 that a machine (a decorticator) was developed to strip the fibers from the plants effectively and separate them from the pulp. The fiber could then be used for rope and cloth and the pulp for paper. More than one giant of big business was threatened by this new invention, as not only the logging industry but the burgeoning petrochemical and paper industries stood to lose billions of dollars if hemp was made easily available.

Also at that time, Ford Motor Company was experimenting with renewable energy sources, hoping to replace the hydrocarbons of petroleum with the hydrocarbons of plants, especially hemp. Lammont DuPont, head of the multinational pharmaceutical and petrochemical conglomerate, joined publisher William Randolph Hearst in a full-steam-ahead campaign to wipe out hemp production once and for all. Both Hearst and Scripps newspaper publisher Edward Scripps from San Diego had substantial holdings in the forest industry, and realized the invention of the decorticator would make hemp pulp available for making paper and other things, reducing the need for timber. The new synthetic plastics industry—which depended on fossil fuels—also stood to lose if the hemp industry thrived, and DuPont began lobbying the federal government for federal legislation banning hemp.

The Marijuana Tax Act of 1937 was the result of a few powerful men orchestrating the destruction of a viable and time-honored industry—all to enhance their positions in life. A variety of people from different walks of life voiced objections to this bill. One was a lawyer-physician from the American Medical Association (AMA) who complained that the bill would essentially destroy the mostly beneficial cannabis-hemp business when there was not sufficient evidence of a marijuana menace. He also differed from Anslinger in that he felt a person who became dependent on marijuana should be considered a patient and not a criminal. His objections were overruled. A major industrialist also objected to the bill, saying it would crush a great industry and it was a "world encircling" measure, as indeed it proved to be.

Harry Anslinger had his eye on international control of cannabis, and he repeatedly pulled horror stories about marijuana out of his hat, defiantly challenging objections from other countries that there was insufficient evidence to back his claims. W. R. Hearst used his newspapers to spread propaganda about an exotic and dangerous drug being used by the Mexicans called "marihuana." Most people were familiar with the word "hemp" for rope and "cannabis" for medical use, but now Hearst's unrelenting yellow journalism popularized the word "marihuana." How many people understood they were all the same plant—the entire plant—leaves, stem, and flowers, and marijuana, hemp and cannabis are all the same, is unknown. The chairman of the senate committee that nominated the bill regarding cannabis was a close friend of DuPont, and the antimarijuana (hemp) bill was quickly pushed through on a Friday when many senators were absent. Only one congressman raised any questions, and he was informed that the AMA supported the bill 100 percent, which was not true. The 1937 Tax Act cleverly put such a high tax on any marijuana transaction—personal or business—it brought to a halt all legitimate enterprises using hemp (cannabis). Years after the bill was passed, one of DuPont's VIPs boasted about the wide variety of products that used to be made from natural sources, such as hemp, that were now made from synthetic plastics.

For a brief time during World War II, farmers were encouraged to grow hemp. During that war literally thousands of acres of farmland began producing the hemp needed for rope and the hempseed oil that was used for aviation fluid. Farmers who grew hemp were exempted, along with their sons, from having to serve in the military. The U.S. Department of Agriculture actually made a film about this enormous endeavor, extolling the virtues of hemp, but in later years when marijuana activists asked to view it the government denied that the film existed. Cannabis can still be seen growing wild in the Midwest, where most of the World War II hemp was grown; it is known as "ditch weed" and has a low THC content.

It is incredible that the laws of the federal government were used to destroy one industry to herald and support others, benefiting the few and hurting the many. In the DuPont Company archives a paper has been identified that refers to this social experiment, remarking on the social reorganization powers of government and its ability to force acceptance of new industrial ideas paid for by the revenue of government. Oddly, the pro-hemp people were Republicans, and those who had engineered the demise of the industry were Democrats. In essence, everyone was duped. The law stated that one hundred dollars an ounce must be paid each time even a small amount of hemp-cannabis-marijuana changed hands, permanently crippling an industry at a time when a new 1937 automobile cost little more than double that amount. One has to wonder how the world might be different if only the Ford Industry had been encouraged to pursue their experimentation with the hydrocarbons of hemp plants.

Once the Marijuana Tax Act became law, doctors who prescribed it were treated as criminals, and people who used it were put away in prison with murderers and rapists. Mayor Fiorello La Guardia of New York City was suspicious of Anslinger and his claims about the evils of marijuana, especially as the little research done had indicated that marijuana had great potential to do good with little indication that it caused serious harm. The mayor had good reason to be concerned about the new tax act that suddenly made users into criminals, as there had been a large influx of blacks from the south who came north looking for work, and they brought their enjoyment of marijuana use with them. Marijuana was part of their cultural identity and Mayor La Guardia knew that this new law could cause a lot of problems.

He set out to find out the truth, joining forces with the New York Academy of Medicine and an investigative team consisting of more than two dozen respected medical practitioners, health experts, and sociologists. Mayor La Guardia also had the full cooperation of the New York Police Department, who trained officers as special investigators to help the medical staff. Prisoners volunteered to be used as guinea pigs, and spent part of their incarceration smoking marijuana regularly, during and after which they were thoroughly tested in every conceivable manner. The results of the study indicated marijuana was a mild stimulant and not addictive in comparison to morphine, and people who had smoked marijuana for years showed no mental or physical deterioration that could be attributed to marijuana. A report on the experiment was published, and Mayor La Guardia even wrote the foreword, so relieved was he with the study's assessment that the smoking of marijuana was not going to be a big problem for his city. In the mayor's study, marijuana had been deemed by psychiatrists and medical specialists alike to be a mild euphoriant, but that didn't stop Harry Anslinger from calling the report "giddy sociology" and "medical mumbo-jumbo." Anslinger set out not only to denigrate the study and its authors but to physically destroy any copy of the report he could get his hands on.

Other studies came up with the same results, yet Anslinger would not relent in his private war against marijuana. He needed money to keep his agency going, and if it was perceived that marijuana was not a problem, he would be out of not only a job but a calling. He decided to go after musicians and celebrities, and the Federal Bureau of Narcotics even started keeping open dossiers on some of their suspects. The FBN also tried to recruit informers from the jazz community, but they found few takers. Anslinger was especially outraged that many of the musicians used their marijuana arrests to get out of military service, and his response was to insist that files be kept on all jazz musicians and their acquaintances who used marijuana.

The great jazz drummer Gene Krupa was the most famous of the FBN's busts; he served eighty-four days in jail for possession of a few marijuana joints. The great Satchmo, Louis Armstrong, spoke of enjoying marijuana but he said the misdemeanor got "meaner and meaner," and he eventually gave it up. Or so he said.

Of course this is what Anslinger wanted, and he continued his methods of harassing minorities. Musicians needed a cabaret card to play in New York City, and the card was taken away if they had a drug conviction, preventing them from working in the jazz capitol of the World. Thelonius Monk was one of many black musicians targeted and harassed by the police; he was falsely imprisoned and lost his cabaret card for six years; he was later found innocent of the charges. Robert Mitchum thought his movie career was over when he was arrested for marijuana possession, especially after he admitted he had been smoking since his youth. His career actually got a boost from the publicity as marijuana, almost unknown to U.S. citizens just a few years earlier, was becoming more familiar to the public after all the advertising by Anslinger and the FBN. Anslinger's zeal was so over the top, he had to be stopped by the U.S. Treasury Department from canceling the passports of all jazz musicians with marijuana convictions—and there were a lot of them. In fact, once he arrested an entire orchestra for marijuana possession.

The mostly black jazz musicians got back at Anslinger with their music, using words and meanings not understood by the average person, and hopefully not by Anslinger or the FBN. In 1943 when Fats Waller sent a recording to the troops overseas singing that he dreamed of a "reefer five feet high," it is possible that only the soldiers of color understood what he was singing about. Anslinger's tactics were actually forcing minority groups to speak in code and form secret societies where they could avoid the cruel and glaring eyes of an increasingly rabid FBN. By attacking their centuries-old custom of using marijuana as a relaxant and social stimulant, Anslinger was further contributing to the isolation and separation of minority groups in America. Putting this mild euphoriant in the same class as heroin and cocaine and prosecuting users as if they were vicious criminals had driven the wedge deeper between the various cultures that populated the country.

Attempting to further vilify marijuana users, Anslinger began linking marijuana to heroin, claiming that smoking it led to use of the harder drug, even though he had said the exact opposite earlier in his career. This was perhaps the most harmful of Anslinger's many untruths, calling marijuana a "gateway drug" when studies not only in this country but in cultures that traditionally use marijuana show otherwise. Marijuana is no more a gateway drug than cigarettes, alcohol, or coffee; most people have used one or more of these stimulants and the vast majority will never go on to use hard drugs. But if you ask a hard drug user if he or she has ever used cigarettes, alcohol, or coffee, most would say yes to all three—making them all gateway drugs by Anslinger's standards. It was this false concept that led to penalties for marijuana as strict as those for heroin and cocaine, and even stricter in some cases than for murder and rape.

Largely because of Anslinger's efforts, legal penalties for marijuana possession increased. In some states a conviction for a second drug offense, whether it was heroin or marijuana, now offered no chance of parole, and even murderers and rapists were afforded parole. Southern states, with the highest minority populations, had the strictest drug laws. In Louisiana you could get up to ninety-nine years for simple possession of marijuana, and in Georgia a second marijuana offense offered the possibility of the death penalty, as did procuring marijuana for minors in many states. Clearly the war on marijuana was a war on minorities, who had somehow, perhaps because they came from a more ancient and horticulturally literate culture, persisted in their choice of the time-honored cannabis plant, and now laws were put on the books to eradicate the cannabis. Or was it the minorities?

Any attempt by reasonable people to salvage the reputation of marijuana and the people who used it was met by harassment orchestrated by Anslinger under the auspices of the FBN. Professor Alfred Lindesmith was a sociologist working with addicts at the University of Indiana, and when he published articles criticizing Anslinger/FBN's stereotypes of people who used substances to alter their state of being, he had his phone tapped, was investigated for communist ties, and for good measure was targeted to have marijuana planted on him so he could be arrested, although the plan never got off the ground. Shamefully, the academic community offered little support for the beleaguered academic; instead they did what they could to protect themselves from persecution.

The Canadians, who seem to have a more clear-eyed approach to these matters, made a documentary film in 1948 that supported Lindesmith's claims that addicts were people, not villains, and that they came from all strata of society, deserving help and respect instead of vilification and incarceration. The film also stated that it was impossible to completely control or restrict the use of drugs, and thus excessively policing the situation was bound to fail and cause significant other problems. Anslinger had the film banned in the United States, while simultaneously encouraging movies that portrayed marijuana use as bestiality, plain and simple. Beleaguered Professor Lindesmith had the support of both the American Bar Association (ABA) and the AMA, who produced a joint paper defending his work and ideas. Anslinger continued trying to suppress and attack Lindesmith and his supporters, who in response ultimately created an independent drug policy institute called the Lindesmith Center, founded to promote science, health, and human rights and to encourage drug policies that help people rather than hurt them. The group has morphed into today's Drug Policy Alliance.

Despite Anslinger's best efforts, marijuana use continued to grow and spread across America, not only because blacks and Mexicans liked it, but also because American soldiers were once again exposed to alien pot smoking cultures—in the Philippines during World War II, and later on in Korea and Vietnam. It wasn't long before marijuana (now called "pot," "weed," "reefer," "Mary Jane," and so forth, and consumed by smoking "joints" and "roaches" and in pipes called "hookahs" and "chillums") could be found in colleges, and eventually, almost everywhere where people questioned the status quo. One of the many things they were questioning and doubting was the wisdom of their elders regarding this much-loved and much-hated roadside weed. Watching movies such as *Reefer Madness*, a ridiculously out-of-touch and hysterical attempt to scare people from trying marijuana, became camp fun for young people who were starting to question other "truths" that had been part and parcel of growing up in America.

The bizarre manner in which the youth in America went about questioning their elders—dressing in strange garb with weird nonhaircuts, inhaling the fumes of exotic plants, blowing bubbles, and reading lore from heretofore heathen nations—had the older generation(s) frothing at the mouth. Literally. And then out of the bowels of the earth came democratic anarchists such as Hunter Thompson and Abbie Hoffman, both of whom confounded all variables and are currently being punished on Mount Olympus. The sedate world of the fifties became a wild space, as the whole world began to learn about our dirty little secrets—white and colored bathrooms, for example. We are nice, decent people and live in the greatest country in the world ever, with freedom and liberty for all. We had said it so many times it had become The Truth, and it was not a popular move to question the 1950s in the sixties. The previous generations had been united by wars, and suddenly we found ourselves in the midst of the wrong war and with the generations also at war with each other. The Anslingers of America were terrified by the surge of newly empowered youth, and it would take considerable effort on their part to create and maintain an international infrastructure to preserve the status quo.

By 1968 the DEA (Drug Enforcement Agency) had replaced the FBN and had declared an International War on Drugs; they soon had ten thousand agents working around the world. Policies that would have been unthinkable before were now de rigueur: the seizing of property and bank accounts, wire and postal (later e-mail) taps, warrant-less searches, freezing and sequestering of assets, and arrest on suspicion. Music was carefully scrutinized; as the antidrug campaign was aimed largely at the young, lyrics of popular songs had to be screened before going on the radio or television. Bob Dylan's lyrics were especially feared by the antidrug zealots because they had to interpret them before offering criticism, and that was tough. MGM violated many musical contracts because of suspected drug lyrics and drug use among their musicians. The middle class began feeling for the first time the effects of persecution, as their sons and daughters were being arrested and sometimes sent to prison for possession of even small amounts of marijuana. Generally, if they were white, and especially if they had power or money, they got off; and if they were of a darker complexion, especially if they had no power or influence, they were fined or sentenced or both.

A National Commission on Marijuana and Drug Abuse, later known as the Shafer Commission, was set up to study cannabis and determine what was fact and what was fallacy concerning this mysterious and controversial plant. After researching claims going back fifty years, the Commission released its final report in 1973. The study found no conclusive evidence that marijuana caused crime, insanity, sexual aberration, or led to other drug use, and recommended that marijuana possession for personal use and the selling and gifting of small amounts be decriminalized. The study's conclusion that smoking marijuana did not lead to the use of other drugs was a crushing blow to the antidrug war. Even though many national public health professionals as well as various religious, legal, and medical leaders supported the findings of the Shafer Commission, Nixon ignored the report and ordered further increases in his antidrug budget.

His successor Gerald Ford preferred more liberal policies and ordered another commission to look at the problem. After all, he had teenagers in the White House. The report from this commission came out in 1975 and agreed with previous findings.

Marijuana use was not a threat to society, and since the government was unlikely to succeed in wiping out the problem, it should concentrate on containing and regulating the problem, and aim to eliminate harsh tactics targeting recreational users.

Around this time, Mexico started worrying that marijuana profits could finance a revolution to overthrow their government. Some farmers in that country had started planting poppy plants between the marijuana plants, which further fueled speculation money was being raised for a rebellion. The DEA, with American funds and technology, gladly offered to help carry out a plan to destroy the marijuana and poppy plants by spraying them with paraquat, a toxin. Unfortunately, paraquat is highly poisonous not only to humans but to other animals; exposure to it can lead to respiratory and kidney failure and even death. It also kills every other plant it touches. The Mexican marijuana growers discovered that if they pulled the plants immediately after they were sprayed, however, they could cut them up into buds and ship them over the U.S. border without anyone knowing the plants had been contaminated.

After discovering that 13 percent of the marijuana tested in the United States contained paraquat, President Jimmy Carter called for the spraying to end. The Mexican government continued to spray the fields anyway, in hopes of fending off a revolution, and soon many Americans began to buy their marijuana from Columbia to avoid possible exposure to this toxin. By 1980 the Columbian marijuana business was employing seventy-five thousand people and bringing in more money than coffee, the country's principal legal export.

President Carter frequently stated that the punishment for a drug should not be more damaging to an individual than the drug itself, and many hoped that with this sensible outlook marijuana would be legalized during his administration. Instead, a backlash against leniency ensued and prohibitionist tactics reemerged. For the first time in U.S. history, marijuana offenses could result not only in life prison sentences but also in property seizure; people could lose everything they owned if they could not prove where the money came from to purchase their possessions. Penalties for marijuana offenses varied in different states, but prison populations skyrocketed everywhere; by 1994, 62 percent of inmates in federal prisons were there for drug-related crimes. In 2002, almost three quarters of a million people were arrested for marijuana possession alone. Certainly this is not what our founding parents had in mind when they risked their lives fighting for freedom.

The modern-day concept of prisons is relatively new; they were originally created early in the nineteenth century as an answer to public outcries against such cruelties as whippings, brandings, and hangings, sometimes just for stealing a loaf of bread. The United States was the first country to develop penitentiaries to house and reform inmates, using techniques such as silence and hard work to encourage reformation. This method of punishment appeared to be successful for more than a century. By the 1960s and 1970s, it became clear the system wasn't working as the population of inmates doubled again and again—from two hundred thousand just a few decades ago to over two million inmates today.

At the same time the prison population was growing exponentially, First Lady Nancy Reagan's intensive "just say no" campaign inspired the spraying of our own national forests with paraquat in an attempt to eradicate domestic attempts at marijuana production. This use of paraquat was in direct opposition to federal environmental legislation meant to protect people, plants, and animals from such environmental toxins. Also, in the 1980s President Ronald Reagan allowed legislation that protected the public from government militarism, the Comitatus Act of 1878, to be roundly ignored.

The Comitatus Act was meant to prevent federal troops from being used to enforce civilian laws, yet suddenly the military was allowed to fight in the drug war against its own citizens. The war on marijuana was so successful in this country, strict adherence to antimarijuana policies led to a scarcity of the substance, and marijuana smoking gave way to using other drugs that were far more dangerous, such as cocaine, heroin, and alcohol.

The 1990s saw a revival of marijuana use as fewer young people were negatively influenced by the inaccurate propaganda surrounding this herb; many felt justified in the risks they were taking to use the drug as they believed current restrictions were unconstitutional. These young people had learned from the experiences of the previous generation that marijuana was less harmful to their bodies and minds than other substances. They were also more aware of the negative aspects of smoking too much cannabis, and labeled those who smoked excessively with pejorative terms. Being called a "pothead" or a "stoner" was not a good thing, even among fellow pot smokers.

A lot more people were able and willing to discern good information from bad where marijuana was concerned, and many wanted to be given the right to choose to use it responsibly. An entire medical marijuana movement evolved from the need of cancer patients to eat and stay healthy; cannabis' role in preventing nausea and increasing appetite had finally been understood by sensible people in the general public to represent a viable way to keep cancer patients alive. Many have been astounded by the absolute resistance (largely governmental) that still exists concerning this health issue, which affects a multitude of suffering people. One book I came upon, called *Mom's Marijuana,* tells of a traditional, nondrug-using mother who learned how to grow marijuana plants in her garden to help her son deal with the negative affects of his treatment for cancer. It's hard to condemn a mother's love for her child, or to feel you have the right to tell this mother she can't do this simple little thing that makes her son eat more and feel better.

Meanwhile, a variety of cultures have collided because of increased travel and relocation opportunities, allowing many people in the United States to learn about other countries in which marijuana use has been a more-or-less accepted part of society. Before the United States coerced Jamaica into implementing laws that criminalized marijuana use—threatening to deny aid to them if they were noncompliant—many of its citizens used cannabis to relax socially and mitigate the ills of life. Many people in Jamaica still believe using cannabis cuts down on alcohol abuse.

In 1970 the U.S. National Institute of Mental Health sponsored a research program on the island to assess chronic marijuana users. The results of the study indicated not only that the use of marijuana went hand in hand with substantially lower levels of alcoholism, but that it did not damage the brain or cause crime, as some had claimed. The study also revealed that within the Jamaican culture there were built-in restraints that controlled marijuana use and abuse. The social rules of Jamaican culture dictated that marijuana should not be used on an empty stomach, when in an unsound mind, or by people who are unstable or have a problem maintaining equilibrium. Various other social regulations concerning marijuana use served as checks and balances, offering assurance that for most people its usage did not become a problem. It became a problem only when the United States made it a problem.

Another study on marijuana was done in England during the Beatles era, when fears concerning cannabis consumption reached a peak in that country. This study, called the Wootton Report (1969), confirmed earlier studies (including one done by the government of India as early as 1893) by concluding that long-term moderate use of marijuana produced no harmful effects. The report went on to say that marijuana was much less dangerous than opiates, amphetamines, or barbiturates, and even less dangerous than alcohol. The report stated that it is the personality of the user rather than the properties of the drug that will determine who will go on to use other drugs. The Wootton Report recommended to the British government that they change their regulations to make it unlikely someone would go to prison for small-scale possession of marijuana. The British government ignored the report and swiftly increased penalties for all cases involving marijuana, because just looking at the Beatles, the Stones, and their followers freaked them out. These harsher penalties did not stop the increase of marijuana use, however; in response to this failure, the English government in 1986 passed a law giving the police the power to seize all assets a "drug dealer" acquired over the past six years if this person was unable to account for their purchase. The seizure did not depend on the amount of drugs confiscated, and it was possible to lose everything you owned for possession of one joint. Reefer madness was alive and well.

The Netherlands' approach to all of this insanity was to revise their drug laws, reducing penalties for possession of marijuana and making it a misdemeanor to possess up to 30 grams of cannabis (considered equal to a three-month supply for a moderate user). Penalties for possession of larger amounts were also reduced, and those for heroin and cocaine were increased, in hopes it would give the message that there were indeed differences among these drugs, and cannabis was simply less dangerous than the others. Marijuana could not be fully legalized because the Netherlands had signed the United Nations Single Convention Treaty, a masterwork of our own Harry Anslinger, which made cannabis use prohibited throughout the world. A country could not legalize cannabis even if it wanted to, and countries were essentially blackmailed into signing it or else face the loss of U.S. money and support. Under this treaty, however, the Netherlands has been able to ignore minor possession of cannabis and concentrate on the reasonable control of consumption and sale of the herb. This allows for the time and resources saved from abandoning the relentless pursuit of small-time users of marijuana to be used for substance abuse awareness and treatment programs. Most importantly, the Netherlands has been able to steer young users away from more dangerous drugs by acknowledging that there are distinctions between drugs, or substances, or herbs, or weeds, and that there should be separate regulations and/or penalties regarding their use and abuse.

Cannabis in the Netherlands is not seen as a deviant and antisocial drug, as it is in the United States, and the young as a result do not feel inclined to rebel against authority by abusing it. They are able to purchase and smoke cannabis in coffeehouses, which are policed on the government's behalf by the owners of the establishments, who don't want the law to be broken because they don't want to lose their licenses. And because they are buying their cannabis in coffeehouses legally, young people do not come into contact with dealers who may be selling more dangerous drugs. Studies have also shown that young people in the Netherlands are usually older when they first smoke marijuana than in countries where it is illegal.

British Columbia has also seen fit to take a more gentle approach to cannabis use, choosing not to alienate its youth by harassing them regarding the moderate smoking of cannabis in coffeehouses. The sale of marijuana in these Canadian coffeehouses is not allowed, so it's sort of BYOM, which unfortunately pushes the acquisition of marijuana onto the street, where problems can arise. The part-legal-part-illegal status in Canada and the Netherlands is not ideal, but it's a start.

CHAPTER 9

Dependency and Addiction

Some interesting literature has come out of Canada (such as *Peaceful Measures: Canada's Way Out of the "War on Drugs"* by Bruce K. Alexander) regarding substance use and misuse. As the charge most often labeled against marijuana is that it is a gateway drug leading to more dangerous substances, Alexander's research is important because it disputes the entire concept of addiction, which implies the addict has an obsession with a specific substance. This new look at addiction views dependency on a given substance as resulting from dissociations in the mind of the addict rather than on the relationship between the addict and the particular substance. From this viewpoint, it stands to reason that the more personal problems one has, the more one will tend toward dependency or addiction, whether it be food, cocaine, heroin, cigarettes—whatever. While certain substances have physically addictive properties, many people can use them and not become addicted, which is why most people who consumed cocaine in Coca-Cola and opiates in over-the-counter medicines earlier in the century did not become addicts.

Eugene O'Neil's great drama *Long Day's Journey Into Night* deals with the tragedy of his mother, who became addicted to opiates. Most people of her era were able to use various medications that contained narcotics when needed and then forget about them. The currently fashionable and overly utilized genetic/disease model of addiction adheres to the belief that a specific substance introduced from outside of the body is the temptation, and a person's inability to resist that temptation is proof he or she has a genetic predisposition and must therefore never go near that particular substance again. Alexander presents an alternative view to the genetic/disease model of addiction, stating that addiction is an adaptation to serious problems or dire situations, and that often addiction is the best a person can do at a particular moment in time. Sometimes the alternatives can be much worse, and the person is literally prolonging his or her life by succumbing to dependency.

This new model of addiction-as-adaptation views dependency/addiction as a failure of psychosocial integration—basically a failure of human relationships, or some aspect of them—caused by a combination of social and constitutional problems, and this failure of integration can happen at any stage of the life cycle (although it is often the result of difficulties with early parental relationships). Even though these adaptations (addictions) are not as satisfying as psychosocial integration (i.e., having a healthy ego and good relationships) they allow the person to survive in the best shape possible under the circumstances that currently exist, leaving the gate open to try again later for assimilation and psychosocial success. What might be considered maladaptive behavior for people who are secure emotionally, socially, and financially can provide hope and distraction from unbearable psychological pain for others who are not so fortunate. Dissociations of the mind are caused by psychological pain, and the addicted person cannot be realistically expected to make a resolution to never use their substance of choice again because it is only one self state that has made the commitment. Only when the addict is treated as a person with many facets, psychosocially speaking, can we begin to deal with the problem of addiction, which is a result of failure or disappointment in the individual human system attempting to survive and flourish in a difficult world.

Alexander even takes on the genetic argument that certain races, such as Native Americans, are highly predisposed to suffer addiction. He believes Native American abuse of alcohol can be explained using the adaptive theory. Other groups of invaded or disrupted peoples, such as Australian aboriginals and American blacks (both when they were first brought over as slaves and when they took part in necessary migrations north looking for a new life), also suffered devastating addictions that have been routinely attributed to genetic inheritance rather than to the many sorrows and upheavals in their lives. Clearly the most disenfranchised of these target groups have succumbed to addiction in the most harmful of ways. The adaptive model postulates that negative addiction, although not a good thing, is often less harmful than the alternatives available, even abstinence in many cases.

Alexander claims that an animal gnawing off its leg to save his life rather than die in a trap is an example of adaptive behavior; it could only be viewed as maladaptive by someone who did not truly understand the alternative. The adaptive model is compatible with evolutionary theory; adaptations can protect the body from severe stress and thus prolong life, but if the adaptation persists for too long, it can cause permanent injury or even death. According to those who believe in the adaptive model of addiction, it is the difficulties encountered in altering a person's life that make addictions so difficult to cure, not a genetic predisposition. Often what is considered a genetic problem is really a problem of bad habits (attempted adaptations) being passed down through the generations because of poor psychosocial integration of individuals, families, and even communities.

Substance abuse must be viewed from the legal point of view as well as from the mental and physical perspective. The disease/criminal model of addiction subscribes to a dual premise that addiction is a disease and the user of illegal drugs is a criminal. Addiction is viewed as a biological process that is progressive and permanent; the drug user is seen as out of control and abstinence is seen as the only remedy. Social stigma and punitive legal practices have made it difficult to differentiate the harm caused by drugs from the multiple psychosocial injuries resulting from various legal and social penalties that come into play once a person has been exposed for using an illegal substance. If one overeats and becomes morbidly obese, help may be sought without being treated like a criminal. Full attention can be paid to the problem without legal/criminal issues interfering, and a setback is just that—a setback. In contrast, the recovering drug addict must deal with competing and overlapping legal, medical, and social professions, all trying to control the addict and the outcome of treatment in some way. Addicts who might choose to obtain treatment are reluctant to expose themselves to bureaucracies that seek to control and punish, rather than to help them in ways that are pragmatic in dealing with their diminished flexibility toward a specific substance.

Critics of the disease/criminal model of addiction believe that, historically, people have always found ways to alter their consciousness, and drug use is part of the daily life of every culture. They believe people have a wide range of experiences with drugs—from positive to negative—and the use of drugs does not necessarily lead to a negative or problematic relationship with their chosen substance. Critics of the disease/criminal model believe drug use is socially constructed, and drug legislation passed in the early 1900s was fueled by moral, racial, and economic concerns. Even today, there is no cultural agreement about which drugs are dangerous. Critics of the disease/criminal model of addiction believe pragmatic rather than moralistic treatment should be sought for users of all drugs—legal and illegal—and addicts should be able to participate in their own goal-setting and treatment choice.

Despite their low success rate, most treatment programs today strive for total "cures"—abstinence is always the goal of treatment. Critics of the medical model believe abstinence is only one option in a wide range of practical choices for drug users. Addicts often complain that current disease models of treatment not only encourage failure and punishment but societal expectations are higher for illegal drug users than for legal drug users. People who try to quit cigarettes or alcohol are not subjected to the same scrutiny as are the users of illegal drugs; they are often viewed as valuable and productive citizens despite their addictions and their failure to control them. Users of illegal substances often feel that treatment strips them of self-worth. Addicts complain that people who work in drug agencies often go home after busting someone for illegal drugs, and drink booze and smoke cigarettes, perpetuating a double standard.

Research shows that drug use is not static and individuals usually move within a continuum, with their patterns of use increasing when times are tough and decreasing as they are able to get things under control. Even positive events such as graduations and weddings produce extra stress that often results in a user's increased use of whatever he or she fancies: food, alcohol, cigarettes, coffee, pot—whatever. Negative events are even more likely to trigger a substance abuse problem. A close friend told me how she literally became a coffee addict after her father died, eventually ending up at the office of her family physician seeking help. At least she didn't have to worry about going to jail, even though a heavily caffeinated person is more likely to be involved with speeding or road rage than someone who has smoked a joint.

Patterns of drug use in people's lives can include abstinence, experimental use, circumstantial use, casual use, regular recreational use, dependence, and addiction. Although addiction is necessarily central to a person's life and supplants other important activities, dependence may remain in the background of a person's life, possibly causing little harm and perhaps adding pleasure and relaxation unobtainable through other means. There are many users of illegal drugs who are not visible users; there is also much diversity with regard to class, race, expectations, social setting, and drug of choice.

Conventional research concentrates on users who are poor, usually minorities from the inner city, while there are many upper-, middle-, and working-class drug users who go unstudied. Many of the characteristics and attributes assigned to illegal drug users have little or nothing to do with drugs, but instead indicate attitudes concerning the user's race and class, and the illegal status of specific drugs. More research must be done to explore the historical underpinnings of the inequalities that shape drug use, thus laying the groundwork for designing meaningful, productive, and pragmatic treatment programs for all people who seek treatment for dependency on drugs, both legal and illegal. The countries that are experimenting with alternative ways to treat substance abuse will hopefully help to shed light on more promising and successful methods of treatment than those currently in place.

According to the adaptive view, the only way to cure substance abuse is to better the lives of the addicted. This doesn't mean just dumping all addicts off at the local welfare department, but seriously dealing with the social injustices that are an integral part of our system. So far, it has been easier to put people who can't cope into jail than to help them build better lives. Ordinary citizens and the powers-that-be in the United States must be encouraged to take another look at our abhorrent methods of dealing with these issues, as the way we control, manipulate, and legislate substances that people use to modify their state of being impinges on the lives of millions.

A recent article in the *New York Times* featured a family who had been greatly impacted by the husband/father's nineteen-year incarceration for selling three ounces of cocaine to undercover cops in 1985. The article spoke of his daughter, who was eleven when her father went to prison, and mentioned the tears in her eyes as she watched him appear in court for the hearing that would set him free early under recently revised drug laws. He had originally been given a mandatory sentence of twenty-five years to life under the draconian New York State Rockefeller laws. His nineteen-year-old-son has never known his father as anything other than an inmate and did not come to the hearing. His wife, who was left with the responsibility of raising their two children alone, had miraculously stood by his side and was anxiously awaiting his release. Considering that according to some, our current president was doing just about the same thing at just about the same time in his life, is there anyone out there who can honestly say this was a fair and just punishment for this man and his family? Imagine living nineteen years in a jail cell because of a stupid, reckless act—but a nonviolent act nonetheless. Are we as a people really that cruel?

It is our greed as a nation that has produced the need for adulterated versions of common plants that have been revered since before Biblical times in their natural state, which now in their adulterated states are many times more powerful and costly than the simple plants ever were. The problems we have created in trying to deal with people's attraction to natural plants such as cannabis, coca, and poppy have greatly surpassed any problems that these plants alone and unadulterated have ever caused humankind.

The Indians of South America have chewed the leaves of the coca plant for thousands of years; chewing the leaves allows small amounts of the substance to enter their bodies, slowly producing the desired effects. These native populations have used and continue to use the coca plant to give them increased levels of endurance and strength to help them deal with the harsh climates and demands of their lives. The problems with the coca plant didn't start until a much more powerful substance, cocaine, was made from its leaves to supply a market created mainly in the United States by its desperate citizens, anxious to augment their frenzied lives. The natives of countries who cherish the coca plant for its beneficial qualities used the plant to address their needs for many years before they were literally accosted by the humongous appetite of U.S. citizens who needed desperately to change the way they felt. By using cocaine they were attempting to adapt to the highly competitive and fast-paced life that was becoming more American than apple pie. European intellectuals had first whetted international curiosity about cocaine, believing it to be a wonder drug and only later coming to realize its dangers. The European cocaine craze was a rather short-lived phenomena experienced by some of the intellectual elite who were generally smart enough to know when enough was enough. Most did not come from financial circumstances that required them to take advantage of the public's desire for the drug by trying to profit from the sale of it, as was the case with the man who served nineteen years for what Freud and other distinguished citizens were able to experiment with and then let go of, moving onto the rest of their lives free from the constraints of jail.

And what about alcohol? A young man asked me the other day why alcohol was legal and marijuana illegal, because his experience was telling him alcohol was the more dangerous substance. It is difficult to tell young people the story of the devious and twisted drug enforcement history in America, and how our own unjust hypocrisy in this matter has gone on to influence the rest of the world. We have used our power to demand of other nations they follow our example in drug matters, or lose their subsidies from us, even when these other countries have come to different conclusions from the United Sates regarding the danger of some of these substances (the unadulterated versions).

Alcohol is an adulterated substance that has been used to help people feel better throughout the ages, medicinally and otherwise. The good and bad properties of alcohol have been with us ever since some prehistoric chef left some fruit out to rot and discovered the changes wrought by fermentation. Although it is hard to find something that everyone in this country agrees on, probably close to 100 percent of everyone would agree that alcohol has caused untold grief for millions, and yet we wouldn't think of prohibiting it again by law, because we know it doesn't work.

The colonizing English learned a harsh lesson about how hard it is to control substances used to alter moods when they tried to tax the alcoholic spirits of the new settlers in America. John Hancock of signature fame was one rebel who reacted by smuggling his own alcohol; he reportedly evaded the king's customs officers with great success. Hancock and others literally endangered their lives to avoid having to pay taxes on whiskey to England; upon one occasion they even dragged a British customs ship onto the beach and torched it. The Revolution began shortly thereafter, and we know who won, but the leaders of our new country emerged from their victorious fray seventy million dollars in debt. And what did our founding fathers decide to do? Tax alcoholic beverages—which makes sense when the tax revenues are going to your own country.

The upside of taxing substances that are considered harmful is that it not only raises money for government services, which hopefully include health care for people who have problems regulating the use of these substances, but it also limits the quantity people will use simply by making excessive amounts unaffordable for the average person. Most people cannot afford to drink in excess for a variety of reasons, and certainly one's financial situation is one factor in determining what one drinks and how much. Drinking alcohol in restaurants and bars has become prohibitively expensive for many people. And the people who can most afford it are assumed to self-regulate their consumption of toxins because they are so happy with their privileged lives that they do not want to die young, and so do everything in moderation, including drinking or drugs. There are exceptions to this rule, of course, and there seems to be no more newsworthy event in America than a rich person or celebrity out of control on booze or drugs. Stories about inebriated movie stars making fools of themselves, particularly if accompanied by arrest photos showing exactly what they looked like in their most out-of-control moment, can easily throw a story about the breakout of war between two countries to the back pages.

The downside of taxing substances such as alcohol is that it has often led to finding ways to purchase the product without paying taxes, such as making moonshine or "rum-running." The American Moonshine Industry was born on the day Alexander Hamilton and his cronies agreed to tax alcohol to raise revenue for the U.S. Treasury following the Revolutionary War. There was a time when there was so much moonshine being produced in this country, it was considered liquid trade in certain territories, just as cannabis was used for barter and legal tender at times in our history. For some people whiskey was how they paid the rent and bought food; they were unable to pay taxes because they did not deal in cash and thus did not have any.

At one point trouble ensued because of difficulties collecting taxes from the moonshiners, and President George Washington called out the military, sending thirteen thousand troops to Pittsburgh. This all-out attempt to establish some control over the burgeoning homespun alcohol industry did not stop the production of moonshine, but the massive effort effectively pushed those who survived it out of the city and into the mountains and the woods where they could hide and continue their way of life. The Moonshine Capital of America slowly emerged from deep in the southern backwoods of Kentucky.

Every time this country has tried to prohibit alcohol use in any way, even by taxation, it has served as a catalyst for making moonshine. The word "bootlegger" refers to a man who sold moonshine during the early history of this country when settlers were known to hide the contraband in their boots. It seems that at times when the consumption of alcohol has either gotten out of control or certain teetotalers think it has, someone always comes along to demand the total removal of this substance, thus creating a destructive want and need far greater than what had previously proved troublesome.

During the 1850s in Maine, a future hero of the Temperance Movement, Neil Dow, helped push through a law banning alcohol sales and consumption for the entire state, whereas before this time alcohol had always been the social drug of choice and acceptance. It is said that as a result of this ban on alcohol, the stills of moonshiners could be seen dotting the hillsides throughout Maine; alcohol was also smuggled over state borders, requiring "criminals" from neighboring states to participate, or creating them when they failed to find any. Many people were only too willing to participate in what had become a large and successful business, albeit an illegal one. In 1855 a mob assaulted city hall in what has been called the "Portland Rum Riot"; a large group of angry residents stole the alcohol stored in the courthouse that was meant for druggist use only. The militia was brought in to tame the unruly crowd, and Neil Dow gave the orders for them to fire; many citizens were wounded in the melee and one of the rebels even died fighting for his right to drink. Other states followed Maine over the years in banning alcohol, and by 1915 over half of the states in the country had adopted this prohibitionist measure. The moonshine business was thriving, as was interstate criminal activity to supply the dry states. By 1919 the moral crusaders had won completely, and the Eighteenth Amendment to Prohibit Alcohol was passed by Congress over a veto by President Woodrow Wilson.

Alcohol distillers who once ran legal businesses found themselves joining the moonshiners in the woods in order to make a living. People out of work turned to growing corn or grain or chopping wood for the distilleries, as the government's policies outlawing booze paved the way for new opportunities to make money. They were breaking laws many regarded as unjust and impossible to enforce anyway. Some opportunists started putting more sugar than corn into their moonshine, enabling them to reap greater profits for an inferior product; there was no central body to set standards for the alcohol produced and no system to test for alcohol content or purity. There were fifteen hundred federal agents who were responsible for busting and destroying bootleggers and their moonshine. Their salaries were poor, and it is said few of the agents were honest. At any rate, it has been estimated they managed to confiscate no more than 5 percent of all of the moonshine produced illegally in the hills and woods of the nation at that time.

Breaking the law became romantic as "speakeasies" welcomed women to come in and drink and listen to the music for the first time; before prohibition women were not allowed in saloons. "Flappers" (people who carried flasks of whiskey) were all the rage as songs glorifying the booze-filled jazz clubs asked, "When will this place be raided?" and singer Bessie Smith bellowed, "Gimme a pig foot and a bottle of beer...we gonna get rousted when the wagons come." The Twenty-One Club in New York City is said to have had a secret buzzer that sent a signal to get rid of the booze behind fake doors if a rousting did occur; similar scenarios could be found in speakeasies throughout the country. A criminal element heretofore unknown in America was encouraged to rise and flourish, as even honest people were enticed into breaking the law. Bad booze became a serious health hazard; watered-down liquor became known as "monkey rum" or "bathtub gin," and sometimes even embalming fluid was used to increase profits. Thousands of deaths were attributed to rotgut liquor as a prohibition program that was doomed to fail limped forward.

There was a large amount of liquor brought into the country illegally—much of it over water in boats of various shapes and sizes. Perilous battles were fought at sea during Prohibition, as huge increases of rum were imported by "rum-runners" who anchored three miles offshore in what became known as "Rum Row." Boats of every kind went out to Rum Row to buy the liquor, and the Coast Guard had a hard time catching them. The rum-runners even filled torpedoes with bottles of alcohol and fired them onto Long Island, which resulted in the government's pushing Rum Row farther out to sea by several miles. The bootleggers used Sea Skiffs that were slow but flat bottomed and could be pushed onto the shore to unload their goods. The U.S. Coast Guard hired the same men who were building boats for the rum-runners to build boats for them. Whose boats do you think these hardworking men built to go just a little bit faster? To further increase their ability to outwit the Coast Guard, the rum-runners added oil to the engines to create heavy smokescreens, especially at night. Angered at the rum-runners' ability to always stay one step ahead of them, the Coast Guard even resorted to opening fire with machine guns on boats they thought were carrying alcohol. It's hard to imagine the government today shooting at a group of people to prevent them from drinking or smuggling alcohol, but it is not a totally unfamiliar scenario in today's drug war.

A huge amount of the alcohol consumed during Prohibition came from Canada via the Detroit River, which was the funnel used by many Canadian breweries to get their alcohol into the United States. When the river was frozen over in the winter, automobiles and trucks were used to drive the alcohol to their desperate neighbors over the ice. Big-time bootleggers bankrolled organized crime and two-bit thugs were made into millionaires overnight. The totally ruthless "Purple Gang" emerged from the chaos in Detroit led by the Bernstein Brothers, who were known to kill anyone who got in their way; hundreds of unsolved murders have been attributed to this gang. In 1927 alone over a half-million cases of liquor were smuggled across the Detroit River from Canada. No wonder it attracted the interest of Al Capone, who came to Detroit, met with the Bernstein Brothers, and with them organized the Valentine's Day Massacre, which was intended to wipe out all competition from Detroit's north side. This bloody slaughter sickened the rest of America, especially as most everyone at this point was ready to admit Prohibition had failed. President Franklin D. Roosevelt finally conceded defeat and repealed Prohibition, ending the thirteen-year experiment that had permanently changed the fabric of America.

Moonshine had become fully entrenched in the United States before the end of Prohibition, and the need for it did not end when the law changed. There were many people who couldn't afford or preferred not to pay taxes on their alcohol; some just liked the taste of moonshine. Automobiles were overhauled to carry large loads of these alcoholic spirits, which were now legal to drink but illegal when they went untaxed; it is said a rebuilt 1944 Ford Sedan could carry 122 gallons of what the moonshiners called "white lightning." The engines on these new rum-runners were also modified for greater speed; the horsepower could be more than doubled, allowing the moonshiners to outrun the police. Reputedly the 1950 Ford Ambulance, already built for speed, was ideal for the moonshiner, especially after a little tampering with the engine.

The world of auto racing and NASCAR originated with people who were moonshiners. Junior Johnson was NASCAR's first winning driver and is considered by many to be the greatest race car driver who has ever lived. The car he drove for his first win had been used just a week earlier to run moonshine. Many other bootleggers were involved in racing their souped-up cars, dividing their time between racing and running moonshine. Junior Johnson was finally arrested one day at his father's still and served almost a year in jail; when released, he went back to both racing and running moonshine. He claims the fastest car he ever drove was a bootlegging car. In 1986 President Ronald Reagan gave Johnson a full pardon for his troubles with the law.

After prohibition ended, tax collectors found themselves in the position of having to track down and terrorize bootleggers to collect money. These organized efforts turned into the Bureau of Alcohol, Tobacco and Firearms. Since the agency has started tracking moonshiners from the sky it has become increasingly difficult to hide large-scale stills and rum-running. Yet moonshine will always exist, not only for people who can't afford the taxed stuff or actually prefer the white lightning taste, but also for many rugged individuals who are titillated by ideas of freedom.

CHAPTER 10

Power and Control

The young man I spoke with who questioned why marijuana use was punished more severely than alcohol use could not have understood all that was involved with this country's attempt to try and control the use of alcohol, and how severely it had failed, creating serious problems in its wake. The governmental and societal logic seems to be that if marijuana were legalized and treated the same as alcohol, with treatment centers for potential abusers, for example, it would somehow increase the number of dysfunctional addicts in the country, rather than decreasing the number by providing a safer outlet for "what ails" than the currently legal alcohol. This young man who questioned the status quo exists in a social culture where many of his peers prefer marijuana to alcohol, and one of the reasons for this is they believe marijuana is less dangerous than alcohol. These young people are currently feeling alienated from a country that is making what they consider to be a false judgment on at least one of their life choices.

My young friend's question about why marijuana was illegal when alcohol is not makes many people nervous because it is so obviously a rational and responsible question, yet somehow it remains unanswered. Why are we allowing millions of people to be maimed physically and psychologically from alcohol abuse while continuing to prohibit a milder and wiser antidote to the human situation, namely cannabis? We are exposed continually to movies and TV scenarios where actors and comedians smoke "weed"; some of these movies glorify its cultivation as well as its use. We live in a culture where an illegal substance, marijuana, is in de facto legal, or so it appears if one is at all tuned into the media. Audiences who would complain like crazy if "normal" people were shown in movies shooting up heroin have grown accustomed to pot-smoking scenes, largely because many of the moviegoers smoke marijuana themselves, or have done so in the past without resultant problems.

Although many of these references to marijuana are tantamount to advertisements, mostly positive in nature, it is also through the media that the downfalls of too much marijuana smoking are explored. Popular wisdom has it that if you smoke too much you can get forgetful, lazy, and eat too much. Responsible media has been enlisted to serve not only as carriers of the current cultural story but also to admonish people to resist excess, much as the Jamaican cultural restraints regarding cannabis use have served that society. Irresponsible media makes light of restraint and encourages excess, much to the delight of the young and inexperienced, some of whom will suffer the consequences. Responsible media helps to balance and add restraint, serving to warn about the various outcomes that await those who do not treat their bodies and minds with the care they deserve. Responsible people pay close attention to these warnings and seek to guide those who might be having problems so they do not burden their bodies with toxins while trying to alleviate the stress in their lives.

The possibility that cannabis could replace antidepressants, at least for some people, seems to be begging for consideration and research. Realistically, there are many people who have already chosen to use marijuana in lieu of antidepressants, usually after they have tried one or more of the pharmaceuticals and did not like the side effects, or just felt the antidepressants did not work for them. For many who make this choice, it is the only illegal thing they do in their lives, and it often makes them feel like criminals (which they are). But they have decided to take the risk for their emotional wellbeing, in much the same way John Hancock and others were compelled to take the risk to smuggle alcohol for their wellbeing. The point is that we as a people are living a lie where the use of marijuana is concerned, and the younger generation is using our response to this issue as a litmus test to see if they can trust the older, in-charge generations on other issues.

The price in trust has been high in order to maintain the lie. In movies and on television young people see marijuana smoked as if it were no big deal, and yet they hear about harsh penalties being imposed for possession of small amounts if someone does not have the right lawyer or is the wrong color, or just ticks someone off. The youngest generation is getting some very mixed messages—many of the people they idolize clearly smoke marijuana and like it, and they don't see anything really bad happening to them. These kids grew up hearing about all the rock stars from their parents' generation who died from drug overdoses—but it was never from smoking marijuana.

When the young man asked me the question about the legality of alcohol versus marijuana, I was working with a group of teenagers. When the subject of marijuana and memory loss came up in our discussion, a teacher's assistant who was born and raised in Jamaica disagreed with the prepackaged conclusion that marijuana affects memory. She told of visiting the island and running into a man she hadn't seen in decades who remembered her name and everything about her and everyone she had grown up with—right down to the last detail. She said he smoked three large reefers every day for almost all of his life, and his memory was sharp as a tack. I conceded it was probably short-term memory that is the problem—like forgetting where you put your car keys.

This Jamaican woman said that when the United States first came to her country and forced them to make marijuana illegal, threatening to withhold aid for noncompliance, over half of the inhabitants of the island used cannabis in one form or another, even boiling the twigs for tea. The islanders were familiar with age-old medicinal recipes and used them frequently. She remembers the horror of the U.S. planes flying overhead to spray the marijuana crops. She recalls the orange dust and how many people were sick afterward, and how all the vegetation was ruined, and how many of the animals that depended on the vegetation were poisoned and died, and how the soils were contaminated for future generations. She said that in Jamaican schools it is common to hold classes outside, and she remembers the planes coming and watching as some of the pilots swooped down and seemed to deliberately spray the children; she holds a picture in her mind of the pilots laughing as they turned their planes back toward the sky. These are the memories of a teacher's assistant in our public schools, and though she has chosen to be in this country because here is where the advantages lie for her family, she never forgets what she has learned about the zeal of the United Sates when it gets a bee under its bonnet.

With all that is going on in the world, do we really want *this particular bee under our collective bonnet* when we should be directing all of our energy toward trying to keep the world from self-destructing? It's interesting and ironic that it is in the part of the world where we were not successful in forcing prohibition of cannabis where we are currently finding most of our problems internationally. Our enemies are a cannabis-permitting alcohol-eschewing people. Do we dare tell them our way is superior to theirs when we have millions of citizens suffering from liver disease and mind rot because of the excessive use of Saint Alcohol?

My son is among many his age who are questioning why an herb they consider less harmful than alcohol is illegal when alcohol is not. His father, suffering from the loss of his brother and best friend, took advantage of our son's legitimate questions about life to lure him into a lifestyle that could, if left unchecked, lead him straight to jail, or worse. Clearly my son's coming of age was having an impact on my husband's behavior, not just because his son was a substitute for his brother, but because he now felt engaged in determining our son's manhood and wanted the mother who had largely raised him to step aside. My final role was expected to be the deliverance of my son to his father for his final stamp of definition, and I could only hope that some of what my son and I had had together over the years since his birth would stay with him.

The new patriarchal emphasis in our family continued having an impact on our daughter as well as influencing our son. At one point she elected to do an internship at a local battered woman's shelter. One day she came home with a pamphlet that listed about a dozen warning signs of an abusive partner. She posted the list on the refrigerator, saying, "My father has every sign of an abuser on the list except one." When I asked her which one he didn't have, she replied, "The one where he says he's sorry and won't ever do it again." She put the list on the refrigerator where it stayed for weeks; it was the only way she felt she could be heard.

I had long known my husband to have abusive qualities, but he had never actually hit me; instead, whenever there was a problem, he would work very hard at trying to convince me it was entirely my fault. He would usually try to accomplish this feat by yelling and screaming at me. Unfortunately, I often felt the only way I could be heard was to yell back, although it never worked as he would always up the ante until I became afraid he would go over the edge and hit me, so I would back down. More than once throughout the years I had actually gotten to the point of telling our children their father and I were divorcing, but they were very threatened by the idea and they always joined my husband in talking me out of it. They wanted a normal family and I always backed down because I wanted to give them one. I had hoped building a house and moving away from my husband's beginnings, a small town lost in the woods where behavior such as his is more acceptable, would improve things. But the death of his brother and our son's coming of age worked as an accelerant on behavior that was already troublesome.

As our daughter matured I could see she was continuing to view her father with very critical eyes. When she started her first semester of college she came home from a psychology course and said, "My father is a sociopath. He fits all the criteria, especially the one about being so charming to people to cover up his bad behavior." My husband could be utterly charming, even to relative strangers, and I often had people make comments to me concerning what a nice man my husband was. My husband could actually be nice and even helpful at times to both me and my daughter, but it was always totally at his discretion, and only when he was in a good mood.

I couldn't help but notice every time I had something really important coming up that involved a lot of work or concentration, he would agitate for a fight, almost as if he were threatened by my possible independence. Although in the end I could usually count on him to come through for me, it was not until he had completely mangled my emotions and left me unnerved and lacking in self-confidence. I grew to not count on him emotionally, and he grew to resent my independence; he became more difficult as time went on, as I not coincidentally became more proficient in removing myself from his emotional tirades.

Sometimes he didn't seem happy until he had managed to really tick me off. I later read in my studies that this is a typical behavior (a defense mechanism) often used by substance abusers called "projective identification." A person who feels a lot of anger projects that anger onto another person, behaving as though that other person is the angry one who needs to be feared and controlled. They behave in ways that actually make the other person angry at them, and then they stand back and act like he or she is the angry person, not them. My husband continually moved from one extreme to the other in terms of his feeling states, and predicting what mood he was going to be in at any given time was almost impossible.

It was extremely difficult for me to deal with the intensity of my husband's mood changes—he could go from acting like a complete maniac, pounding his fist through a wall, to enthusiastically offering to help me dig a trench for some flowers he knew I wanted to plant. In fact, there was no better time to have him do a project than right after one of his flipouts; I didn't even have to ask. Unable to deal with his outbursts in an authentic manner, he would become the do-gooder running around trying to fix things that had needed fixing for months. At that point I was so angry, I usually wasn't speaking to him. It was his way of turning things around and starting over; like Sisyphus, he became expert at rolling the rock up the hill and then having it roll back down again, with nothing ever changing or progressing. I knew in my heart it was never going to get any better and finally gave up trying. There were moments when I felt sorry for him and us because he was seemingly unaware of the connection between his actions and my feelings toward him. He believed love was loving someone anyway—despite everything. Life just doesn't work that way.

In his book *Why Does He Do That? Inside the Minds of Angry and Controlling Men*, Lundy Bancroft says men who abuse women represent every personality type and come from all walks of life. Contrary to their often-used excuses, these men are aware of what they are doing to the women they are trying to control—unless they are extremely mentally ill and their reality testing is off. Bancroft is a counselor to the male abusers of women, and claims cultural training, not childhood deficits, are the key to why men abuse women. His work with abusers has led him to believe that role models and peer groups are more apt to determine whether or not a male becomes disrespectful and abusive to females than whether or not a man was himself abused as a child.

Bancroft goes on to say that abusers are drawn to power and control, and part of getting it is to be charming in public so they will look good and the claims of their abused women will not be believed by others. Often women do not reach out for assistance or tell anyone what is going on because they feel no one will believe them, especially if their mate has done a good job of convincing others he is a great guy. Sometimes I would almost gag watching my husband drool all over someone—male or female—I knew he didn't care one whit about but was trying to impress with his charm. People are very susceptible and responsive to this kind of sycophantic behavior. Once at a family reunion, my husband saw me speaking to a cousin who I had met only a couple of times in my life and barely knew. He assumed that since we were cousins we must have had a long history of intimacy; he came up and started telling her how often I had spoken of her and so forth. My children and I were dumbfounded, and everyone standing there—except him—knew that what he was saying had no bearing in reality. We all said nothing, letting the space fill with awkward silence after he finished speaking. In his effort to be charming, he never let truth get in the way.

Once I returned to graduate school, I had the opportunity to focus on issues that related to various problems I was experiencing in my own family; I became especially interested in doing research on women who were the victims of domestic abuse. I learned that my feelings of shame and disappointment were normal, as women in particular have a psychic investment in creating the ideal home space, and when it doesn't work out, they feel like they have personally failed in their mission. The warm bosom of the hearth and home had become increasingly chaotic and unkind once I began to assert myself against an increasingly volatile husband. I had to learn to take care of myself so as not to absorb all of the guilt and all of the blame; this simple mission turned out to be one of the most difficult endeavors of my life.

As I tried to piece together exactly what had happened in my life to bring me to this difficult place, I realized that, as with all people, I was simply the product of all that had gone before me, not only within my original nuclear family but without in the broader space of the world. Raised in a midsized conservative city known more for cornstalks and pork bellies than culture, I used my first opportunity to flee by going away to college on the West Coast. Conflict slowly emerged as I grew a new identity alien to the rigidly narrow expectations of my past. My leitmotif for the next couple of decades was to try to become an authentic person and not be totally rejected by people with whom I was already on thin ice—my conservative, strict, and powerful parents. During the time I was growing up, the future for young women was pretty bleak, with few opportunities other than marriage and childrearing, or perhaps nursing or teaching. Many parents believed it was their job to break the spirits of those daughters who had stars in their eyes and wished on the moon, just so they wouldn't be disappointed.

I was a young woman in college when a cultural revolution emerged from the chaos of the civil rights and anti–Vietnam War movements, eventually morphing into the women's movement. This second wave of feminine values was essentially born out of the frustrations women felt while dealing with the arrogance and disrespect of the males who they encountered while trying to participate in the civil rights and anti–Vietnam War movements. A proposal by women read at a Students for a Democratic Society (SDS) convention in the 1960s demanding full participation was greeted with hoots and catcalls, while the president of the Student Non-Violent Coordinating Committee (SNCC) responded that the only position in the movement for women was prone.

As a female entering adulthood with all sorts of fears and apprehensions, I was immediately attracted to the new feminine movement and was more than happy to blame all of my problems on sexist policy—past and present. When I moved to the country from the big city after graduating from college, I found myself living amidst a time warp where the women's movement had yet to appear. I tried hard to fit in—learning to grow vegetables and can tomatoes—but when the Equal Rights Amendment (ERA) was being debated, I couldn't help but get involved, going door to door for votes.

After it was defeated, a woman neighbor told me upon seeing my sadness that even though her husband had told me he was going to vote *yes,* he didn't and never had any intention of it; he had lied rather than disappoint me. Although at that point I felt betrayed by the whole world, I was touched by his concern for my feelings and learned to live with the defeat, until a so-called "snuff" movie arrived at a theater in a nearby town. I immediately joined a motley group of nuns and lesbians and Latinos (the purported victim was from South America) to picket the theater, and we actually succeeded in getting them to stop showing that horrible movie. There was little else to do but adjust to the time warp and grow cabbages the size of watermelons with pure cow shit shoveled by hand from a pickup truck.

At first I loved being outdoors and not always thinking. By the time I met my future husband, I had abandoned the identity of an intellectual city girl and was happy to meet the epitome of a healthy, handsome male from the culture I had partially adopted. I felt that as a woman I could counterbalance some of the ingrained patriarchal stuff from my culture by being with a man who had been raised with different expectations about male and female roles. I had grown weary of the stuff of early feminist battles—trying to gain ground inch by inch with men of my ilk: white, privileged males born with silver spoons in me-first mouths, who truly believed it was their right to always be in the driver's seat. My new beau was salt of the earth and did not appear to be threatened by the kinds of issues that had proved troublesome in previous relationships. I believed there was a greater possibility for equality in the male/female arena because of our cultural differences. It didn't hurt that he was five years younger, which also helped balance the male/female power differential inherent in patriarchal cultures. I was not about to accuse myself of being naïve or lacking in circumspection, particularly living in the middle of nowhere, which was the only place I could afford on the paltry income of a starving female artist.

At first it was a relief to live a life devoid of the intellectual arguments raised by men threatened by the slowly changing status quo. I felt more freedom in not really belonging to my surrounding culture than I had in supposedly belonging, and it was freedom I wanted—freedom from the ten million constraints that had been forced down my gullet by every person, situation, or institution I had had dealings with since the day I was born. I was such a misfit among the natives in my new land, they had few expectations of me and I of them. Away from so-called civilization, I was able to ignore the fact that most other "liberated" women were busy getting careers together. The low cost of living enabled me to concentrate on my art, which I honestly believed mattered in a world saturated with the work of male artists. What I didn't understand was how thick and low the triple thermopane glass ceiling was for women in the fine arts; I bumped my head on it getting out of bed every morning for the next few decades. Those decades included giving birth to and raising my two children, which reduced not only my time in the studio but my ability to be an advocate for women's issues. Time passed and as my needs changed due primarily to the advent of motherhood, I began to be more aware of how differently from my husband I experienced the world.

As the years went by, my discontent grew and festered in proportion to my growing sense of isolation and helplessness. I grew less interested in being part of my husband's world, which centered increasingly on his obsession with marijuana. When issues concerning my husband's excessive use of pot became problematic in our relationship, he became more difficult and controlling, keeping me in line with the mantra that I couldn't go for help because it would threaten his job. His modus operandi was that he was not about to let me or anyone else tell him what to do. Period.

Bringing professional help into our lives had seemed the only option but now that I had taken that route, I found myself in the biggest mess of my life. How could I have trusted the police? How could I have believed in the therapist who repeatedly encouraged me to go to the police? The reality was that my husband's increasingly bizarre behavior had pushed me into a corner and I felt a tremendous pressure to fix things; since nothing that I'd done on my own had any impact, I was forced to trust people outside of my sphere of influence. I had never before been intimately involved with the law, and had lived peacefully for decades obeying the "don't ask, don't tell" rule that seemed to apply to moderate marijuana consumption. Not only did the media, the modern-day temple of worship, give tacit approval for this attitude and behavior, but an extra wink was given to artists as though to condone this accepted boon to creativity. That those five marijuana plants and a first-time offense could completely destroy the lives of an entire family was not a possibility I had considered on that fateful day when I finally broke down under the strain. What kind of government would be so cruel as to take away a person's income and benefits from more than twenty years of hard work when what the person obviously needed was treatment—not just for excessive use of a substance but for the complicated mental health problems that caused the misuse in the first place?

What I had not understood as a white, middle-class citizen was that the so-called war on drugs was quite literally a war, and that as often happens during a war against another country, normal peacetime rules of law had been suspended. Had I not spent the year following my husband's arrest doing research, I probably would have chalked our horrendous experience up to bad luck. But any innocence I once had was lost upon learning more about how our government has misbehaved and harmed not only so many of its own citizens but the peoples of the world as well—creating havoc by influencing economies and policies around the globe with punitive and atavistic drug policies. With all the looking the other way and winking and media endorsements throughout the years, I had actually grown so naïve as to believe that marijuana was moderately tolerated in our society. Many adults no longer became hysterical when they discovered their adolescents smoked marijuana; some perhaps even preferred that their teens experiment with pot rather than cigarettes or alcohol. These adults were, after all, the first generation to have actually tried all three of these substances and knew more about the relative dangers of each.

In general, it was the people who had persisted in smoking cigarettes and drinking alcohol excessively who were having the health problems now. The moderate smokers of marijuana I knew were among the healthiest people around, usually paying close attention to all they consumed. I began to understand that my family had joined hordes of other victims in one of the most hypocritical, self-serving (by the privileged few) frauds of our time. Drug war propaganda resembles real wartime propaganda in that its mission is to frighten and control, not inform. The violence and repetition of messages in both kinds of war are extraordinarily simple and effective: Hate thy enemy.

The relationship of the drug war to ethnic minorities is clear as we fill our prisons with people of color who have violated the rules of society. Their crimes are often related to drugs—generally to the problems created by the prohibition of drugs rather than to the drugs themselves. We have allowed ourselves to take a serious look at the unhealthy relationship between alcohol and crime. Now that problems relating to the prohibition of alcohol are largely in the past, we can clearly see how the Mafia was formed and other criminal activity came about as a result of trying to enforce an unenforceable law.

There are still many crimes that result from alcohol intoxication itself because of the way alcohol affects the body. We know the overuse of this substance can lead to aggressive and/or dangerous behavior, putting not only the drunk but others in harm's way. Yet the jail time for an accident that occurs under the influence of alcohol, even one resulting in serious injury or death, is often less than that for possession of a small amount of marijuana because there are many powerful people who drink alcohol and who could possibly find themselves or a family member in the horrible position of having committed vehicular manslaughter. Drunk driving is usually a white man's crime; first of all, you have to own a car. The laws support and protect the actions and activities of those in power, and assist in persecuting those who question the righteousness of rules meant to control and punish the disenfranchised.

What interested me most during my research on substance abuse was the idea that addiction is the result of the failure of an individual to make it in their environment on some level and that addiction can serve as an alternate lifestyle for a person until something better can be worked out, often saving him or her from worse harm. In the case of severely down-and-out people, this may be never—and may even result in death. But for the majority of people, addiction is often a temporary refuge that allows for the ego to be safeguarded, thus preserving body and mind and defending them against worse afflictions such as insanity or suicide.

Research shows that most people are able to avoid addiction and are able to use substances in ways that are positive and nonthreatening (e.g., a glass of wine or two with dinner). A person could go on living with a habit like that for decades, and when he or she eventually dies, nobody is going to say it was the wine that killed him or her. When people are so down-and-out they are dangerously using a substance, their problems are usually so deep-seated one can often sympathize with their choice to numb themselves. It is clearly a failure of society that we have so many citizens who want to numb themselves—even to the point of death.

Bruce Alexander's book advocating "peaceful measures" to deal with mind-altering substances promotes the adaptive model as the only reasonable explanation for addiction, stressing that integration failure is actually a precondition of addiction. The "identity achievement" stage that takes place in adolescence is the most dangerous time for the adoption of a "negative identity" such as addiction. It is at this time that delinquency, alcohol, cigarettes, drugs and totalitarian thinking (such as cults) have a special allure. The task for the individual at this juncture in life is to create a healthy boundary between childhood and adulthood, where a sense of wholeness and inner identity allow one to integrate personal and public identities.

This task is so overwhelming and difficult for young people who are trying to leave childhood behind, societies actually allow for a "moratorium" from adult responsibility while this (hopefully) successful transformation is taking place. During this period of time, much is overlooked and forgiven as adolescents flounder in their attempts at social integration, sometimes taking temporary refuge in substitute identities that are condemned by society. A prolonged identity crisis can be relieved by finding like-minded people with whom to share a deviance, whether it be dressing all in black, body piercing, or substance abuse. Research has found that those who rely on these negative substitute identities most often have more than one risk factor to propel them toward integration failure. Everything from having experienced physical or sexual violence, too much or too little parental control, a reduced attention span, and/or heightened emotionality can push one toward integration failure. Most young people make it out of the minefield of adolescence and proceed with their identity formation tasks to become mature and responsible adults.

Yet even those who have achieved successful integration in adolescence can be at risk later in life if they should happen to divorce, lose their job, or suffer from any number of life's unfortunate events. Even minor biological abnormalities have been found to be associated with substance abuse. It has been found that any deficit, however small, can produce sufficient stress to cause integration failure to some degree under the right (or wrong) circumstances.

If the adaptive model is correct, people are not out of control when they choose a negative addiction but are purposefully choosing (although they usually don't realize it) what they consider to be the lesser of two evils at that moment in time. Many addicts have been taught by Alcoholics Anonymous–type groups to believe they are completely out of control where their drug of choice is concerned, but even chronic alcoholics generally do not drink to oblivion, unless undergoing a severe crisis in their lives. Studies show that alcoholics will self-moderate their consumption of alcohol for many reasons, and in a controlled setting will not consume all of the alcohol available to them. They generally vary their consumption at will, showing that alcoholic behavior is under the same kind of control as other behaviors. Addiction as a behavioral response has been part of the human story for a long while, and evolutionary biologists generally consider such stable behavioral responses adaptive rather than maladaptive. If addiction were not sometimes the best option available to a person in trouble, it would have stopped being such a popular option a long time ago.

Alexander compares addiction to the costly adaptation process of hibernation, during which time an animal cannot meet the demands of the winter environment and survives by adopting a diminished mode until the harshness of the surroundings comes to an end. This yearly event leaves the animal weak and a target for predators, yet alive. It is interesting that hibernation is made possible by the release of opiate-like endorphins, which help the animals to relax and sleep, and ends when anti-opiate substances are released into the bloodstream to end their "drugged-out" state.

Heroin addicts often choose to withdraw in order to find relief from a life that is too harsh, and if their chosen drug is not available, they tend to use alcohol and/or valium—or anything they can get their hands on. Poly-drug abuse—when people misuse many different types of drugs, particularly when their drug of choice is not available—is more common than abuse of a single substance, and addictions tend to cluster in certain individuals, supporting the adaptive theory that it is not a particular substance that grabs hold of the mind and body of the user, but it is the user who is drawn toward negative addiction.

When people become exercise addicts to the point where they are physically harming themselves, unable to heed warning signs or admonitions from doctors and friends, it is not the jogging that is causing the trouble—it is the state of mind that is telling them they must jog. When people are overweight to the point of endangering their health, we do not blame the food. We do not say everything was fine until he or she happened upon those creamy donuts: Let's ban creamy donuts. Is eating a donut, made with trans fats and other adulterated ingredients, any better for you than having a glass of wine or sharing a joint? It all depends on the amount, the excess, the addiction.

Alcohol and drugs often figure into the moratorium that adolescents hide behind when they get into trouble, at home or with the law. It has been pointed out that this teen-years moratorium, which suspends expectations and sometimes punishment for youthful offenders, primarily functions as protection for the ruling class. Black and other minority youth are more apt to serve jail time or get probation for offenses that for white perpetrators are often considered youthful folly and written off as a hard lesson learned. Both state and federal budgets have significantly reduced funding for programs to help young people stay out of jail, often turning around and putting the money saved by closing down daycare or after-school programs toward building new prisons. Our jails are teeming with people of color. Jails that began as humane protests against harsh treatments, such as floggings and hangings, have since become organized sadism. I refuse to believe all of our current prisoners are incorrigible or need to spend such huge portions of their lives in jail.

The war on drugs has created a fast track to prison for the segment of the population that is economically disadvantaged and restless. "Keep them there for the duration of their youthful energy and much disaster will be avoided" seems to be the idea—disaster caused by outrage, not by drugs. When white housewives were taking opiates and cocaine in their medicines, they were not being sent to jail for bad conduct. If overindulgence became a problem, the situation was likely handled with sensitivity and tact, as nobody was threatened by a bunch of bored housewives who had discovered that cold medicines helped more than just their colds. In fact, they probably didn't help their colds at all.

Methadone maintenance programs are evidence that treatment programs requiring total abstinence do not work for many people, as taking methadone is pretty much the same thing as taking heroin itself. Methadone was developed by the Nazis during World War II when supply lines for morphine were cut; it is chemically similar and basically serves the same function—to combat pain. While many addicts cannot discern the difference between methadone and heroin when one or the other is injected intravenously, others can tell the difference between the two and some actually prefer methadone, saying it gives a better high. Others prefer heroin, some because of the high but others because they claim there is a more excruciating withdrawal from methadone, and heroin addicts must always keep that in mind because of the possibility of being cut from a methadone program for relapsing or violating parole, or just because they are unable to comply with the rigid scheduling imposed by many methadone maintenance clinics.

Methadone maintenance programs are difficult to get into and stay in, as there are specific requirements and time slots that must be met. If participants go off the wagon just once, they are usually out of the program and must then endure an agonizing withdrawal from this copycat drug. Even with this major drawback, Alexander calls methadone maintenance a humane suspension of the war on drugs for people who have shown they cannot be coerced into accepting treatment that involves total abstinence. Under the auspices of the disease/criminal model of addiction, even treatment for the willing often fails, and it is commonly believed that as many people will get better spontaneously without treatment as will be helped by treatment. It has been found that the remaining third will not get better at all. Methadone maintenance programs reveal that even the professionals acknowledge the fact that some people will never get better, and they will need some way of coping with the grave disappointments in their lives.

Although methadone is a drug similar to heroin and is offered free by the government for those who qualify, very few so-called normal people would willingly take advantage of the offer. Most people do not want or choose to use such a drug, even if it were given to them for nothing. This fits with the adaptive theory that the majority of people will not be affected by the availability of drugs as they do not need or want them. They are able to handle troublesome situations as they arise without resorting to dangerous drugs or addictive behavior. People do seem to be attracted to substances that temporarily alter their consciousness but do not take over their lives. For many, alcohol and marijuana fit into this category, and most can use them successfully without fear of dependency or addiction.

CHAPTER 11

Hypocrisy Unlimited

Citizens who obey the antimarijuana smoking laws often think of those who break them as deserving of whatever punishment they get. After all, how hard can it be to go without it? If a person is that weak-willed maybe he or she deserves to be punished, possibly even by going to jail for a long time. The government's attempts to harness individual freedom of choice regarding marijuana use is even more hypocritical when one considers the toxins they not only allow but encourage U.S. citizens to consume, such as the chloride and fluoride many local governments add to their water supplies. U.S. citizens have also been encouraged en masse over the past few decades to eat margarine instead of butter, to use hormone replacement therapy to combat aging, and to ignore the real and potential dangers of pesticides and irradiated and genetically modified foods.

Americans have also been pushed to sign up for more vaccinations for our children than their little bodies can adequately handle, leaving many damaged for life. The issue of vaccinations has recently been the focus of attention as a possible (or probable) cause of autism because of the mercury added to the inoculations as a preservative. Although there is only a minute dose of mercury in each vaccination, multiple doses of mercury from the many vaccinations now required of school-age children add up to a toxic and dangerous dose. The lives of many children were destroyed before someone finally did the math and compared the symptoms these children were having with the symptoms of mercury poisoning.

There is nobody more popular these days than a kid with chicken pox among holistic people who resist vaccinating their children because of the inherent dangers. Parents line their kids up for play dates in hopes their child will catch the now-rare chicken pox virus and thus build immunity the natural way. These parents are choosing to take their chances with chicken pox rather than with a medical establishment they have learned not to trust. To those who claim that doing away with vaccinations could bring on terrible epidemics, they should be first in line fighting for the right of parents to resist the excessive list of vaccinations now demanded of children by schools and institutions so perhaps a more reasonable number would suffice to ward off major epidemics. Perhaps resistant parents would feel differently if vaccinations were carefully monitored so years did not pass once again with the people at the epicenter of disease control in our country asleep at the wheel.

Trust is the issue that prevents many Americans from relying on their government for accurate information regarding health issues. For how many years were susceptible Americans told to stay away from butter and encouraged to use margarine instead? Margarine is little more than plastic oil and now decades of relying on it has most assuredly affected the health of millions who routinely trusted the powers-that-be who falsely claimed margarine was not only safe but *safer* than butter.

Only recently have we begun to hear a lot about trans fats in the media, even though the health food journals have been warning against these hydrogenated fats for years. Thank God, butter, used in moderation, has once again come back into vogue, and people can stop damaging their bodies with the use of its plastic version. But hydrogenated oils are in practically all processed foods, as well as in most cookies, crackers, chips, and breads, and now manufacturers are even putting them in many cereals, some of them marketed specifically for children. Products often say "cholesterol free" to attract customers, because it is true that hydrogenated oils do not have cholesterol—but hydrogenated oils are worse for you than cholesterol! Cholesterol is produced by the liver and is actually good for you in the proper relationship to other natural substances found in the body.

Food manufacturers seem to go out of their way to confuse the issue of fats so they can sell their products, which are quite harmful if they contain hydrogenated fats, and not necessarily harmful if they contain cholesterol. The issue with cholesterol is one of moderation, not switching to plastic oils that will hopelessly gum up your body. The people in our government who are responsible for making sure the foods we eat are safe have known about the issue of trans fats for years, yet they have permitted the use of these toxic fats in food production because they prolong the shelf life of foods, thus assuring big business more profit. A package of graham crackers sitting on a shelf in a deli for six years will still be "good" to eat when it's finally purchased; after all, it's been laminated. The diseases that result from the fats we consume will no doubt be an obsession of the new millennium, once people realize their bodies have turned to plastic. Yet men and women are languishing in jails for smoking marijuana.

Fluoridation of the water supplies as a means of preventing tooth decay and osteoporosis has been a hotly debated topic for more than fifty years, and it looks increasingly like the public has been duped on this issue, too. Data coming in from what has essentially been a huge research experiment with hapless citizens as guinea pigs has revealed that fluoride's benefits were exaggerated, to say the least. For starters, sodium fluoride is rat poison, plain and simple; it is literally used to kill rodents. This controversial substance is a waste product of aluminum mining, and it was the aluminum producers themselves who had the brilliant idea that fluoride might reduce cavities, and they even funded the research to "prove" it. Instead of having to find a way to rid themselves of their manufacturing waste, these geniuses of industry were able to spawn an offshoot moneymaking bonanza by convincing people they should be grateful to have fluoride added to their water supplies.

Are we to believe they did not know that millions of people in India and China suffer from skeletal fluorosis, a crippling bone disease caused by moderate to high levels of fluoride that occur naturally in the water supplies in certain areas of their countries? Chronic joint pain is one of the first indications a person is developing skeletal fluorosis, which could possibly help explain the epidemic of arthritis in our country after a half-century of experimentation with this toxic substance. Fluoridation of drinking water also causes mottled teeth, or dental fluorosis, which today occurs in two or more of the teeth in 30 percent of the children in areas where fluoride is added to their water. There is also disturbing evidence from studies done on rats that fluoride possibly enables aluminum to cross the blood-brain barrier, as amyloid deposits like those found in Alzheimer's patients were elevated in the rats that were exposed to fluoride in a study, as compared to the control group of rats. Fluoride is also a known depressor of thyroid activity, and has even been used therapeutically to help lower overactive thyroids.

Could it be possible that at least some of the twenty million people in this country who are now treated for low thyroid functioning are suffering from the effects of fluoridation? Drinking water is not the only source of fluoride; food processing and especially beverages that are made by mixing water with concentrates often contain fluorides, as do dental products and residues in the air and water from the emissions of fluoride industries. Studies reveal that fluoride is also a hormone disrupter and may reduce melatonin production as it tends to accumulate in the pineal gland. There is also evidence that fluoride might cause bone cancer in male rats and perhaps in young men, and that brain function and IQs have perhaps been affected as well. The tragedy is that the addition of fluoride to the water supply has shown very little gain in tooth-decay prevention, as the incidence of cavities has gone down to a similar level even in areas that do not fluoridate their water supplies because of a general promotion of dental care. In addition, eighteen studies undertaken since 1990 have found an association between the fluoridation of water and an increase in hip fractures in the elderly. It has been estimated that perhaps fifty thousand people die each year from osteoporosis-related hip fractures, and yet there is no public outcry about the possibility that fluoridated water is contributing to some of these fractures.

Chlorinated water is thought by many to be an even bigger culprit than fluoridation, as 75 percent of the water consumed in this country has been treated with this industrial waste product. Although adding highly reactive chlorine to water treatment systems has greatly reduced the incidence of infectious waterborne diseases, this can be accomplished using other treatments that are safer and cheaper, such as hydrogen peroxide or ozone treatments. Chlorinating the water supply also creates free radicals that encourage the development of cancer, destroys immune-strengthening acidophilus in our digestive systems, and destroys essential fatty acids, which are the building blocks of the brain and nervous systems. Chlorine is highly destructive to living tissue, which is why it is used to kill bugs in swimming pools. Once chlorine is ingested and carried into the bloodstream, it begins to attack the arterial walls. The body then tries to repair the damaged blood vessels by laying down a layer of cholesterol, because cholesterol is produced naturally by the liver to do just that—repair damage to arteries. As the damage continues because of continued exposure to chlorinated water, the repair jobs involving cholesterol become thicker, giving cholesterol—instead of the chlorine—a bad name, while it is chlorine that is causing the problem in the first place.

Doctors look at the problem and see only that the arteries are clogged, and they tell their patients to reduce their consumption of cholesterol rather than to drink filtered water (although chlorine can also enter through the skin while bathing). Autopsies of soldiers killed in Vietnam showed a buildup of cholesterol in their arteries that was greater than in same-aged young men who were killed in automobile accidents. The difference was significant enough to warrant a study, which revealed that the soldiers had been given water purification tablets made of chlorine to disinfect the water before they drank it in Vietnam, thus creating a cycle of arterial disturbance. Not only are hydrogen peroxide and ozone relatively inexpensive when used to purify water, their only byproducts are pure oxygen and hydrogen. The chemical companies that tricked the United States and Canada into chlorination of their water supplies not only did not have to pay to get rid of their waste products, they were able to make huge profits by dumping these toxins in American waters. The French and Germans, less controlled by their chemical industries, now only chlorinate water in emergencies. We, on the other hand, are letting government and industry get away with mass murder by once again accepting their version of what is safe to consume without having all the information necessary to make such decisions.

Hormone replacement therapy (HRT) for women is another example of how industry and government have influenced people to buy products at the expense of consumer health. The recent flurry of backpedaling by the various powers that encouraged the use of estrogen replacement therapy does not include any apologies or even acknowledgment of wrongdoing. Many women surely died after following the advice of their physicians to take estrogen, a known carcinogen. Nutritionist Adelle Davis advised women against the use of estrogen in her 1965 well-read classic *Let's Get Well*, revealing that estrogen had been used in studies to induce cancer in mice and rats. She also quoted a doctor in the book who warned that the use of estrogen by a woman who already had cancer might activate dormant cells to a malignant state. Other doctors and nutritionists also spoke out against the use of estrogen during the decades when pharmaceutical companies were getting rich filling prescriptions made largely from the urine of pregnant horses, but accurate information on HRT was largely confined to health food stores and the books sold within.

Nutritionist Dr. Linda Page has written about what happens to mares raised exclusively in horse factories to produce urine to make Premarin. In 1997, for example, she wrote that there were almost five hundred of these hideous factories in Canada and North Dakota, with around seventy-five thousand of the poor animals chained to stalls where they could barely move as they were hooked up to machines to collect their urine. After being artificially inseminated; the mares were forced to spend their eleven-month pregnancies in stalls so small they could not turn, and if they tried to lie down, their heads were jolted upright by their bridles. They are forced to stand and live miserable lives with droopy ears, a known sign of horse misery. Many become crippled from the agony they must endure.

They are also given little water so their urine will be thick and contain lots of estrogen; they often get sores from the pee bags that are strapped to them in an uncomfortable manner. If they are not kept as replacements, the foals are removed from their mothers a month or two after birth and shipped sometimes long distances without food or water to slaughterhouses. They are then forced to stand in line and wait to be killed by a bolt through the forehead; the little foals seem to understand what is happening as they reportedly tremble and pee on themselves while standing in line. When the mares can no longer become pregnant and produce estrogen containing urine, they also are sold for horsemeat.

Native American Indians have known about black cohosh, vitex, red clover, and other herbal remedies that help balance women's bodies hormonally. While no doubt many women have died as a result of estrogen replacement therapy prescribed by their doctors and pumped up by the pharmaceutical companies, there is also a growing number of females who have heeded the advice of those who advocate natural remedies to relieve discomfort during menstruation and menopause. By the time the headlines announced around the turn of the millennium that estrogen replacement therapy was dangerous, it was old news for the many health outlaws who had been paying close attention to what was happening to truth in a world consumed by dollars.

These same people who have resisted the erroneous advice of professionals in government and private industry are also rallying against irradiated and genetically modified food and fighting for the right to know which foods have been tampered with when shopping at the supermarket so one can choose to "just say no." The campaign for a Europe free of genetically modified foods has collected declarations from thirty-five hundred areas (similar to counties or municipalities) in twenty-six European countries stating they will not grow genetically modified food products, even though they are under intense pressure from the United States and the World Trade Organization (controlled by who?) to keep European markets open for genetically altered foods.

A 2001 ABCNews.com poll found that 93 percent of Americans say the federal government should require labels identifying genetically modified foods, and 57 percent say they'd be less likely to buy genetically modified foods. Health food stores have sprouted up across the country to aid persons who no longer trust that their government will protect them from unscrupulous businesses. These stores have been so successful in helping people to lead better and healthier lives, they have engendered the jealousy of industries who can see they are not able to entirely control the pocketbooks of all consumers.

This envy has set off what some have called "the vitamin C wars," which has resulted in the introduction of a bill in Congress called Codex Alimentarius, which if passed will make it illegal to use, buy, or sell most vitamins, minerals, and herbs without a doctor's prescription. According to the Natural Solution Foundation in New York, if Codex Alimentarius, or C.A., passes, only eighteen supplements will be allowed and at dosages that are too low to have much clinical impact. All other nutritional substances will become illegal—like heroin. Vitamin C at dosages above 200 milligrams, for example, will be illegal.

Although this bill has been voted on and defeated by Congress several times, it has been defeated by a smaller margin each time. With the current composition of Congress favoring big business and pharmaceutical companies, it is a frightening possibility this bill will pass, even though there has been an enormous grassroots outcry against it. Petitions have been organized that beseech Congress to act as staunch defenders of the interests of Americans rather than kowtow to a pharmaceutical industry that understands a healthy populace spends less on prescription medication than does a populace with no access to effective natural prevention and treatment. Some signers of the petition against the bill believe Codex Alimentarius has been engineered not just to control the burgeoning vitamin industry but to force ill health on our citizens in order to sell their own medical products. I am not looking forward to experiencing what would happen if the safekeeping of vitamins and minerals were put into the hands of big government and the pharmaceutical companies.

To add to the list (which is endless) of what our government allows in terms of legal toxins, one cannot overlook the enormous health problems brought on by analgesics (pain relievers) such as aspirin and Tylenol. Medical problems from ingesting these toxins include kidney and liver damage, addiction, and many deaths, yet nobody is calling for analgesics to be dispensed by prescription only. Over-the-counter pain relievers can inhibit the immune system by interfering with antibody production, causing innumerable problems in the body if used on a regular basis, Many people are doing just that, however, and sometimes permanently injuring themselves without ever learning that what they are doing is dangerous.

The Bayer Company introduced aspirin commercially in 1899, only a year after the company had introduced heroin into the marketplace. Aspirin and aspirin-like analgesics have today become the most widely used medicines in the world as they can relieve mild to moderate pain without interfering with thought or concentration. Although they cannot cure any disease, these analgesics can reduce pain, fever, and swelling and can thin the blood and reduce the formation of clots. These qualities make them "indispensable" for many individuals on a daily basis, who often do not realize the harm they are causing their bodies until it is too late. The most common complaint of regular users of analgesics is abdominal discomfort in the form of heartburn or nausea.

The fact that intestinal damage can occur even when these meds are injected led to the discovery that it is not just local irritation causing the discomfort but the inhibition of prostaglandin synthesis in the stomach. Over half of the patients taking aspirin and compounds with aspirin regularly will have blood in the feces produced by gastrointestinal bleeding. It has been estimated that almost three-quarters of the people who use these analgesics on a regular basis will lose about a pint and a half of blood a year from intestinal bleeding. Prolonged use of these over-the-counter pain medications often reveals no detectable symptoms until permanent kidney damage has resulted, which is often referred to as "analgesic abuse nephropathy." Although complete kidney failure can and does occur in some cases, a substantial portion of regular users will show at least moderate loss of kidney function.

Loss of normal immune function protection and even deaths from overdose are yet other problems associated with drugs people commonly take to relieve pain. Overdose deaths from acetaminophen are usually the result of liver failure. Although the war on drugs is busy targeting marijuana, a drug for which there have been no known overdose deaths, our government casually allows people to make their own choices regarding potentially lethal over-the-counter pain relief products. Although most people use painkillers carefully and in moderation, it is not uncommon for people to become dependent and negatively addicted to them. It has long been known that some people use analgesics recreationally to produce a psychoactive effect, yet there is still no public outcry or government crackdown.

A 1979 article in the *New York Times* concerning Howard Hughes's death quotes his personal physician as claiming the famous millionaire's decline was because of the ingestion of massive doses of aspirin, to the tune of up to twenty or thirty tablets a day. Alexander writes about Canadian factory workers washing down handfuls of aspirin with Coca-Cola to give themselves a lift. A Swiss study showed that people who overused over-the-counter headache medication were usually deeply troubled—insecure, depressed, and isolated. The study concluded that these over-the-counter drugs were abused because they were easily available and purported to be safe. People using them often did not realize the harm they were doing to their bodies until it was too late.

Another study of fifty-six patients with kidney failure attributed to aspirin-type drugs revealed that only two of these patients initially had a detectable medical reason for using the drugs. Most dependent people also greatly underreported using analgesics, and many continued their habit despite opposition from family and friends. In some cases, shopkeepers who sold these over-the-counter painkillers refused to sell them to certain people they had grown to view as addicts; but some users simply sent relatives or children to buy them instead. Clearly analgesics can be addictive and lethal.

Recent news coverage has finally brought much-needed attention to the prescribing of speed to children so they will sit in their seats and behave. Current articles reveal that about 10 percent of ten-year-old boys are now on Attention Deficit Hyperactivity Disorder (ADHD) drugs, most of which are derived from powerful stimulants, including amphetamines. That's one out of ten little boys! Four percent of ten-year-old girls are on these drugs, and adults are also joining in on the rush to be always alert. The horrifying part is that these kids are not able to choose to say no; they are given the pill at breakfast with their orange juice and the parental hope that it will help them climb the ladder, now in gym and later in life. The Food and Drug Administration (FDA) was forced to take notice after receiving reports of deaths linked to these drugs, as well as other serious health consequences, usually involving the cardiovascular system. According to *USA Today,* the FDA has narrowly voted to put stronger warnings on the widely prescribed stimulant-type drugs. Meanwhile, the leading ADHD drug, Adderall (an amphetamine), raked in 974 *million* dollars in 2005. We should all be ashamed for sitting back and allowing this travesty to happen to innocent children—especially the drug companies.

Why is Congress so concerned about controlling vitamins, which are essentially just concentrated foods and herbs stuffed in a pill or capsule, yet mum on the problem of analgesics that kill thousands annually from internal bleeding and kidney and liver failure, and ADHD drugs that are cardiovascular time bombs? The pharmaceutical companies are major lobbyists whose influence is enormous if one is to judge by the obviously dangerous and even lethal medications that have been allowed to slip by the government's radar screen. People in government who rely on the support of these companies for reelection have been reluctant to regulate painkillers and are even remiss in disseminating information that would help people who care about their health monitor their own use of these substances more carefully. If Codex Alimentarius passes, you can be sure that the pharmaceutical companies will soon turn products that are now beneficial to your health into irradiated vitamins and minerals with toxic fillers and artificial flavors and colorings. By the time they finish with vitamins/minerals/herbs, they will no longer be healthy to consume. By then Congress will be no more interested in the "threat" of vitamins than they are in the maladies caused by vaccinations, hydrogenated oils, chlorinated and fluoridated water, irradiated and genetically altered foods, and dangerous pharmaceuticals.

Part III

In the Beginning

CHAPTER 12

Connecting the Dots

I began to realize there was an eerie connection between what was happening in my life and what was taking place in the insane and brutal world surrounding me. At first glance the two spaces did not seem to be related, but it soon became apparent there were common themes and strains that tied them both together. The perceived threat of violence that had sent my daughter and me scurrying to our therapist and finally to the police had been a long time coming. It was evident my daughter and I were losing power in our family; it was just not clear why this was happening. I certainly wasn't ready to attribute or connect any of our difficulties to the overtly masculine, aggressive, and controlling patterns and influences that leaped at me from everywhere, including television and movie screens, the Internet, magazines, billboards, and conversations. Even though I knew rationally and realistically that women had made many advances over the years—at least in this country—I also believed that important feminine values and influences had been slipping in areas where they should have been more securely grounded by now.

The emphasis, for example, on female physicality over and above any other qualities that might make a woman desirable as a person had become the norm for too many people—male and female. I had noticed for some time that male-inspired jokes and songs were increasingly denigrating to women, setting the tone for much else in the media that served as a funnel, continuously pouring its misogynistic contents into homes around the world. While everyone was pretending women were having it all and were now so powerful they should be able to take a little ribbing about their perceived (from a masculine point of view) faults, in many homes the females were experiencing a decline in power as the ubiquitous women-bashing blather burrowed further into their psyches. Their mates and other family members were picking up the same messages regarding the diminishing value of femaleness, and it should not be surprising they were also influenced by the never-ending drone of negativity.

To further complicate matters, it seemed that just as my children were entering adolescence there was a worldwide explosion of pornography—something else they were going to have to contend with as they labored to construct post-childhood identities. When I thought of all the kvetching by women over the past few decades regarding their not wanting to be viewed and experienced as mere sex objects, I could not understand how the message had become so completely skewed as to have engendered the exact opposite response. It seemed women were now viewed more as sex objects than at any other time in history. Our nation's obsession with pornography has increasingly put women and children in danger all over the world. We are obviously trendsetters with money, continuously brainwashing other cultures with the nonstop promotion of our seedy standards using technological advances that allow for words and images to travel instantly almost anywhere and everywhere on the planet.

A recent Link TV documentary on child prostitution in Indonesia showed the rescue of two young girls who had been lured away from their small towns with the promise of jobs, only to find themselves prisoners in a house of prostitution, unable to escape. When they were kidnapped, these prepubescent girls had not even begun to menstruate; sadly, they were always chosen first over the other women by the men who came to the brothel because of their childlike appearance. They had to service many men in a night, and both girls had boils on their vaginas by the time they were rescued. Few are so lucky as to be rescued.

How can we say we are not partly responsible for the fate of women and children in third-world countries when our culture sets the standards for what is desirable and what is not—no matter how degrading and damaging the results may be for everyone everywhere, even those of us who only stand by the sidelines and silently bear witness. We celebrate models and females who look like sexy children rather than the luscious women on the walls of art museums, who if they'd had no flesh on their bones would most likely not have been chosen by artists to paint or sculpt. By continuously showcasing extremely young, thin females instead of girls and women who are more representative of nature, the media and big business are both aiding and abetting the increase in sexual crimes against children. Persistently accenting and celebrating the youngest, thinnest, and usually weakest members of the female sex has become a veritable social pathology that must be studied and dealt with. Instead, we tolerate misogynistic comments and jokes and promote any trend that comes along that celebrates youth over maturity, such as the new craze in total pubic hair removal for women, encouraging them to look as prepubescent as possible.

I began to think a lot about the world's entire patriarchal setup, which is essentially based on one-half of the human population having more power than the other half. After this first division of humanity between male and female, it becomes more complicated as many other divisions and layers of power follow, often obscuring the patriarchal reality as there are many rich and powerful women in the world who have power over lower status males. But ultimately, the most powerful males hold vastly more power than their female counterparts. I had become interested years ago in civilizations that predated the stories from the Old Testament. There was a time before Yahweh when females had more interesting and powerful roles in societal mythologies, and a growing number of archeologists and scholars are in agreement that these ancient myths spoke of a very real time when the balance of power between women and men was complementary yet equal. For years archeologists steeped in the patriarchal system were simply not able to recognize the multitude of clues supporting the existence of these equal partnership societies.

It is not surprising that ancient people would consider females to be powerful and even miraculous because they were able to bear children, bleed without an injury, and produce milk from their bodies. It was also noted by the ancients that the menstrual cycles of women were somehow related to the cycles of the moon, and when women lived together their menstrual cycles became synchronized. The relationship between women and the moon was an extraordinarily powerful and influential concept for many thousands of years. The moon held significance for people who not only treasured its light at night but who had observed that the movements and phases of the moon coincided with the growth cycles of living things on earth. The powerful observation that women were somehow connected to the moon, and thus the universe, gave them as individuals and as a group a lot of power, especially mystical and religious power.

I began thinking a lot about a book I had read several years earlier. It argued convincingly that the changeover from ancient equal partnership societies to the patriarchal systems now in evidence throughout the world was due largely to the invention of the alphabet. In *The Alphabet Versus the Goddess: The Conflict Between Word and Image,* surgeon and author Dr. Leonard Shlain maintained that the introduction of any new form of communication has always resulted in a reconfiguring of society. He further wrote that the invention of writing has had the most profound effect of all, completely changing the power balance that had existed for tens of thousands of years between the sexes because reading and writing unwittingly emphasize left-brain, masculine values. Dr. Shlain also wrote that the newest electromagnetic revolution in communication, much of it visual, is playing a major role in the current struggle between masculine and feminine influences. It is helping to rebalance the power in society between the sexes, although not without extraordinary upheaval and chaos, just as was experienced when the introduction of the written word brought about similar kinds of turmoil.

According to the doctor's theory, today's madness is to be expected as the gears shift and turn slowly but inexorably back toward right-brain values and influences—and hopefully toward embracing a more egalitarian future. Before I came upon the doctor's book, I had spent enough time reading about early Goddess-worshipping civilizations to wonder why I had heard so little about this time period in my history classes at school. Even when a rare mention was made of goddesses, they were usually portrayed as wispy fairies in a fake religion that came before Real Religion—never as having symbolized the cherished position of feminine values that actually existed at one time in the world.

Until I read *The Alphabet Versus the Goddess,* I had always felt saddened by the male-female situation, which I basically viewed as men being physically stronger than women and capable of controlling them to make sure their offspring were really theirs. It all seemed so simple and hopeless. Apparently my lot as a woman was essentially to accept this inequity and try to make the best of it; I was supposed to feel lucky I was not born in a country where women suffered much worse fates than my petty complaints of injustice. I thought that no matter how hard we tried to resist, we females had been conquered, were still being conquered, and would always be conquered. As a woman, trying to regain lost power was exhausting, but necessary if one was to have any dignity at all. I felt the dichotomous and unequal relationship between men and women had destroyed the possibility of real human happiness, as I believe a sense of true equality is necessary for relationships to be healthy and flourish.

Looking at my children, now almost adults, I could see the insidious effects of this split between the male and female was difficult for both of my children, not just my daughter. Problems and issues that kept me awake at night were lately more about my son than my daughter. She, of the "weaker" sex, often seemed the stronger of the two. I had spent many years dealing with the patriarchal system and what it had meant in my life and the lives of other women, my daughter included. I was now forced to look critically at what this overtly masculinized system was doing to my son. While during my depressed and pessimistic moments I woefully acquiesced to the possibility that things were not going to change substantially in my lifetime, I knew in my heart this was not the way it was supposed to be. I always held out hope that someone or something would appear to rescue us pathetic humans from our own suffocating petard. Certainly no God or Goddess would wish for such an injustice as inequality between the sexes, and if there were deities who so desired this state of affairs, I certainly wouldn't be so naïve as to worship them.

Ancient Goddess Worship

Dr. Shlain's extensive research on ancient civilizations convinced him that in every local in every part of the world, the discovery of an alphabet brought about a time of disruption because learning to read and write unbalanced the right-left brain equilibrium in humans that had taken thousands of years to perfect. Anthropologists and archeologists concur that around ten thousand years ago groups of hunter-gatherers began settling down in various parts of the world, such as around the Mediterranean basin, forming small groups that farmed the land and kept animals for food. The women who had for thousands of years been the primary gatherers of plants and berries became responsible for planting crops, and the men for the most part exchanged their hunting of wild animals for animal husbandry. All of these earliest societies worshipped an Earth/Mother Goddess who was *the* principal deity. In Sumer her name was Inanna; in Egypt her name was Isis; in Canaan her name was Asherah; in Syria her name was Astarte; in Greece her name was Demeter; and in Cyprus her name was Aphrodite. The Grand Goddess in each of these early civilizations was considered the source of all food and the nurturer of all life. She was also responsible for death.

These goddesses were often shown with a male consort—a lesser being who was smaller, younger, and weaker. The Egyptian Goddess Isis and her consort/son Horus are eerily similar to the Virgin Mary and her son Jesus, and the many statues of Isis nursing her son presaged by many centuries the ubiquitous images of Mary and the Christ Child. In Egyptian mythology Isis gave birth to Horus without the aid of male insemination (immaculate conception), and Horus was also, like Jesus, considered an intermediary between humans and the divine. Jesus's birth date, while historically unknown, is celebrated at the time of the Winter Solstice—the day the Goddess gave birth to the Sun in ancient religions—which usually falls between December 21st and the 24th. Jesus's resurrection every Easter symbolizes the regeneration of nature as did the Death and Rebirth celebrations involving other sacred offspring of the Goddess in earlier times. There are many other connections between earlier goddesses and the Virgin Mary. Legend has it that Mary even traveled to the largest shrine consecrated to a female deity in the Western world—the Temple of Artemis at Ephesus (considered one of the "seven natural wonders")—when it was time for her to die. What was the connection between Mary and goddess worship in the ancient world?

Dr. Shlain became interested in early goddess-ruled societies while vacationing in the Mediterranean in 1991; he noticed that shrines originally consecrated to female goddesses had almost always been changed to honor newer male gods. Clearly something of monumental importance had occurred in ancient times to cause this dramatic cultural shift. As the doctor began to question and study, he realized the situation he was observing in the Mediterranean was essentially the same everywhere on the planet. Every civilization he studied had arrived at a juncture in their history where the primacy of goddess worship was relinquished in favor of masculine gods, and eventually one God in most locals around the world. After years of painstaking research, the doctor came to the conclusion that the final toppling of the Goddess in favor of one male God and the consequent devaluation of all things female was primarily a result of the invention of the "modern" alphabet. He observed that all around the world the appearance of an alphabet and universal literacy brought with them the rise of patriarchal societies with their structured and hierarchal relationships of unequal status and power, especially between men and women.

Anthropologist Claude Levi-Strauss was one of the first to comment that the appearance of writing in all parts of the world coincided with the establishment of hierarchal societies in which one part of the population is made to work for the other. Because we normally associate literacy with progress and the good things in life, it feels preposterous at first to try and grasp the concept of patriarchy and misogyny going hand in hand with reading and writing.

Dr. Shlain is a vascular surgeon in his other life, and his knowledge of the brain's structure and the effects of neural pathways on different kinds of learning led him to speculate that the advent of literacy, which has much to do with the left side of the brain, eventually overpowered the influences of the right side of the brain and actually caused right-brain influences to diminish in value over time, to the great detriment of all humanity. The doctor's observations from the findings of antiquity led him to believe that the uniquely human nervous system had developed in response to the specific needs of nurturer-gatherer/hunter-killer societies and to assist humans in the evolution of speech. This eventually resulted in the war between the sexes that has been fought on all battlefronts to this day.

Around a million years ago our human ancestors' (hominids) bodies and brains gradually began to increase in size, beginning the long evolutionary journey that eventually produced homo sapiens, the wise human. The human brain that emerged around a hundred thousand years ago had acquired an extra pound of neural tissue and was now divided into two lobes, apparently so one lobe could be wired to accommodate speech. All vertebrates now have a bilobed brain, but in most species the two halves are symmetrical. The "new" hominid brain veered from the anatomically mirror-imaged hemispheric lobes developing in most other vertebrates to acquire what is called hemispheric lateralization. What this means is that although the two different sides of the brain appear to be symmetrical, they are in actuality functionally different. The two different sides of the brain have different functions, but they are dependent on one another and can work together.

While some other vertebrates have this feature to a certain extent, it is more pronounced in humans as is evidenced by their development of speech and a preference for the use of one hand over the other. After years of studying stroke victims, researchers now know that each side of the brain has attributes distinct to its own hemisphere and each side of the brain controls the muscles of the body's opposite side. If the left side of the brain is damaged, muscles on the right side of the body will be paralyzed, and speech and abstract thinking will be affected. If the right side of the brain is damaged, the left side will be paralyzed, and the person's ability to solve spatial problems, recognize faces, and appreciate music will be diminished or lost.

Researchers have discovered that women have more connecting neurons between the two sides, which helps them keep better track of what the other side is up to (of the brain, that is!). Women are more influenced by the right hemisphere and are often better at multitasking, while more left-hemispheric men are better at honing in on a single task and not allowing for distractions. The right side of the brain is the older side and develops first in the fetus; it is familiar with early animal communications such as sucking, cuddling, touching, and crying, and, more than the left side, generates feeling states such as love, humor, and aesthetic appreciation. The right side of the brain is associated with the left hand and left side of the body and experiences things all at once—gestalt-like. The right brain does not participate in speech but helps in the comprehension of the spoken word by listening carefully and deciphering content.

The left brain's functions are opposite and complementary to the right brain's functions; the left hemisphere's agent is the right hand and its symbol is speech; in right-handed people, 90 percent of their language skills reside in the left hemisphere. Words are associated with the left hemisphere of the brain and are not only directed outward to communicate with others but are implements of thought within the brain. In understanding speech, the left brain's task is to separate letters, words, and sentences into separate parts and view them in linear progression in order to understand what is being communicated. Communication is not understood holistically—gestalt fashion—as it is with the right brain, but in an ordered, logical sequential fashion.

It is important to remember that all normally developed humans have continuous access to both sides of their brains, and the influences of one side over the other are different in each individual; women and men are each a unique blend of feminine (right-brain hemisphere) and masculine (left-brain hemisphere). According to Dr. Shlain, the power imbalance between men and women that exists today is due to the preponderance of left-brain activity at the expense of right-brain activity because of the overwhelming impact of literacy that has taken place over the past five thousand years. This imbalance of brain activity has created an overly masculinized point of view and state of affairs everywhere people are literate—basically everywhere. This does not mean that reading and writing are bad, as they obviously have brought much good to humankind, but people need to be aware that the emphasis on left-brain activities that comes with literacy has a downside and currently threatens the destruction of life on earth as we know it with its overtly aggressive and masculinized point of view. The good news is that because of image-based photography, movies, television, computers, and so forth, a rebalancing is underway. If we can all survive the insanity that is taking place because of the right brain making a comeback and the left brain resisting, there is a good chance we can get our brains rebalanced in time to save the world.

Having two sides of the brain working together to gather information increased the ability of early humans to respond intelligently to situations and gave them a distinct advantage over other animals. Amazingly, the rods and cones in the human eye also evolved opposite and complementary tasks in correspondence with the functions of the right and left sides of the brain. Within the retina of each eye are two different types of cells—rods and cones, and both report to both hemispheres of the brain. Rods are associated with the functions of the right side of the brain, are evenly distributed throughout each eye, see in dim light, and are able to see the totality of a visual field, perceiving reality all at once. Cones are associated with the functions of the left side of the brain, are clustered in the center (macula) of the eye, and are able to appreciate color and intensify clarity as they concentrate on one aspect of the visual field at a time. The eyes see reality in a figure/ground scenario, with the cones able to best see figures as the rods best visualize ground. Rods, aligning with the right side of the brain, have an older ancestry and are available for a baby to use within days of birth; cones do not fully develop for months. The left-brain cones are better suited for focused vision while the right-brain rods see more holistically. The cones isolate and view in sequence sections of the visual field, seeing objects one at a time, whereas the rods see better in the dark and take in more at one glance.

Human hands have also become specialized to go with the functions of the brain. The left hand is controlled by the right brain, and in most people its movements are clumsier and not as well coordinated as the right hand, which is aligned with the left brain. Dr. Shlain comments that the left hand is generally used to carry a shield or hold a baby, while the right hand is used to carry a sword, wield a hammer, or write a poem. Nature encouraged the survival of humans by dividing the brain into two parts, differentiating the functions of the retina, specializing the two hands, and helping them all work together. This specialization developed over a period of many thousands of years and allowed humans to be both hunter-killers and nurture-gatherers; these two strategies for survival are still found in all of us. The precise division of these functions determines how each person perceives and manipulates the world around them—to what degree each individual is influenced by the feminine (right) brain and the masculine (left) brain. Societies can and do accentuate and reward one way of responding to the world over the other by responding positively to certain traits and not others. Left-brain values are clearly more highly valued by civilizations of today than the complementary right-brain feminine influences that were equally cherished in ancient times.

Left-Right-Left

This right-left brain stuff was the thesis of Dr. Shlain, and I was slowly beginning to understand my thesis, which was that my family was simply a microcosm in and of an all-encompassing, all-powerful left-brain-dominated masculine culture. The symptoms currently experienced by my family were part and parcel of what was happening in society at large—a sort of reactionary masculine madness as feminine influences continued to regain lost power. With all that is at stake in the world at present, it is no wonder some of the tension has trickled down into my own small family and into the lives of many other families around the world as well.

I had read Dr. Shlain's book several years before my family began undergoing its own intense reconfiguring, and although I had related positively to what he was saying the first time around, the second read convinced me his theory made more sense and explained things better than any other story I had ever heard about why women are dominated by men everywhere in the world. In his book *The Alphabet Versus the Goddess*, the doctor makes the case that the invention of an alphabet, which first occurred several thousand years ago, slowly but surely shifted the balance of the brain in humans to a left-brain dominance that has resulted in the elevation of masculine values and influences and the devaluation of things right brain and feminine. According to the doctor's theory, what is considered culturally normative everywhere on earth—the domination of the female by the male—is a relatively recent development for the human race. Dr. Shlain believes the invention of writing unwittingly served to unbalance the ancient human brain, which in turn created inequities in the sexes that have become a permanent part of our landscape.

The now ubiquitous written word continues to challenge the way men and women view themselves and each other. Although most people believe women have come a long way, at least in the United States and especially since the second wave of feminine-values movement of the 1970s (the first was earlier in the century and resulted in women finally getting the vote), many also perceive the gains achieved by women as having encouraged a backlash. Dr. Shlain contends that this repercussion is due not so much as a result of women's gains but more because of the many new styles of communication that have arrived on the scene, constantly flooding our brains and senses with visual stimuli. This new visual way of communicating is causing humanity to go crazy for a while as the brain accustoms itself to the onslaught of right-brain stimulation and influences.

With all of the new types of communication that have emerged over the past hundred years, it is no wonder we've had such a bloody century (the rise of fascism in Europe after World War I was enabled by the use of the new radio technology). Yet this century has also seen enormous progress. If we could harness that progress before it destroys everything and everyone on the planet, we could use it to finally create the life many of us really want, with no part of humanity one up and no part one down. The world of images that surrounds us because of the advent of movies, television, computers, and so forth, serves to strengthen right-brain functions and feminine values. But because the media is so overwhelmingly controlled by men and the patriarchal left-brain system, the visual technology is also being used to reinforce negative stereotypes by objectifying women and attempting to reduce them to their physical form only. The newest rebalancing of the brain because of right-brain image-based influences is causing a societal hysteria in many parts of the world that will need to be dealt with successfully before things can settle down and progress can be made toward the formation and revitalization of egalitarian civilizations.

New research studies indicate that today's media, with its ubiquitous portrayal of stereotyped and highly sexualized females, is heavily complicit in many new age illnesses such as anorexia, bulimia, cutting, and substance abuse. That old standby—depression—is still a favorite of girls and women who are forced to accept lives that are not of their choosing. Some scholars have noted that throughout recorded history, whenever men have tried to reassert their control over women who are actively striving for equality, it is an indication that a period of regression and bloodshed is settling in. This period has already begun, and the sequestering and veiling of women on the one hand and prancing them around naked on the other have become symbols for each side in this great battle, which threatens to become the greatest and final battle of all. The emphasis on manliness emanating from my husband that began at the onset of my son's puberty had greatly disrupted the harmony of my family, and if the news I was paying attention to was accurate, my family was not alone in reflecting the overtly masculine, warlike values of our surroundings.

CHAPTER 13

Written in Stone

Archeology as an official science has been around for little more than a hundred years and has been almost completely dominated by males since its inception. Conventional archeological wisdom has it that writing first began with the Sumerians and Egyptians around five thousand years ago to help keep track of commercial goings-on—how much food was in storage and so forth. More recent evaluations of archeological evidence dispute the commercial emphasis placed on humanity's first scribblings, suggesting instead that the first written communications between people were spiritual and related to Goddess worship. Tablets and pottery with inscriptions dating back seven thousand years have been found in sixty old European sites, showing a rudimentary form of linear script that appears to have been an outgrowth of the earlier use of art as a kind of visual shorthand to communicate. Symbolic signs of the Goddess such as whirls, circles, and multiple lines are incised on figurines and tablets during a time when the Goddess was the Supreme Being, and men and women were considered equal partners in society. Male and female were considered complementary halves, each necessary for the completion of the other.

Archeological findings reveal that a patriarchal bias first began to emerge around five thousand years ago, at around the same time humans began to make more sophisticated representational marks on stone and clay. Highly pictographic ideograms (cuneiform) were first made by the Sumerians in about 3200 B.C. by gouging marks in wet clay. The invention was reputedly to help record the amounts of food and grain that were in storage and to keep track of what and how much had been offered various temple deities. The Sumerians believed cuneiform was a gift from the goddess of grain and storage, and the pictograms were a unique way to store thoughts. Scribes had to learn a large number of characters, and this difficulty prevented the average person from learning to use this new form of communication. Excavations of the earliest royal Sumerian tombs reveal that queens shared equal power and wealth with kings at this time in history; records also indicate that the common woman's status was high. The early Sumerians principal deity was the goddess Inanna, who controlled the fate of mortals and was also the goddess of wisdom; she had no domestic responsibilities and lived a carefree live rendering judgments and having adventures.

The agrarian Sumerians had long revered the feminine principle, which makes the creation myth that emerged four hundred years after the invention of cuneiform and which replaced the earlier creation story of the Great Goddess Nammu (representing water) creating an earth goddess and a sky god, appear unusually misogynistic in comparison. This new creation story was a 170-line poem that starts by introducing the Great Goddess Tiamat and her lesser male consort Apsu. Apsu is murdered by other male gods, including the god Marduk, who then go on to trick and murder the Great Goddess herself by rupturing her bloated (pregnant?) stomach and splitting her heart. According to the new myth, the god Marduk believed the goddess Tiamat was too haughty and needed to be reduced in size.

After the victorious slaying of the Great Goddess, Marduk dismembered her body and created the universe out of its pieces: her buttocks became mountains, her breasts became foothills, her tears became the Tigris and Euphrates rivers, and finally, her pubic mound was used to support the sky. Marduk blamed the late Tiamat's death on her worshippers and then sacrificed the Goddess's favorite son Kingu to atone for their sins. He then ordered the flesh and blood of the Goddess's son to be kneaded and sculpted into mortals, who were forever condemned to crawl over the surface of Tiamat's carcass toiling to provide food and wine for the gods. The Goddess's divine son suffered and died for the "sins" of his people, and they would forever be burdened by guilt as they owed him—their martyred God—their very existence. Sound familiar?

While virtually all ancient societies had oral creation myths that changed over time, this new Sumerian myth, called "The Seven Tablets of Creation," was distinctive for its time not only because of its antifemale bias but because it was the first creation myth to appear in written form. The date of the myth's creation coincides with the life of Hammurabi, the ruler of Babylon who is famous for having executed the world's first written laws. Dr. Shlain believes the decline in feminine power, revealed by the changing myths of the Sumerians as well as in the stories of other ancient societies, was because of a feature unique to the use of writing as a form of communication.

Although speech appears to come easily to young children who are surrounded by reasonably intelligent, caring people, writing is another story as it takes many hours and even years of hard work to learn. Writing changed the very nature of communication as it replaced intuitive and spontaneous oral communication with a reality that is rigid and unyielding once it has been set down on stone, clay, parchment, or paper. Writing something, whether it is the truth or not, makes the words permanent, unlike oral traditions that are continuously subject to change and revision. Once something was written down, the "thoughts turned into words" became authoritative and absolute—the antithesis of the more feminine oral tradition, which included the possibility of change as a necessary ingredient.

Hammurabi's Code of Laws written in 2350 B.C. began by forbidding women more than one husband (polyandry had heretofore been an accepted practice), with punishment by stoning if the law was disobeyed. A full one-quarter of Hammurabi's new written laws related to restrictions on women's rights, including an edict that sons honor their fathers but not their mothers. Eunuch chaperones for women and the veiling of the female face were introduced for the first time as the goddess Tiamat was replaced by the god Marduk.

The great Egyptian civilization of antiquity came up with a more sophisticated form of picture writing called hieroglyphics at around the same time as the appearance of cuneiform in Sumeria. Each picture, or glyph, was able to represent a thing or action, stand for the sound of a syllable, or clarify the meaning of adjoining glyphs. Because the hieroglyphs were not able to express certain concepts, the Egyptians eventually invented twenty-five icons to represent their language's spoken consonants, thus allowing a person to sound out a word, although it is not clear how much this alphabet was actually used. During this period of experimentation with written communication, Egypt saw the rise of patriarchal values and the replacement of its earlier creation myth of two females intertwining to bring forth life. The new creation myth told the story of a male god Atum, who masturbated into existence eight powerful gods and goddesses. Once more the appearance of a written form of communication coincided with the devaluation of all things female—beginning by negating her role in giving birth.

Beginning around 1500 B.C., the half-human, half-animal gods and goddesses of the Egyptian pantheon started assuming human form only, and in another significant departure from earlier divinities, one manifestation of the god Amon was invisible. He had no face, becoming the first God without an image at the same time Egyptian writing was going from pictographs (icons) based on images to symbols based on abstractions. In an equally bizarre departure from the earlier divinities, a relatively obscure Goddess of nature and fertility, Maat, was elevated to a high position in the pantheon. She was unusual because she was now completely divorced from nature in that she represented the abstractions of truth, order, and justice. The majority of the common Egyptian people, however, continued to worship Isis with her reverence for nature and for her gift of resurrection each spring; the new divinities with their strange abstractions were generally worshipped only by royalty and the wealthy who could better afford the divorce from nature.

Another unusual event occurred during the Eighteenth Dynasty of Egypt's New Kingdom when the Pharaoh Amenhotep IV (whose wife was Nefertiti) ruled that his subjects were allowed to worship only one god, and that god was Aton, who like his rival Amon had no image. Amenhotep attempted to completely change the order of things by renaming himself Akhenaton and making it a crime for anyone in his kingdom to worship the older deities. Akhenaton would have been the very first monotheist, but he relented under pressure and allowed Maat to be the female consort of Aton and operate as a complementary goddess figure. When Akhenaton died after seventeen years of rule, his successor King Tut ordered Amon reinstated and Aton worship was dismantled; the common people continued to worship Isis, the Great Mother Goddess, and her pantheon of deities.

Women in ancient Egypt managed to hang onto higher positions in society for a little longer than did their counterparts in Mesopotamia, but as literacy increased in both civilizations, feminine power and values suffered a precipitous decline. Dr. Shlain believes information received by means of viewing linear, sequential symbols (left brain) contributed to a radical upheaval in gender relationships, and the scale was further tipped toward left-brain values once a new, easier to learn, twenty-odd letter, totally abstract alphabet came on board. The reading of cuneiform demanded the learning of over six hundred characters and understanding hieroglyphics required knowing six thousand icons plus learning rules for applying them (grammar). It is no wonder scribes were necessary to carry out what the common person could not or did not want to master. During these times the pantheon of gods and goddesses underwent changes but nothing so drastic as what was to occur once the average person—even children—could learn to read and write using symbols that were fewer in number and easier to master.

With the invention of a new, less cumbersome alphabet, suddenly for the first time ever, a law could be written down that almost everyone could read, understand, and obey. In time, all of the cultures that adopted an alphabet (and most did) rid themselves one by one of their pantheon of deities and chose instead to worship One God—one masculine God, and societies were all reorganized according to His newly written laws. Although there were many good things that came out of the advent of the written word, the new alphabet-using mindset was also abusive of nature, devalued feminine values, and glorified war and imperialism.

The new abstract-symbols-only alphabet that replaced the more pictorial cuneiform and hieroglyphics systematized knowledge and encouraged abstract thinking, leading to many discoveries that have been beneficial to humankind. Unfortunately, once totally abstract symbols began to represent individual letters and the left brain was fully engaged in comparison with the right brain's partial engagement, feminine power and influence began to slip rapidly. It is important to remember that the brains of both men and women were influenced by this change in the balance of the right and left hemispheres of the brain. A woman's brain would also have been pulled to the left, so to speak, and she would have begun to see things differently. She would have taken part in the devaluation of herself and other females, possibly being the first to criticize the mores or abilities of other women. Her sense of her own importance and the importance of other females would have been undermined at the same time her male counterparts were also beginning to doubt the value of feminine/right-brain characteristics.

The uniqueness of the alphabet in comparison to cuneiform and hieroglyphics is that in the former each letter has only a single sound and no representative meaning in and of itself. The meaning to words can be deciphered only when letters are strung together in a row and read sequentially.

The word "bull" is no longer represented by a pair of horns, but instead can only be understood by reading a four-letter word one letter at a time, with each letter having no meaning in common with the other letters.

When young children learn to read, they are leaving their right-brain world of all-at-once perception and entering into a new, abstract, and unnatural world of one-at-a-time perception. The importance of rods that are oriented to the right brain and see images all at once is supplanted by the hegemony of left-brain oriented cones, which focus one-at-a-time and in linear, sequential order. This unbalancing process of the brain takes place in every male or female who learns to read and write, and upsets the innate right-brain view of the world that is part of the innocence of infancy and early childhood. This was also part of the innocence of our early ancestors who had not yet dealt with literacy issues.

As the right hand (controlled by the left brain) became the hand that for most people held the pen that wrote, left-brain dominance was further encouraged in both men and women who became literate. Writing down words as well as reading them reinforced the left-hemispheric values that were already changing the way people saw themselves and others in relation to the world. As the alphabet flourished people began to turn away from worshipping divinities that represented nature and began believing in an abstract, faceless, natureless God who was able to be everywhere at once, but who was also nowhere to be seen. The Great Mother Goddess was forced, along with the fairies and nymphs of the forest, to take a backseat to an invisible yet all-powerful masculine God.

The early Egyptians used a picture of a snake in their hieroglyphic system for the word Goddess. Before the appearance of the written word, the snake had represented all-powerful female energy, sexual and otherwise. Since the snake regularly sheds its skin to begin anew, it was seen as immortal, as was the power of the feminine. After the advent of literacy, the snake as quintessential female symbol became reviled in patriarchal cultures and eventually became the evil presence (Satan) that tempted Eve in the Garden of Eden. Clearly the new patriarchal order was not happy with just usurping the goddess, and needed to vilify her to keep the masses from returning to her as in the past.

Although "protestant" basically means anyone who protests, the word is normally used to denote a protest against certain religious practices. Dr. Shlain claims the first "protest" reformation took place in the Sinai Desert almost four thousand years ago when members of a small desert tribe revolted against the worship of multiple deities and images, the Egyptian belief in an afterlife, and the use of rituals to substitute for individual morality. This first protestant reformation was accompanied by the appearance of the Ten Commandments—brought down the mountain by Moses as a gift from the God Yahweh to His "chosen" people. The first two commandments were unique in that (1) Yahweh forbade the worship of any God but Himself, and (2) He banned the making of all representative images—no pictures of *anything!* There is no archeological record of any previous civilization banning the making of representational images. This upstart male God forbade His tribe to make pictures of birds or animals or anything that people had used as totems in their religious past—no pictures of beautiful plant or animal life that represented bountiful Mother Nature, and certainly no pictures of other deities, whoever or whatever they might be.

Dr. Shlain questioned why the first two commandments were considered by Yahweh to be more important than murder, theft, lying, coveting, slandering, and adultery—issues that were dealt with in the last six commandments. Yahweh wanted these powerless, nomadic Israelites to learn to read the Commandments that were written down on the slabs Moses brought down the mountain. To encourage the revolutionary accomplishment of universal literacy, Yahweh (Moses?) forbade these Semitic wanderers from worshiping their old gods and goddesses—and even from visualizing any of their features; He also prohibited his followers to envision His image, instead commanding them to concentrate on His *words* only.

Sometime after Moses's visit with God in the desert, after a reasonable number of people had learned to read, the first book ever written in an alphabet appeared: the Old Testament. The appearance of this first Holy Book was soon followed by the sharp curtailment of women's rights.

Approximately two thousand years later a second "protest" reformation took place in Rome, which rejected not only the Old Testament's Judaism but the polytheism of the Romans in favor of a new religion that would come to be represented by written words in the second sacred alphabet book: the New Testament. Christianity was originally based on the kind and loving words of Jesus—words that were twisted and defeminized and then used by various male writers and patriarchal church officials to justify their restriction of women's rights and the banning of goddess worship and image making. Once again, words were of paramount significance in the new religion and all distractions had to be eliminated in order for people to concentrate on the relatively new abstract symbols strung together in a row.

A third protest reformation took place in the Arabian Desert and produced the third sacred alphabet book: the Koran. Around six hundred years after the birth of Christ, the (future) Islamic Prophet Mohammed was instructed by the Angel Gabriel in a dream to read so he could take the words of Allah and bring them down the mountain to his people. These words essentially instructed them to worship only Him (Allah) and rid themselves of all other divinities, which were largely goddesses at that time. The ancient desert civilizations of Arabia had long venerated the goddess, a fact that was noted by the ancient Greek historian Herodotus during his travels there one thousand years before the birth of Mohammed.

Mecca was the Arab people's holiest city long before Islam, and three out of the four stone images that ringed the famous Kaaba shrine, a large black gender-neutral cube venerated by pre-Muslim Arabs, were female deities. Even after the rise of Islam the priests who attended the Kaaba shrine in Mecca were referred to as "sons of the Old Woman." Mohammed declared that the people must abandon their worship of deities and icons and adopt the worship of an imageless monotheistic God.

Before Mohammed's visit from Gabriel in a dream, he had traveled a lot and noticed the Jews and Gnostic Christians he met along the way seemed more unified than the preliterate Arabs with their pantheon of deities and political disunity. The "miracle" in the Arabian Desert was that Mohammed was given the gift of literacy by the grace of God so he would be able to take His words to the people and convince them to worship only Him, Allah. To sweeten the deal, Mohammed promised converts to Islam life after death in exchange for their repudiation of all other divinities. Like Jesus, Mohammed never wrote down any of his words; loyal followers would take on this task at a later date. All three of the great monotheistic religious movements—Judaism, Christianity, and Islam—became popularized at the very time literacy was introduced to the general populace and involved the exclusive worship of an imageless, male god, followed shortly thereafter by a sharp curtailment of women's rights, the outlawing of goddess worship, and the banning of representational images.

The Semitic alphabet is the oldest known alphabet that was actually used enough for us to have found early evidence of it; a script resembling Hebrew letters that dates back to around 1800 B.C. was found at the site of an Egyptian temple dedicated to a goddess in the Sinai Desert. Dr. Shlain believes it is more than a remarkable coincidence that in one of the most inhospitable spots in the world, where nothing significant had ever happened before, two major revolutions occurred at exactly the same time in history: the adoption of one supreme male god and the advent of literacy. Both were *major* developments that have changed the world forever. According to Dr. Shlain, there must be a connection between these two major developments. He believes the incredible success of the first monotheistic religion, which has now blossomed into three major religions, had everything to do with the written word and its enormous power and ability to influence. The Egyptian ruler Akhenaton had tried to establish monotheism but failed as he lacked one essential ingredient: literate subjects who could read the words of God.

Archeological research tells us that most ancient polytheistic people created sacred sanctuaries—a tree, a rock, a cave—where they could go to worship their deities. The Hebrews left no sign—no temple, no shrine—of exactly where it was that Moses brought the Ten Commandments down from Mount Sinai; they were a nomadic people and apparently not interested in building and maintaining a permanent shrine. They created a God they could take with them everywhere they went; they did not need a specific grove of trees or pile of rocks in order to worship or sacrifice. Instead, they built a wooden box and carried the Ten Commandments of Yahweh around with them as they moved from place to place; this Ark of the Covenant was their temple.

Moses commanded that all of Israel become literate in order to read the holy words contained in the ark that basically instructed the Hebrew people to worship One God and lead moral lives. The laws prescribed by the Ten Commandments presaged the Magna Carta and the U.S. Constitution by demanding the universal application of laws that attempted to implement a justice system that pertained to all (except, of course, women and slaves). Dr. Shlain's research led him to believe that the invention of the alphabet was the miracle that happened in the Sinai Desert almost two thousand years before the birth of Christ, and that this incredible innovation led to the emergence of successful monotheisms in the form of Judaism, Catholicism, and Islam, eventually obliterating most of the older, oral, and more holistic-based religions.

These older polytheistic religions had evolved over a long period of time and had a way of changing with the circumstances of the people, as change is inevitable in life. The ancients borrowed gods and goddesses back and forth from their neighbors and trading partners, and even blended the responsibilities of deities when necessary. Once laws were spoken by One God and written down for all to read, there was no more changing that could be done without breaking one of the laws. Writing down laws instead of speaking them was the beginning of religious warfare not only between the three major religions but among them. The first-known slaughter of a people because they did not worship the assigned deity occurred when Yahweh ordered Moses to kill all the Canaanites—except for the virgin girls—as punishment for worshipping other gods and goddesses.

Not only did the new monotheistic religion of the Hebrews have no special shrines as did the multi-deity religions that came before it, but its God discouraged many sensual influences of the older polytheistic religions that were appreciated by the right brain, including music and dance. Eventually the first religion based on an alphabet would abandon bright colors, drums, dance, and cymbals as well as goddesses and images. Early orthodox representatives of Judaism, Christianity, Islam, and Protestantism all dressed in drab colors, usually black and/or white, and scorned music and dance, believing they distracted from the words of their respective sacred books.

Although the Hebrew religion espoused compassion for many who had been unprotected before—such as the women of fallen armies and slaves, determining that such women should not be raped and slaves should be set free after seven years—it also introduced religious intolerance, the notion that one religion, the Hebrew religion, was superior to the others. The Israelites clearly felt superior to people who worshipped a pantheon of deities that represented and mirrored human society; these early deities had personalities as well as images and paralleled humanity in that they had families and adventures that were similar to ones in the lives of the common people. These very early polytheistic societies had personal gods, family gods, local gods, and gods for a variety of specific purposes. There were sometimes skirmishes over land or horses or women, but not because someone believed in a different deity and/or wanted to impose their religious belief system on others.

Civilizations that were conquered or gradually overcome by invaders would absorb some of the divinities of the conqueror as well as the conqueror incorporating gods and goddesses of those they now ruled.

Once there was One God with One Book there was no longer room for the constant evolution and exchange of deities; the same words were stuck in the same book, never to move or change—well, not much anyway. People knew exactly what words they were fighting for because they were "written in stone," unlike the casual give-and-take of earlier oral polytheistic societies. Clever people who created a workable, easy-to-learn alphabet and system of reading and writing had unwittingly created the monster of religious intolerance—the Written Word. To date, the combined Written Words of the Old Testament, the New Testament, and the Koran have inspired more killings than any other force in the long history of humanity.

The Loss of the Goddess

When mostly white male Christian archeologists were first confronted with multitudes of female figurines unearthed during excavations of prehistoric sites, they assumed they had found evidence of minor fertility goddesses or remnants of man's early pornography! Considering the overwhelmingly patriarchal world from which they were coming, it is not surprising these archeologists could not even imagine a civilization that worshipped a Goddess as their primary deity and that was responsible for the production of all those female figurines. Excavations little more than one hundred years ago on the Mediterranean Island of Crete surprised many archeologists by revealing a socially and technologically advanced god/goddess worshipping civilization that existed six thousand years before the birth of Christ. It seems nobody was prepared to believe that paved streets, hot and cold running water, and a drainage system could be part of people's everyday life thousands of years ago. The art of these Minoan people from the Island of Crete was beautiful and elegant, depicting many pleasurable activities enjoyed by both males and females, who were portrayed as equals. The murals in the palace at Knossos on Crete celebrated life and nature rather than extolling the virtues of war or offering tributes or memorials to powerful leaders.

It wasn't until the 1950s that information started coming from excavations at Catal Huyuk and Hacilar, early farming communities in southern Turkey that existed around the same time as Minoan Crete, some several thousand years before the birth of Christ. The archeological evidence from these sites discovered some fifty-odd years ago reveals that these societies were also incredibly sophisticated and egalitarian.

These early civilizations venerated a primary Earth Mother Goddess as part of a "religious" worship that permeated their entire lives from birth to death. They would not have understood our erudite discussions on the separation of church and state. It was not until excavations on the Island of Crete and in southern Turkey were thoroughly studied that it became clear women had most likely created and dominated Neolithic religion and agriculture.

The oldest known shaman's or religious healer's grave was discovered in the Czech Republic only within the last century and dates back to the last ice age. Since they had long imagined early shamanistic healers to be members of an all-male club, male archeologists were shocked to discover that the painted-red skeleton buried ceremoniously under the shoulder blades of a mammoth with a fox in hand (clear indications the person had been a shaman) was a woman. The tradition of females as givers of life, wisdom, and health remained an integral part of all early civilizations as they moved from traditional hunter-gather societies to a more agrarian way of life. There is no evidence from any of the early archeological excavations of goddess-worshipping cultures to support the existence of a specialized military or central authority; archeologists have never been able to show that these primitive people fought in organized wars. Archeological evidence clearly gives support to the belief that the multitude of female figurines and statues from theses early cultures were icons/symbols of the Neolithic people's major religion. Since these agrarian-equal-partnership civilizations appear to have been successful, fruitful, and long lasting, what happened to make them all go away?

One by one every civilization, as they adopted and used an alphabet, experienced the erosion of feminine values and the eventual loss of the goddess. When the Greek city-states adopted the Ionian alphabet in 402 B.C., literacy rates soared. This monumental happening was accompanied by a revolutionary change in the Olympian Golden Circle of Twelve Deities after hundreds of years of stability: Hestia—Goddess of hearth, family, and children—was suddenly ousted in favor of Dionysus, God of wine, sexuality, dance, and madness. With the rise of alphabet literacy, the Greeks needed a God to represent the inexplicable insanity that was happening all around them because of all of the changes taking place. They replaced the Goddess of hearth and home with the God of wine and debauchery, which says a lot about what was happening to feminine values at the very time in history when the Greeks were becoming alphabet literate.

It was also unusual that Dionysus became the only member of the Olympian Circle to die, and he also became the first god who was able to resurrect himself each spring, promising salvation through rebirth; many believe Dionysus's resurrection was the model for the future story of the springtime resurrection of Christ. There had been earlier resurrections such as Persephone, who spent six months of each winter in Hades (as punishment for eating six pomegranate seeds), resurfacing each spring in time for the growing season and harvest, but Dionysus was a male god, making the connection more direct between the story of his resurrection and that of Christ's. The emergence of the Dionysian cult followed the Greeks' Golden Age of classical culture; words dominated the social/political scene and women suddenly became feared and despised by their learned male counterparts. Homosexuality, especially among men and young boys, was rampant. New Greek myths spoke of frightening stories that involved evil women killing their husbands and lovers, although in real life women were rapidly losing power.

Depression among females resulted from this loss of power, and suicide became common among women in classical Greece, reaching epidemic proportions in some areas. In one desperate effort to stop the rash of female suicides, the king of the city-state of Miletus proclaimed that any woman who killed herself would be carried naked through the streets. The downfall of the Golden Age of Greece occurred after universal alphabet literacy arrived on the scene; the city-states were so weakened by the internecine warfare between rival city-states and the removal of women from public life, they were unable to resist the Macedonians who invaded from the north. It is said that after the final battle of the war, which ended Greek hegemony, the plains near Thebes were littered with pairs of corpses as male warrior-lovers fought to their deaths at each other's sides. Just as the alphabet triumphed in Greece in the fourth century B.C. their democracy floundered, a casualty of abstract political beliefs.

It was at this mad time in Greek history that Socrates was condemned to death for his Ideas, a new concept in crime. Greek leaders feared his Ideas would incite riots in the young who would in turn overthrow their fragile democracy. It was also at this time the playwright Euripedes wrote *The Bacchae* as an allegorical tale that instructs us not to ignore our darker, intuitive side in favor of reason and the written word. In this prescient story, King Pentheus rejected Dionysus despite warnings he should honor this popular god. The king wound up being torn to pieces and eaten by his wife and mother while they were under a Dionysian spell and did not recognize him. The moral of *The Bacchae* is that we all have a feminine and masculine side, and both of these sides are further divided into a dark side and a light side; if we ignore either half of our masculine or feminine natures we will have to pay the price, which can be severe.

There is no doubt that we are at this moment dealing with the darker side of humanity, and that a rescue is essential if we are to continue living at all. When large numbers of people are willing to tie bombs to their bodies and die unspeakable deaths along with their victims—victims they usually don't even know and might even like under different circumstances—it is time to go inside of ourselves instead of looking for answers from the outside. It is clear we must rescue ourselves. How can One God decide who should win when He is ostensibly in control of and rooting for members of all three of the world's major religions, just under different banners and with slightly different stories and regulations? Yahweh, the Holy Trinity, and Allah all sprung from the same source, and we must go to that source to undo the damage that has been festering ever since rabid-monotheistic-word-idea-oriented systems became the rule of the day.

CHAPTER 14

Literacy Run Amok

Most people consider suicide bombing to be an act of madness and cannot imagine themselves doing something so unbalanced, yet the long history of monotheistic religions going crazy in the name of God is replete with such acts. Some early Christians were so eager to martyr themselves that they refused the help of Roman law counselors trying to get them off the hook for the crime of believing in Christ. These very counselors most likely paid tribute to any number of deities and could not see the sense of dying for any one particular god. A number of Christians who had been arrested were given the opportunity to renounce their faith in place of death, but refused; one group was even given a thirty-day reprieve to think it over but turned down the opportunity to live and begged for martyrdom. One counselor, who was unsuccessful in trying to help some would-be Christian martyrs, referred to them as miserable creatures, wondering sarcastically if there were enough ropes and cliffs for them if they really wanted to die so badly. Christian leaders understood that the blood of martyrs was seed for the cause, and they encouraged potential martyrs to give up their lives for their religion.

Sound familiar? This early Christian martyrdom was the first time in known history that people were willing to commit suicide for an Idea. The world of these early Christians had recently experienced the onslaught of universal literacy. People's brains were under renovation and somehow dying for a bunch of words seemed logical to them—this despite the fact that Jesus never wrote down any of his words or asked anyone to martyr themselves for him.

What we do know of Jesus has come from firsthand and secondhand oral accounts. Even Paul, the first Gospel writer, never actually met Jesus. Many say it was Paul who really created Christianity, as he is responsible for making it attractive to the masses by renouncing the painful circumcision of the Jews and by promising an afterlife, which the Hebrews did not believe in. Both of these changes served to make the new religion of Christianity more appealing. Unfortunately, Paul may have been a good businessman but his personal life was dour and dark. He apparently was married once but in actuality he spent most of his life traveling in the company of men. Jesus was known for his compassion and love for women, and they participated freely in his life up to his last day on earth and even afterward, when he reputedly rose from the dead under their watch. Paul rid himself of women in the new religion of Christianity using the Eve excuse: Women could not participate in the new religion because Eve was responsible for all the sins of mankind because of the apple-eating incident, just as the Greek Pandora was responsible for letting sins out of the box and making all of her people suffer forever. As an old departed friend used to say, "Blame it on Mame."

The early Christianity based on Jesus's oral teachings was popular partly because it allowed for women to return to the church on a variety of levels, a significant departure from the patriarchal harshness of Judaism. Once again the masses found themselves drawn to the worship of a female deity, this time in the form of Jesus's mother, Mary. The Hebrew god was a very masculine and singular god who was often punitive and unyielding, without the nurturing qualities of the goddess. Even when Saint Augustine pronounced that the worship of Mother-Earth goddesses was obscene, monstrous, and wicked, he was not able to prevent the seduction of the masses back into worshipping the goddess in the form of Mary, Mother of God. Sightings of the Virgin Mother seemed to increase in response to patriarchal pressure to conform to the new religion honoring a divine all-male trilogy.

The worship of Mary has ancient roots. The very name Mary, "Maria," *la mer,* means "the sea." Seawater, the universal substance of life, had long been the quintessential symbol of the goddess and all things feminine. The earliest creation stories of ancient civilizations generally began with a Great Goddess of the Water creating the Universe out of Her Ineffable Essence. The Church was undeniably concerned about the popularity of Mary, the worship of whom was growing rapidly without the benefit of words since very little had been written about her. Paul never mentions her and she is mentioned only a few times in the other Gospels. Yet during Medieval times, literally hundreds of churches and cathedrals were dedicated to her. The important Feast of the Assumption on August 15th was also named in the Virgin's honor. It took place on the very same day pre-Christian pagans had honored the goddess Artemis, the virgin huntress and moon goddess. Medieval calendars in France and England were even recalibrated to begin the New Year on the Day of Our Lady, March 15th.

At the beginning of the Dark Ages, Pope Gregory voided the Second Commandment that forbade the making of representational images when he realized visual aids were needed to convert the illiterate masses and keep them interested in the Catholic Church because they could not read the words in the Bible. The first painting the Church not only allowed but commissioned was a portrait of the Pope receiving the symbols of his station (insignias of power) from Mary—not from God, Jesus, or a male Saint, but from a female who was barely spoken of in the Bible and who was merely the mother of Jesus! Images of Mary were everywhere—in homes, churches, shops, and pageants; her gentle image led every medieval procession. Sightings and apparitions of Mary increased as her cult grew, while there were only rare sightings of Jesus and none of the Father or Holy Ghost. As the Marianism cult grew and threatened to undermine the all-male Holy Trinity, the Church invented the devil to help combat the obvious tendency of the common people to revert to Goddess worship. Earlier civilizations—Sumerians, Egyptians, Greeks, Cretans, Romans—all had some deities who possessed a dark side, but no society heretofore had ever conjured up a being who personified the abstraction of Pure Evil and nothing more. The Fathers of Christianity got together and created a diabolical red-colored, cloven-hoofed creature with a tail and horns who carried a triton.

Red has always been considered the color of female sexuality. Female primates high in the trees signal the male during estrus with their flaming red vulva and buttocks, triggering an exciting anticipatory neurotransmitter response in the brain of the male primate, which leads to a sexual response and the procreation of the species. Red has long been associated with female power and sexuality, most likely because red is the color of life-giving menstrual blood, which was considered full of divine power because of its association with the lunar cycle. Blood from a young woman's first menses was considered auspicious as it was believed to increase connections to the spirit world, and as such was highly valued. Reactions are buried deep in the human psyche and feelings of passion and vitality can still be triggered by the color red, which is why men like red lipstick and women receive scarlet letters.

The snake and the bull had been the goddesses' most powerful totems for tens of thousands of years—since the beginning. They represented female power and knowledge, and the ability to bring forth life and sustain it. In images created by the Church the devil's tail looked like a snake and the tip of the tail resembled a serpents head. The horns in Satan's images look like the horns of a bull. While today we think of the bull as representing male power and energy, early humans considered the bull to be a feminine symbol as the frontal view of a bull's skull resembles the female reproductive system—a uterus with fallopian tubes, à la Georgia O'Keeffe. The Church fathers were clearly aware of the primitive association between bulls and the female sex and were trying to forge the association between females and wickedness in the minds of their brethren by putting horns on their image of the devil along with a snakelike tail.

In Greek mythology, Zeus fought a terrible serpent in a battle to see who would win control of the universe. Zeus won, as did other male gods who fought the great serpent and won at the very time their cultures were first experiencing alphabet literacy. The male god killed the serpent along with its representation of female sexuality, power, and wisdom. Even Medusa did not survive literacy, as her powerful snake-hair image was destroyed along with the other she-serpents.

The two oldest known passages in the Old Testament (Psalms 74 and 89) tell different versions of a creation story, both in which Yahweh kills a sea serpent and becomes ruler of the universe. These psalms, which predate Genesis, imply that Yahweh did not create the universe—that it was already there, and he conquered it by killing a snake. It is implied in these Psalms that the universe was created by a sea serpent, which at that time in history represented feminine power and values. The advent of the written word brought disaster to both the snake and the bull as they began to represent sinister behavior (snake) and lustful yet frightening virility (bull), leaving their more creative and benevolent female associations in the past.

The triton that was associated with various primal water goddesses from ancient times became a fiery pitchfork in Hell under the direction of the Church, completely reversing its earlier association with watery (feminine) substances. In *The Alphabet Versus the Goddess* Dr. Shlain calls the cloven-hoof addition to the Church's personification of evil a masterstroke of male propagandists attempting to eradicate female power. A pig's footprint in the mud looks like the ancient vulva sign painted (at least as far back as Paleolithic times) on rocks and in caves; this image of the oval with a cleft running up from the bottom had been the universal symbol of females and feminine energy for many thousands of years. Probably because of this, pigs were considered sacred to the Goddess. To have the most evil creature ever summoned in the minds of man leave a cloven footprint, which was practically identical to the ancient symbol of the Earth Goddess, was clearly the patriarchal church's attempt to erode female power.

Try as they did to eradicate female values and influence, the hundreds of churches built in honor of Mary—from Notre Dame in Paris to Saint Sophia in Constantinople—attest to the tenacity of ancient beliefs in goddesses and the feminine. The many saints that eventually came to people the Christian religion were similar to the pantheon of gods and goddesses from earlier times, and sometimes things didn't seem to be very different. Women during the Dark Ages played a central role in religion and were even at times able to officiate over major sacraments. There was little fuss over heretics or witches, and celibacy was discarded in favor of a lustful life, if that could be arranged—even by members of the priesthood.

Witch Hunts and Other Insantities

It was not until words were written down by men (Yahweh in the Old Testament commanded, "Ye shall suffer no witch to live!") that women who were considered knowledgeable and wise found themselves in danger of suffering unspeakable brutality and death. Archeological evidence indicates that at the time Yahweh reputedly spoke these harsh words, there had never been a civilization that hunted and killed its women: not the Egyptians, the Mesopotamians, the Jews, the Greeks, the Phoenicians, the Muslims, the Hindus, or the Chinese. Little more than two thousand years later, in 1468, the papacy in Rome declared the crime of witchcraft a *crimen exceptum*, meaning that suspected witches could be officially tortured prior to a trial. In 1484 the papacy for the first time in the fifteen-hundred-year history of the church declared that witchcraft was a threat to Christianity. So infectious was the hysteria that it eventually reached the shores of our early democracy; the witch trials and executions that took place here in America are still the subject of controversy and befuddlement. How could it have happened?

Dr. Shlain posits that it was the invention of the printing press that created a climate ripe for the wholesale brutality of women. In 1457, Johannes Gutenberg published his Bible with movable type in Germany and copies of this first type-printed book were read all over Europe; soon afterward many duplicate type presses appeared in other countries (patents and copyrights did not exist at the time). In 1460, just a few years and a few miles away from Gutenberg's printing plant in Frankfurt, twelve "sorceresses" were burned in Heidelberg's public square, the beginning of much more to come.

This witch-hunting insanity began at the very time the printing press began to turn out not only Bibles but other religious propaganda. The church commissioned a guide for exterminating witches called "The Hammer of Witches," published in 1487, and it became a bestseller. It was a basic how-to book—how to distinguish a witch from a God-fearing Christian and what to do about it. This instruction manual basically said that women were more apt to be seduced by the devil because they were silly and gullible. It described women as having insatiable carnal lust, which caused some to desire fornication with the devil. Suspicious women were stripped, blindfolded, and tortured until they confessed they were indeed agents of Satan; they were forced to give names of other women who were so-called witches and after all that, they were burned at the stake. Their children were often beaten and forced to watch as their mothers writhed and screamed in agony as they burned. The inquisitors would then round up the women whose names they had gotten from torturing their last victim.

Nothing so singularly antifemale as witch hunting and burning had ever taken place in the history of the world, and this horror of horrors occurred in the midst of the Humanist Renaissance! Leading humanists such as Erasmus and Thomas More (of *Utopia* fame) and scientists such as Francis Bacon, father of experimental science, and William Harvey, physician to the King and discoverer of the secret of blood circulation, all supported the purge of witches. Heretofore, both men and women had always acknowledged the abilities of women as healers; the greatest physician of the age, Paracelsus, said he learned all he knew from a woman healer, a sorceress. Women had been the repositories of knowledge concerning nature and its ability to heal since the beginning of human life.

During the so-called Renaissance, appointed Church officials went from town to town throughout Europe in search of witches; tens of thousands of innocent women died gruesome deaths at the hands of these religious men. According to Dr. Shlain's research, by the time officials finished searching for witches and exterminating them in two particular villages in Germany, there was only one woman left alive in the whole of the two towns combined!. Women were hunted like animals, and even young girls were not immune to the torture and murder that occurred, as it was assumed a mother passed her witchcraft down through her daughters. Entire lifetimes were spent in fear of being called a witch, or alienating a neighbor; it's amazing women even ventured out of doors or learned to trust anyone ever again. It certainly answers the argument of male supremacists as to why women were not accomplishing things at the same rate as men during the Renaissance. They were too busy hiding.

At the same time the Church felt the need to purge its kingdom of so-called witches, the depravity at the Vatican became so egregious that inevitably complaints became bolder and louder among the flock. Sexual license and promiscuity in the Church and around the countryside had reached epidemic proportions, as sodomy, prostitution, and adultery ruled the day. Syphilis ran rampant as moral values and behaviors sank to new levels. During the fifteenth and sixteenth centuries, the Popes lived like emperors and were the richest men in the world. Men of the cloth throughout Europe kept mistresses and fathered children.

Individual officials of the Church made much of their money from selling "indulgences"; for a fee, a person could have all of their sins wiped away. Ordinarily, a Christian who committed a mortal sin would owe seven years' penance in Purgatory, but it was possible if one gave the right amount of money to have one's slate wiped completely clean of sins. People could also buy their deceased relatives' way into Heaven. They were told that once the coins hit the bowl, the person for whom the penance was paid would fly straight out of Purgatory and into Heaven. One particularly ambitious monk sold sealed letters that claimed forgiveness for sins a person had not yet committed, but might be thinking about. In 1517, in an attempt to raise money for a war against a particular duchy and to rebuild St Peter's Basilica, Pope Leo held a bargain sale for indulgences, officially offering absolution and remission for all past sins and "preferential treatment" for future sins. Once a man of the cloth had his foot in the door of the papacy, he held it open long enough to get many of his family members lucrative positions in this incredible money machine, which witnessed peasant families starving themselves in order to get departed relatives into Heaven.

The most notorious papal family to reside at the Vatican was the infamous Borgias, a Spanish family whose wild orgies and incestuous relations brought disgrace and contempt upon the Catholic Church. Borgia Pope Alexander VI brought depravity to a new level with his rumored incestuous relationship with his daughter Lucretia, who was also rumored to be involved sexually with both of her brothers. When one brother's body was found dead floating in the Tiber River with nine dagger wounds, most assumed it was the other jealous brother who did it, as both apparently wanted their sister all to themselves. When a son was born to Lucretia, her father the Pope decided to make the child legitimate by issuing two papal bulls. The first identified Lucretia's son as the offspring of her still living brother and an unknown woman, and the second bull acknowledged that the baby was his (the Pope's!) with the same unidentified woman. Many believe the baby was really the offspring of the Pope and his own daughter.

In his book *A World Lit Only by Fire*, William Manchester writes about one of Pope Alexander's more memorable Vatican parties called the Ballet of the Chestnuts. After a sumptuous dinner, fifty of the city's most beautiful prostitutes danced with the guests in front of the Pope and his children. The whores then removed their clothes, and squatted and squirmed among chestnuts which had been scattered all over the floor, attempting in ingenious ways to pick up the nuts. The guests who were interested then stripped off their clothes and joined the prostitutes on the dance floor, "coupling" in front of all onlookers. Servants traversed the room in an effort to keep track of each man's orgasms, and a prize was given at the end to the man with the greatest ejaculatory capability, as this was a quality greatly admired by the Borgia Pope.

Amidst all of this squalor certain Popes still managed to have the good sense to support some of the greatest artists in history—Michelangelo, Leonardo, Raphael, Botticelli, Titian—artists who were allowed to explore their talents because of the tainted money they received from the Church. The Popes' motives for supporting the arts were largely selfish (although they had good taste), as they realized these wonderful works of art would bring people into the Church and thus into the greedy clutches of the clergy. At any rate, it was a far cry from the banning of images.

Despite the artistic wonders made possible largely because of the extravaganzas of the Vatican, the deplorable circumstances resulting from the excesses of the Catholic Church reached such a debased level they could not possibly have continued unchallenged. Machiavelli noted in 1513 that the proof of how decadent the Church had become lay in the fact that the nearer people were to Rome, the less religious they were, and anyone studying the principles of Christianity could see how widely divergent they were from current practices. Several years later the Protestant Reformation began in earnest when an obscure monk named Martin Luther nailed a complaint about the sale of papal indulgences onto the door of his local church in Wittenberg, Germany. Because of the printing press that had been recently invented in Germany, the new "Protestants" were able to spread their ideas quickly by printing pamphlets using their native language. The Catholic Church had always claimed that only a few high-level priests were capable of interpreting the New Testament, which was printed in Latin. Augustine's declaration that there was "no salvation outside of the Church" was used to bully people into believing they needed the Church to get into Heaven. Copies of the Bible had always been carefully guarded, sometimes even chained to desks to make sure no one tried to kidnap the book and determine the meaning of the Scriptures by themselves—if they could read Latin, that is.

The Catholic Church, meanwhile, having done away with God's second commandment banning images, had become comfortable with mega rituals that included fabulous visual images rich with music, color, and pageantry. Luther objected to this ostentatious debauchery. He believed the words of the Bible alone should influence faith, and individuals should be able to examine the teachings of Christ themselves by reading the New Testament in their own language. He hoped they would be transformed by His words to act in a righteous manner. Although Jesus never wrote down any of his words, what we have been told of what he said is that he never mentioned original sin or Eve's special role as Despoiler of Humankind, nor did he forbid the making of images or advocate burning anyone for their beliefs. Luther, a dour and pessimistic man, unfortunately chose the darkest passages from the Old Testament to emphasize in his writings, portraying God as the harsh and avenging Yahweh rather than the loving and forgiving Jesus of the New Testament. He urged people to resist the Catholic Church and join his new Religious Protest movement.

Luther also believed in Saint Augustine's strange vision of Predestination, the belief that all humans are born sinners and the vast majority were predestined to go to Hell while they were still in the womb, before they were even born. Augustine was a peculiar Christian who had been troubled since his adolescent years by the nature of sexuality, which he later concluded was so involuntary and vexing it must be controlled by Satan himself. Born more than three hundred years after the birth of Christ, Augustine's faith in God (his mother was a Christian, his father a hedonistic pagan) and his excellent writing skills allowed him to work his way up through the hierarchy of the relatively new writing-based religion. The future saint introduced several controversial interpretations of Christianity that had nothing to do with the original teachings of Christ. Augustine wrote that God had contaminated Adam's seed and the seed of future generations as punishment for his sin in the Garden of Eden. Men's semen was polluted by this original sin, and every newborn baby from that day on was born a sinner. Augustine claimed Jesus was the only exception to this "rule" as he was conceived through Immaculate Conception. According to the New Testament, Jesus never mentioned original sin nor did he say anywhere that sex was sinful. Even the dour Paul, who considered Adam's misstep to be a sign of the weakness of the flesh, did not think this "sin" should haunt the future of all mankind forever.

Augustine was a peculiarly morbid fellow, who interpreted God as punitive and unyielding; his new mythology of Christianity completely twisted Jesus's words to eradicate the more right-brain feminine sentiments of forgiveness and mercy so evident in His Message. According to the belief systems of St. Augustine and Martin Luther, every human was born with original sin and required the help of an official of the Church to help mediate the severity of their sinful nature. Augustine decreed that only baptism at birth and later the sacrament of confession could free a soul from sin and allow for its admittance into Heaven; he maintained that only a priest of the Orthodox Church could perform these sacraments, thus securing the place of the Church and its many (male) officials in the lives of all Christians.

Augustine's concept of original sin wiped out the common-sense free-will version of sin, in which a sin is committed by a free and willful act. Several important Christians challenged Augustine on this dark interpretation of

Christianity. One British monk argued that God would not undo His perfect creation (referring to Adam and Eve) to make man alone evil among the animals; he also argued that only a person who actually committed a sin should be punished. This feisty British monk even organized a campaign to try to thwart Augustine's position on original sin but the future saint sent lobbyists to Rome, followed up by eighty costly Arabian horses that were distributed to key voters on this hot issue to influence them in his favor. The controversy over the concept of original sin was such that there were actually riots in the streets of Rome, but Augustine was victorious and little more than four hundred years after the birth of Christ, the disgraced ex-communicated monk from Britain, who had dared to challenge the future saint, saw his fervent belief that humankind was born innocent and without original sin condemned as heresy.

Martin Luther was attracted to Augustine's dark and pessimistic outlook on humanity; he believed virtue and charity could not help a person at all—only absolute faith in the story of God's sacrifice of his son to save humanity allowed for possible redemption. Luther believed mankind was essentially evil, and even in the noblest person the evil far outweighed the good. It is not surprising the depressing philosophy of this fourth "protestant reformation" went hand–in-hand with the world's first wholesale slaughter of female "witches."

By the time of the fourth "protest" Reformation, goddess worship had been largely eradicated or driven underground, although there were still some pockets of Europe, and definitely areas beyond, where polytheistic traditions prevailed that included the worship of female deities. What distinguished this fourth reformation was its ability, largely because of the invention of the printing press, to bring the words of the Bible and other religious writings to a multitude of people in their own language by providing numerous inexpensive copies. Add the influence of Martin Luther and you have a reformation and the advent of Protestantism. Besides having a dark and pessimistic personality, Luther disliked nature and was one of the most prolific writers in German history. Words combined with the invention of the printing press once again severely curtailed women's rights and powers and encouraged a stark world of black and white, devoid of the luxurious religious rituals and images of the Catholic Church that had managed a comeback despite various restrictions. Never before in history had so many newly literate people been inundated by so many words—words in their own language they could understand. The impact of these words in terms of brainwashing (or brain unbalancing) haunts us to this day.

Things only got worse when the Protestant torch was passed to John Calvin, who continued to give the new Christian "protest" religion its masculine edge, tainted with unyielding discipline and cruelty. His emphasis on the harshest ideas from Judaism and Catholicism helped turn back the burgeoning Renaissance and produced the blueprint for an exclusive male hierarchy of ministers, deacons, and elders, who were all to hold sway in the newly reformed churches of the Presbyterians, Puritans, and Huguenots. Calvin pretty much completely got rid of right-brain, feminine influences such as rituals, images, and sacraments; gone from the Church were all celebrations involving joy, laughter, beauty, color, and mercy leftover from earlier pagan days of worship.

Calvin believed in a theocratic state where religion and politics were blended into one, and when he founded his Ideal City of God in Geneva, Switzerland, he implemented harsh rules of government to ensure the obedience of his brethren. In 1541 he ordered church elders to visit every house in the area and keep dossiers on everyone, which contained private information gleaned from conversations, observations, and hearsay. Excessive tardiness or absences from Church could bring about banishment or even death; children were encouraged to spy and report on their parents in this new world of reformed Christianity. Calvin's Church forbade dancing and singing and any kind of music other than church hymns. Playing cards, burning incense, and frivolity of any kind were also banished. These were the days of public stocks and executions for all kinds of crimes: Failing to give your baby a Biblical name; wearing jewelry, lace, or any kind of interesting or colorful clothing; being caught with a rosary; being caught with an image of the Virgin Mary—all could and did receive harsh punishment. The more serious crimes such as adultery, idolatry, blasphemy, or witchcraft usually resulted in torture and execution. Unmarried girls who were found pregnant were routinely drowned; this practice led many young women to hide their pregnancies and then abandon their babies at birth rather than face the brutality of the all-male courts. Anyone who dared criticize the severity of the new Church was branded a heretic; one former friend of Calvin's who was accused of criticizing him was tortured for thirty days and then his feet were nailed to a stake before he was beheaded.

The reign of terror that followed this fourth reformation, which centered around "sacred ideas" printed in books for all to read, included religious wars against: pagans, Jews, Moors, former Jews (Conversos), former Moors (Moriscos), Anabaptists, Huguenots, and peasants. During the Peasant War in Germany in the 1500s, Martin Luther opined it would be best if all the peasants were killed as punishment for revolting against their oppressors without divine authority. In the 1600s the Lutherans and Calvinists finally had a go at each other in Germany's Thirty Years War, wiping out over a third of the population of the country before it ended; fighting over the interpretation of God's words and intentions in that long war resulted in so much destruction it took over a century for Germany to recover.

The Sacred Book of Arabia

The third sacred book of monotheism, the Koran, was the first book ever written in Arabic prose, and there are many who say it is still the greatest example of Arabic writing. At around the same time the Ten Commandments were introduced to the Semites in the Sinai Desert, an advanced civilization was being constructed by the Sabaean people (of Queen of Sheba fame) in the deserts of Arabia, replete with impressive monuments and advanced irrigation techniques. The pre-Islamic culture that developed out of these early beginnings in time created an alphabet of its own. This alphabet did not initially gain acceptance with the people, however; the only literary tradition that seemed to take hold for a long time was the art of poetry. Since it took a while after the development of an alphabet for a system of writing to develop, poetry and proverbs transcribed from oral recitations were the first written expressions of pre-Islamic Arabian ideals of courage, loyalty, and generosity.

The poet in these ancient times was the orator and historian of his people; he was well versed in their genealogy and folklore, including family rights, pasturelands, and borderlines. This was an important role as it was said that these nomadic people were always ready for a fight but not necessarily eager to be killed, and a good poet could help sort things out before bloodshed occurred. The poet's job was to keep these skirmishes and the recollection of its heroes alive for centuries, while at the same time providing well-kept information when necessary to help settle disputes honorably yet safely.

Persian and Hellenic influences had long been woven into the poetry of pre-Islamic Arabia, and it was inevitable that ideas gathered from various contacts with the Jews and Christians who had settled in Arab lands would also find their way into the local poetry, ballads, and proverbs. Nascent Islam no doubt sprung from a mixture of these ideas and is still evolving under the same multicultural influences today. The future prophet Mohammed was one of many pre-Islamic Arabs exposed to the poetry and verbal exchanges of the bards. These poets became indispensable to the masses because of their talent for filtering ideas and sentiments and weaving them into stories of romance and intrigue.

The vast majority of pre-Islamic Arabians were illiterate; even Mohammed was unable to read until the visit in his dream from the Angel Gabriel. Allah gave Mohammed the gift of literacy so he would be able to bring His words to a matrilineal, tribal people whose worship had long centered around multiple deities of both sexes and a large black meteorite sheltered in the Kaaba at Mecca, the Arab's holiest city. Annual pilgrimages and sacrifices were made to deities at this holy site in Mecca. However, little is known of these gods and goddesses since after the advent of Islam, efforts were made to erase all traces of this earlier period, which Muslims later referred to as the "Age of Ignorance." Little has survived this pre-Islamic era, but archeologists and anthropologists have pieced together enough information from this early Arabian past to reveal a culture in which both men and women were able to come and go as they pleased, own property, and run businesses. Also, both men and women participated in a vibrant spiritual life that had evolved over thousands of years from the simple worship of nature and its symbolic deifications and personifications.

Little is known about the early life of the Prophet Mohammed, founder of Islam, except that like Jesus, he came from humble beginnings. Mohammed was orphaned at the age of six and was raised by his grandfather until he died, then by his uncle. When he was twelve he accompanied his uncle on a caravan trip to Syria, where he met a Christian monk; this was perhaps his first exposure to Christianity. When Mohammed was twenty-five he married a woman fifteen years his senior; she was a widow and a successful businesswoman. Mohammed was so devoted to her that he remained monogamous until after her death twenty-six years later, although by law he could have had more than one wife.

Mohammed's exposure to Judaism and Christianity during his travels had opened his eyes to the possibility that people could unite under an idea rather than because of shared bloodlines. Perhaps he wondered if this idea based on the worship of One True God could unite the warring Arabian factions that were always doing battle to rectify some insult to themselves or their kin. Mohammed observed that the respective sacred texts and belief systems of the Jews and Christians seemed to provide them with a sense of cohesion that the Arabs lacked, prone to bickering as they were. Mohammed brought his radical message to the Arabian people after his terrifying dream in a cave on Mount Hira. He proclaimed that there was only One God and that God was Allah; that worship of all other deities must cease if one wanted entry into the Kingdom of Heaven; and that continuing to worship other gods and goddesses would consign a person to Hell forever.

Scattered remnants of written words made from oral recitations were collected after the death of Mohammed to become the third great sacred text by the end of the seventh century after the birth and death of Jesus. The Koran has probably influenced more people than the Old and New Testaments combined because it has been used not only for worship but to teach Muslim students to read. Muslims believe the Koran reveals the words of Allah exactly as Gabriel passed them on to Mohammed, and all Muslims are supposed to live their lives according to the many rules and regulations in this sacred text. Most of the stories in the Koran have Biblical parallels and names, borrowed from both the Hebrew and the Christian Testaments, although other stories are related to older Arabic or Persian tales. Old and New Testament personalities such as Adam, Noah, Abraham, Moses, and Jesus all have parts to play in the Koran. It is interesting that Jesus's mother Mary is actually mentioned more in the Koran than in the Christian Bible.

Beginning in the eighth century A.D., soon after the life and death of Mohammed had transformed Arabia, the Islamic world experienced a Golden Age, which lasted around five hundred years, during which time science, medicine, mathematics, and philosophy flourished. The discovery of paper from the Chinese made books and libraries possible. New Islamic laws were compiled that formed the "shari'a," and a new sacred book to follow the Koran was written called the Correct Book, which contained stories from oral memory (hadiths) about the life of the long-dead Prophet. This book, like certain parts of the Gospels written long after Jesus's death, did not always seem to ring true to the egalitarian and woman-loving attitudes Mohammed had espoused during his lifetime. The position of women and representative art once again suffered while literacy spread among mostly male Arabs. The appearance of sacred texts written in their own language created a religious zeal that not only encouraged Muslims to conquer others outside of their realm but also to overpower the population of women within it.

It was at this time literate men first demanded their women wear veils to cover their faces. As the image of the face is perceived by the right brain, not being able to see each other diminished the collective power of women as well as reduced the sense of individuality that expressions of the face make possible. Women who had prayed with men in mosques during Mohammed's time were at first segregated from the males and later expelled from the mosque altogether. As literacy and Islam grew, many women were forbidden to leave their homes, and in some areas male slaves were castrated in order to gather food and supplies that had been the traditional realm of women for thousands of years. By the fourteenth century, one Arabic male expressed pleasure with his pious elders because they had proclaimed a woman should leave her home only three times during her life: when she marries, when her parents die, and when she goes to her own grave. As with other cultures, the beginning of literacy brought a certain madness, and the more recently a Muslim territory had become literate, the harsher were the restrictions on women. Among peoples who had a long tradition of literacy such as in former Mesopotamia, Persia, and Egypt, practices against women such as sequestering, veiling, and genital mutilation were less severe than with Muslims in East African tribes, who had more recently been exposed to the alphabet.

The pre-Islamic, preliterate cultures of Arabia had also, like their Jewish and Christian counterparts, evolved from an ancient Mother Goddess culture that had feathered out over time into pantheons of gods and goddesses, each with their own duties and jurisdictions, much like the Christian saints of today. Evidence of residual fertility rituals could still be found in preliterate areas of southern and southwestern Arabia as late as the nineteenth century, where the practice of "sexual hospitality" was observed. Dr. Raphael Patai's classic study of Arab culture, *The Arab Mind*, reports on a tribal group in which it was customary for the wife to pass the night in the bed of a male houseguest, and if he did not meet her expectations she was to cut off the bottom part of his cloak; apparently an intact coat at breakfast time was a signal for the guest to be treated with great honor. Other local customs that lingered from ancient Arabia into at least the nineteenth century also encouraged exogamy (sexual union outside of the tribe) to ensure fruitfulness; women were encouraged to engage in sex before marriage and in some tribes even relationships after marriage were favored to ensure a good mix of genes.

Later, once literacy and Islam had become firmly entrenched, Arabia saw women's rights restricted to the point of becoming injurious to procreation in some areas as women were forbidden to mate outside of their tribe for fear that their sons would grow up and serve the patriarch (and kin) of another tribe. Arab males in some kinship groups began viewing endogamy (mating with relatives or near relatives) as a matter of honor and survival; the most preferred marriages were between the children of two brothers, so all of the children resulting from the union would be members of the same extended family and thus increase the power and prestige of the familial tribe. A woman's job was to serve her family honorably and produce many sons so if a tribal skirmish did occur, there was a greater chance of survival. With several wives busy at once producing sons to fight and daughters to deliver offspring, the tribe had a good chance of prospering.

Within a century after Mohammed's death, the third great monotheistic religion, Islam, had evolved into an empire that spread from the Atlantic Ocean to China. This fast-growing yet traditional Arab-based empire became largely responsible for the awakening of the Renaissance in Europe, and many of the ideas Europeans were eventually credited with, such as the "blasphemy" of Copernicus's astronomical observation that the earth revolved around the sun rather than the other way around, were made possible because of the cultural reach of the Muslims. The triumphant success of Islam was no doubt largely because of a sacred book written in a common language for all those who could read (mostly males). As happened in the first two great monotheistic religions, literacy became power; but literacy also brought about decay tainted with madness.

Years of stagnation followed the Golden Age of Islam as dogma and fundamentalism replaced the creativity and adventurous search for knowledge that had for so long defined the Arab mind and spirit. The Muslims have never forgotten their glorious past, and much of their traditionalism has been blamed—or credited—with this longing for the past. The once-glorious Arabian empire fell into disrepair and misery, and poverty set in among the Muslim people; they were ripe for the picking when Europe began its era of colonization. Some historians believe that the people of Islam were not able to take greatness beyond the fourteenth or fifteenth century because they got bogged down in traditional studies of language and religion, and could literally not move beyond the dictates of the rules of grammar and prayer.

Authors in Raphael Patai's *The Arab Mind* discussed the Arab absorption with the past, saying it was like a chronic disease, and the Arab stagnation that followed centuries of glory was not simply the result of feudal excesses or colonial rule but was due in large part to the roots of female oppression. The authors stated it was no wonder the Arab world remained so backward when the position of its women in society was so low. Once again, the advent of literacy and the lowly position of women walked hand-in-hand.

Conflict and divisiveness were an integral part of the pre-Islamic heritage of the Arabs, probably because of the intense group cohesion necessary for survival in harsh circumstances, which placed the interests of kin and lineage above the interests of the individual or the larger society. Honor was given the highest priority, and retaliation was considered a dutiful response to any injury (real or imagined) suffered to protect the family name. Pre-Islamic competition between blood groups generally consisted of verbal matches under the watchful guidance of kin; actual physical combat usually never went further than the use of sticks or stones. Insults were often used—almost ritualistically—with the women encouraging the fighting with shouts and songs. If injuries or deaths did occur, neutral members of the kinship groups would become immediately involved to negotiate peace before animosities were allowed to escalate further. The purpose of the fights was generally not to kill or be killed but to show "upper hand," and mediators always took care to make sure both parties were able to walk away from the fight without suffering dishonor or shame.

Once sacred laws were written down for all to read, interpret, and obey, something changed in the way the different blood groups fought with each other in order to regain their "honor." The newly literate Arabians as a group began to develop a reputation for fierce, blood-revenge militaristic approaches to conflict. Before Mohammed delivered Allah's sacred rules of society written down for all to read, perceived loss of honor was dealt with by using exaggerated self-praise and boasting as a way of lifting a person up out of "dishonor." Other methods had developed as well to help rebalance a relationship that had gone sour and regain honor without resorting to bloodshed.

The concept of honor in the Arab world is difficult to understand for those who live outside its jurisdiction. Although it seems there are a variety of ways a man can lose his honor, and even get it back, there is none that weighs more heavily upon his soul than the loss of honor because of a female blood relative's loss of her honor, which essentially means any sexual conduct (even a "look") outside of marriage. If a woman behaves in a way that risks losing her honor (or is reported to have done so) she also causes her male blood relatives to lose their honor, and some Muslim men believe the only way they can get it back is to kill her. If a woman, for example, were to have an affair outside of her marriage, her husband's honor would not be affected to the same degree as would be the honor of her father and brothers. The husband can regain his honor by divorcing his adulterous wife, but the honor of her male blood relatives is permanently damaged unless they murder her (worst-case scenario). A man, however, can have a number of wives and/or concubines according to the laws of the Koran without dishonoring himself or any of his family members. Honor killings take place in many parts of the Muslim world to this day.

From the point of view of this harsh, masculine code of honor, it is somewhat understandable, yet absolutely unacceptable and horrifying, that ways have been found to ensure the virginity of a daughter before marriage. The veiling of the face and extensive covering of the body, even in the hottest weather, is clearly enforced to reduce the temptation of the male, who in the Muslim tradition is not even supposed to glance at a woman other than his wife (or wives). The sequestering of the female, making sure she does not go out of the house, is another effective way to deal with young lust.

Female circumcision, the removal of the sexual parts of the woman not necessary for childbirth, also contributes to the ability of families to keep their daughters chaste as it attempts to remove desire. One of the many problems that results is that a woman's ovaries still produce hormones to create the desire, but the genital mutilation leaves her unable to be fulfilled. But to be as sure as one can reasonably be that a daughter will be a virgin on her wedding day (even if her husband-to-be is a disgusting old coot with three other wives and numerous concubines), infibulation is sometimes performed, which not only removes the clitoris and outer portions of a woman's vulva, but sews together the remaining "sides" leaving only a small hole from which urine and menstrual blood can escape. On her wedding night, the "healed" wound must be cut open in order for her husband to have intercourse with her. Observers have noticed that this horrifying procedure is so shocking to the young girl she often never recovers, and if she does not die because of some horrible infection resulting from this drastic homemade surgery, she often becomes permanently numb with grief.

It is no surprise that in a culture where women have often been so powerless, their literacy rates have lagged seriously behind those of not only Arab men but other women throughout the world. United Nations data shows that as late as 1962 in three Arab countries—Saudi Arabia, Yemen, and Somalia—the illiteracy rate of women was 100 percent. These Arab countries had the distinction at this time in history of being among the only countries in the world where not one of their women could read!

Part IV

Out of the Darkness

CHAPTER 15

East Meets West

Western exposure to Arab culture became significant when Muslims began crossing the narrow strip of the Mediterranean between the continents of Europe and Africa (the Straight of Gibraltar) during the expansion of the Islamic Empire during their Golden Age. This invasion of Muslims is similar to what is happening on the southern border of the United States today, except that initially there was more fire play involved on the southern tip of Europe as desperate citizens on the Iberian Peninsula tried to prevent the incursion of Muslims from Africa. The Islamic hordes kept coming, and eventually they were able to overpower the mostly Christian lands of Spain and Sicily.

In 1492, the Muslims, or Moors, were finally expelled from Europe after almost eight hundred years of rule. It is an easy date to remember because it was the same year Columbus set sail for America. Columbus had gone to King Ferdinand and Queen Isabella of Spain to ask for their patronage in funding a trip to search for a passage to India, but they turned him down because they were busy fighting the Muslims in Granada, the last stronghold of the Moors. Legend has it he hadn't gotten very far away when he got the message that "Los Reyes Catolicos" were finally victorious in kicking the Moors out of Spain and they were ready to finance Columbus's mission. It is said that Boabdil, the defeated Muslim ruler, turned back to have one last look at the glorious city of Granada as he fled with his people; his mother, upon witnessing her son's tearful glance, admonished him not to weep like a woman for what he could not defend as a man.

No one who has ever traveled through the magnificent Andalusia (El-Andalus) region of Spain and spent time at the wondrous Alhambra will wonder at Boabdil's tears. There was not only beauty in the magnificent surroundings, natural and manmade, but relative peace and harmony prevailed between the various peoples and faiths of Spain during the time the Arabs ruled. Civilization reportedly flourished in every way and three alien cultures (Christian, Muslim, and Jew) lived side by side with respect and tolerance for each others' religious and ethnic differences for more than seven centuries. El-Andalus was home to some of the most wonderful cities the world has ever known, where scholars and intellectuals of all faiths were able to communicate their ideas; the Jews had a special role as translator between the Muslims and the Christians, as both cultures were familiar to them.

The Christian world was coming out of a dark age and was able to receive ideas from Greek, Persian, and Indian science via Arabic texts. Europe owed the Muslim world its access to Arab medical, agricultural, mathematical, navigational, and astronomical knowledge as it emerged from the Middle Ages. Can it be mere coincidence that the rabid Christian fervor that suddenly felt the necessity to expel all infidels—especially Arabs and Jews—from Spain in 1492 after such a long, peaceful coexistence came shortly after the invention of the printing press, which produced large quantities of pro-Christian/anti-"infidel" sentiments distributed throughout Europe?

In 1492 the indigenous peoples of what was to become the Americas were living a relatively peaceful existence reminiscent of earlier Neolithic peoples of Europe; in many tribes native women enjoyed power and influence and nature reigned supreme. The natives could not possibly have been prepared for what lay ahead—the invasion by Christian fundamentalist nation builders who were doped up on words and were prepared to mow down anything that got in their way—and did.

The role of Arab women began to change once the Prophet Mohammed was given the gift of reading so he could teach his fellow Arabs the words of Allah. While he was alive, the Prophet taught that every human was equal in the eyes of Allah, and in his era women were considered equals to men legally and otherwise. Mohammed was like Jesus in many respects; he apparently lived a simple, gentle life—always available to his people. He was responsible for the generous laws pertaining to orphans, slaves, and the weak, possibly because he himself was an orphan. Like Jesus, Mohammed was also persecuted for daring to threaten the status quo.

Unfortunately, years after his death individuals of lesser stature were busy writing down thousands of oral traditions ("hadiths") that were attributed to

Him; some of these hadiths praised women (the "three most precious things in the world are women, fragrant odors, and prayers") and others denigrated them, blaming life's ills on their very existence. It seems clear that the words of more than one person made up the Correct Book of hadiths, a book whose purpose was to augment and explain the Koran in the way that the Talmud followed the Old Testament in order to answer questions not covered sufficiently in the first Hebrew holy book. The Koran does not forbid the painting of images, for example, but a later hadith claimed that the Prophet declared in a conversation painting or sculpting images (including of Himself) was forbidden. Since Mohammed was illiterate before his dream where Gabriel commanded him to read, it makes sense that words transcribed from oral tradition many years later when literacy was well established would, like elsewhere in the world, contain misogynist sentiments not found originally in words attributed to the Prophet's oral recitations.

The religious community the Prophet founded became the state of Islam and was the first Arabian attempt to organize society according to an ideology/religion rather than around blood ties. According to the new rules of Islam, no matter what kinship/tribe a person was from, everyone who adopted Islam was considered brethren. Mohammed's emphasis on One Religion overriding blood ties proved to be a clever addition to monotheistic ideology. Substituting the abstract notion of faith for the deeply cherished values and beliefs inherent in ancient Arabian blood ties and tribal kinship was a stroke of genius. The new religion of Islam was to have no hierarchal structure or priesthood; once again, the written word—the Koran—was to be given primary significance in place of the rituals that had been such crowd-pleasers in the days of illiteracy. The imams, reputedly infallible and sinless descendants of Mohammed, had sole responsibility in leading the faithful in prayer as well as in leading Muslim armies against the outside world, if necessary, and this included against other Arabs who were heathens. Thus, political Islam has been part of the Muslim faith almost since its inception.

CHAPTER 16

Politicizing Religion

The concept of jihad that currently threatens Western cultures essentially began once the disciples of Mohammed were left with the chore of trying to remember the Prophet's words so they could write them down. The disciples were responsible for continuously interpreting and reinterpreting these now written words. The challenge of all three monotheistic word-based religions is the same: What are the words? What do they mean? What is to be done with them? Just as there is room in both the Old Testament and the New Testament for the interpretation of words that encourage the extermination of people who have sinned against God, usually by not believing in Him, there is room in the words of Islamic texts that allow for a jihad against oppressors or nonbelievers. In his book *Good Muslim, Bad Muslim,* Mahmood Mamdani traces the emergence of militant Islam to jihads that were originally fueled by efforts to expel invaders and right wrongs. The author claims there were only four major jihads in the twelve hundred years of Islamic rule before the Afghan jihad of the 1980s, a jihad first aimed at Soviet infidels and finally morphing into a jihad against the infidel West and its values, especially the values of the United States.

The first jihad, or "just struggle," was in response to the invasion of Christian Crusaders beginning in the eleventh century and produced the Kurdish hero Saladin who successfully reconquered Jerusalem during the second Crusade; to this day he is celebrated for standing up to the West and winning. Christians are taught in Sunday school that the purpose of the Crusades was to rid the Holy Land of "infidels," and the Muslims are taught that the West was—and is—the infidel. The first Crusade to expel the infidels from Jerusalem began in 1096 and the Christians prevailed largely because they were able to take advantage of a period of weakness and anarchy in Arab history (post-literacy madness?) and combine it with the zeal that comes with Papal encouragement and the reputed finding of the lance that speared Christ's side during the Crucifixion. Many of the Crusaders were little more than rabble-rousers and adventurers who were escaping devastating economic and social situations in their own countries; they were happy to take up a cause—any cause. Other crusaders were merchants hoping to exchange commodities or were romantics hoping to conquer some land on which they could settle down and start over.

The Crusades also represented the reaction of Christian Europe to the aggressiveness of the Muslims, who had pushed for expansion into Europe since the seventh century and who were still largely in control of Spain and Sicily at the beginning of the Crusades. Although some historians like to divide the Crusades into numbered invasions, others believe the Crusades were essentially one long continuous invasion. The Christian justification for the Crusades was to wrest control of "their" Holy City of Jerusalem from the Arabs, who also considered Jerusalem to be one of their holiest cities. When the Crusaders first approached the walls of Jerusalem, they marched barefoot around the city blowing their horns in hopes the walls would fall down as they reputedly had done in Jericho. It was a long month before they were able to storm the city and massacre the Muslim infidels indiscriminately, including women and children; there were piles of heads and hands and feet on display throughout the holy city.

The Crusades became the model for a militant Christianity—from knights to missionaries—which would erode a sense of goodwill and tolerance that had accompanied numerous other experiences between Muslims and Christians in the past. The Crusades symbolized the West's first attempts at colonization of overseas territories; for a couple of hundred years as towns and cities were captured and recaptured by both sides, attempts were made by Christian settlers to make the conquered area their home. Muslim rule of Christians and Jews in Spain and Sicily since the eighth century had not provoked undue conflict, once conquered, and people of all faiths had lived side by side in relative peace and harmony; everyone was permitted to worship and live as they pleased, with the exception that non-Arabs had to pay a special head tax (which encouraged many people to convert to Islam). The implantation and rule of Christians in Arab territory did not work out as well; both sides became more hardened to each other because of conflicts over religion and land.

The second Islamic jihad was in response to the widespread violence and decay in north African-Arab societies in the fifteenth century because of the slave trade and the toxic dealings with Europeans who participated in that enterprise. Mamdani believes militant Islam as an actual movement originated as a direct result of the negative effects of the slave trade on Arab society, which was sort of caught in the middle between the Europeans buying slaves and the captured slaves themselves; it was inevitable some Arabs would become middlemen. The vice and decay that resulted from having such immoral dealings in their midst occasioned a militaristic jihad in response to European encroachment that found Arab support when some of the Islamic aristocracy began selling their own people to the European slave traders. Unfortunately, what began as an earnest attempt to thwart cruel aggression ended in anarchy, with the new leaders raiding their own neighborhoods for slaves to sell to the highest bidder—all in the name of jihad. What had started out as a moral quest ended up as a moral failure.

The third jihad was in the mid-1700s in response to occupation by fellow Muslims, the Ottoman Turks, and resulted in an alliance between Great Britain and the House of Saud (Wahhabism). The fourth Islamic jihad took place in the late 1800s in resistance to two occupiers, Turkish/Egyptian Muslims (fellow believers in Allah) and British colonial occupiers (infidels); once again an honorable fight for liberation degenerated into slave raids and anarchy.

There were no more attempts at jihad for nine decades until the middle of the twentieth century when the writings of Pakistani Abul A'la Mawdudi and Egyptian Sayyid Qutb inspired ideological passion for a reformed Islamic cultural/political state that was without borders and under the rule of One God, Allah. Mawdudi viewed jihad as a necessary and relentless pursuit to abolish the rule of man over man, staking your life, if necessary, to achieve that purpose. This popular journalist and politician was the first to claim that armed struggle was necessary and was the first to call for a universal jihad to promote the ideological state of Islam.

The shift from colonialism to a postcolonial world proved difficult for the Arab world, especially as many Muslims felt confused by the Western values they had incorporated into their Eastern/Islamic identities. The Society of Muslim Brothers arose in Egypt to meet the new challenges of Muslims. They originally advocated the creation of an extensive nonviolent welfare organization; this idea took fruit and eventually grew so large it provided its own hospitals, schools, armies, and so forth. This organization was eventually seen as a threat to the already unstable national governing bodies and was outlawed. Reformist Muslims became radicalized and interested in armed conflict only after Arab armies were defeated and the State of Israel was created in 1948.

Sayyid Qutb was a member of the Egyptian Brotherhood, and was jailed for years and eventually executed during Nasser's regime. He became a martyr for the new Islam searching for a Muslim modernity amidst the rubble of democracy, socialism, and communism. Qutb called for a radical rejection of Western civilization, believing Islam had an obligation to resist servitude and create an environment of freedom for all men and women. He wrote that the democracy of the West was sterile and the very real danger faced by humanity of annihilation was just a symptom of the real disease of moral decay and all of the manmade ideologies had lost their ability to sustain healthy life. He believed Islam had the needed values for humanity. He is probably most responsible for the radically reformed notion of jihad that inspires many Muslims today, largely because of the effect of his letters, which were smuggled out of prison by his sister and which have became a manifesto for a radical, political Islam.

In *Good Muslim, Bad Muslim,* Mamdani traces the movement of this political Islam along the intellectual fringes of society where he believes it might have remained relatively inconsequential, even dissipating over time, but instead entered the mainstream of Islamic politics because of U.S. interference and the promotion of infidel (i.e., Soviet) hating. The Soviet Union was a godless society, or at least the Communist ideology announced that it was, and the United States believed it could encourage religious fundamentalism and jihad against Soviet infidels because both the U.S. and the Muslim world believed in God—or at least most people from these cultures did. By the time the Soviets invaded Afghanistan, the neoconservatives in Washington and the Central Intelligence Agency (CIA) had perfected the use of mercenaries and proxy wars after much practice in Asia, Africa, and Latin America; they were ready to take on their arch nemesis using Islamic mercenaries.

Proxy Wars

The Vietnam War debacle had left the people of the United States weary and suspicious of fighting the ideology of communism with foreign wars. U.S. Congresspersons newly elected on antiwar platforms were gun- and money-shy when it came to any skirmish involving the domino theory. The motto du jour (the Nixon Doctrine) pronounced that Asian boys fight Asian wars, and so forth, yet funds from government sources were used to encourage and enable decades of covert actions and military operations aimed at combating the ubiquitous and hysterical threat of communism. These fears were based partially on the very real atrocities and mass executions that had taken place under Communist rule, especially in the Soviet Union and China. But the socialist/communist ideology that threatened the Western capitalist way of life—and especially the pocketbooks of the rich—was also used as justification for illegal and covert military actions against regimes considered "unstable," that is, apt to fall down with a bunch of dominoes. No one could deny the savagery that had taken place to promote Communist rule under Stalin, Mao, and others. Evidence of U.S. covert operations to reduce the spread of communism around the world has revealed that savagery upon savagery is no better.

The CIA, under the auspices of someone in the U.S. government, began waging secret wars totally removed from Congressional and public scrutiny. Unknown to most Americans who were watching the war with Vietnam unfold nightly on the network news, the United States was also secretly bombing Laos (home of the Ho Chi Minh Trail and communist guerillas) and funding Hmong mercenaries to fight communist guerillas.

The idea of using secret proxy wars to fight our anti-communist battles solved the problem of dealing with the public outcry from U.S. citizens who had been instrumental in bringing about an end to the Vietnam War. If proxy wars were not acknowledged, political leaders did not have to go before Congress to get permission to start or fund them. Most Americans were relieved to finally be out of Vietnam, and did not want to make the connection between the U.S. and various rumblings around the world. It was easy to convince them we were involved only in handing out "humanitarian aid" packages to poor countries.

As Western colonialism in third world countries continued to unravel, the United States became frantically worried that the surge of worldwide revolts against capitalistic colonial oppressors would lead to communists in charge of emerging and fragile nation states. It was determined by a rising group of neoconservatives in Washington that this fear alone was justification for further interference with emerging post-colonial governments. The assassination of Prime Minister Patrice Lumumba of the newly independent Congo reputedly took place out of fear he might become an "African Castro." Lumumba's followers were outraged and fought back as best they could with bows and arrows and bicycle chains against U.S.–backed aerial bombing missions. Mercenaries hired to defend white privilege from an emerging African identity were responsible for torture, rapes, and executions in the Congo, Angola, and apartheid South Africa, even while post-Vietnam antiwar sentiment in the United States led to the passing of the War Powers Act of 1973 and the Clark Amendment of 1976, both of which were committed to ending U.S. military involvement in other countries. Fear of communism led to disastrous alliances with right wing dictators who were only too happy to take U.S. aid to help them keep down their oppressed masses yearning to be free.

It was not long before the use of mercenaries and proxy wars led to the general acceptance among neoconservatives of CIA–inspired terrorism's legitimate use to weaken and eliminate any threat to Western so-called democracy. Low-intensity combat routinely targeted civilians in what was to become known as "collateral damage," a term implying that the death and destruction of nonmilitary targets, including innocent people, were accidental byproducts of war. Mamdani claims that, in actuality, the public's fear of "collateral damage" led to a deliberate strategy to create anxiety among a population, any of whom could be targeted at any minute for no personal or political reason whatsoever. After a while the frightened populace were apt to choose the terrorists to be their leaders to get the terrorism to stop—the terrorists of course being friends of the United States.

Our nation even opened the School of the Americas (SOA) in Georgia, financed by U.S. tax dollars, to teach the tools of terrorism to whomever we were backing at the moment. Each year a group of concerned Americans stages a protest in front of the school, which usually results in arrests and jail time for some of those determined to end U.S. involvement in the torture, execution, and subjugation of others. Recent attention has also been focused on land mines, which have been used extensively in a number of countries as a way of permanently terrorizing and controlling people, even after the war is over. With secret proxy wars and terrorist tactics, the war is never over and it becomes clear the collateral damage done to ordinary people is the aim of terrorism, not just the result of it. *Scare the shit out of 'em and they'll shut up.*

Americans were forced to look at the reality of their democracy when the Iran-Contra scandal broke in 1986, revealing that the United States sold arms to Iran and used the profits to fund the Contras, a CIA–backed group of terrorists in Nicaragua. People in the United States were shocked to learn that funds for terrorist atrocities in the Americas were being generated by the sale of arms to Iran, a country that had expressed hatred and vengeance toward Americans and had even kidnapped hostages from the U.S. embassy in Tehran. The United States, after all, had formed an alliance with Saddam Hussein in the 1980s and encouraged Iraq's invasion of Iran, even training Iraqi soldiers and giving them chemical weapons and aerial maps to make their work easier.

According to Samantha Powers, who wrote about America's relation to genocide in her book *A Problem from Hell*, these chemical weapons came back to haunt the United States when their own Gulf War veterans began suing U.S. companies and banks that reputedly helped Iraq with its chemical weapons program in the 1980s. Veterans claimed that permanent bodily harm resulted from the bombing of storage facilities containing these U.S.–made chemicals during the first U.S. invasion of Iraq.

Afghanistan entered into a relationship with the United States in the 1980s, allegedly because it had been attacked by Soviet forces. But documents seized during the embassy takeover in Iran revealed that the United States began meeting with rebel mujahideens from Afghanistan before the Soviet military invasion ever happened. Former CIA director Robert Gates confirmed that this was the case, writing in his memoir that he had warned President Jimmy Carter these covert meetings with Afghan rebels might cause a Soviet military response. When Ronald Reagan became president, the plan congealed into one of making a war with Afghanistan the "Soviet's Vietnam," and everything was done to make sure this happened. The result was the eventual collapse of the Soviet empire.

Although the Islamic world had not witnessed an armed jihad for almost a century, they were encouraged by the CIA to despise the godless Soviets who had invaded their country after being taunted from across the Afghan side of the border by secret agents of the United States. The Afghan jihad was really an American jihad whose goal was to fund a proxy war relabeled a holy war that would attract millions of Muslims to Afghan soil to fight and destroy the Soviets. Author Mamdani claims that radical ideological Islamists were lightly scattered across the Muslim world before the Afghan war with the Soviets, but became mainstream after years of fighting a holy war against Soviet infidels with the use of American advisers and weapons.

Muslims from all over the world went to Pakistan to train with the mujahideens, and Islamic moderates were ignored and set aside while the United States helped to create a network of terror. Reagan's enthusiasm for his new anti-Soviet proxy soldiers was over the top, and he even introduced visiting mujahideen (possibly in the United States for training) on the White House lawn, comparing them to our "founding fathers." When the Soviet empire collapsed after ten years of fighting in Afghanistan, these highly trained Muslim soldiers went back to where they came from, bringing to their homelands a new revolutionary and fundamentalist Islamic zeal.

Islamic schools called *madrassahs* were formed to teach sociopolitical ideology along with religious teachings that would inspire students to overthrow the left-wing Afghan regime backed by Moscow. Mamdani reports that some of the textbooks used in these madrassahs were designed by the University of Nebraska and taught students math by asking them to add and subtract dead Russians and to calculate how many seconds it would take for a bullet to strike a Russian's head traveling at a specific speed from a given distance. He also claims in his book that U.S.–sponsored textbooks can still be found in Afghanistan and Pakistan that instruct children to pluck out the eyes and cut off the legs of their enemies. When Afghanistan's Communist government collapsed and the Soviets withdrew their troops in 1989, more than one hundred thousand radical Muslims had been exposed to CIA–backed training, learning more than sixty deadly skills, including the know-how to make and use sophisticated fuses, timers, and explosives. They added this knowledge to their local skills, which included throat-cutting and disemboweling.

A *Los Angeles Times* reporter investigating the effects of the Afghan War found that every major terrorist attack since this period has been carried out or orchestrated by key members of a former CIA–trained Afghan jihad; one Algerian sociologist told an *L.A. Times* reporter the United States had participated in creating a monster that has now been turned against the entire world. The Afghan anti-Soviet jihad turned out to be the largest covert operation in CIA history, with an estimated three billion dollars of secret aid for the mujahideen—more than all the other covert CIA operations during the 1980s combined. With the collapse of the Soviet Union, the United States had won the role of sole superpower in the world. What it lost was much of its own self-respect and the respect of the rest of the world. The shame is that so many Americans slept through most of it, believing we were at war with no one.

The ideological assault on communism that reached its zenith during the Reagan years presented itself in newspapers and on television as a response to attacks on democracy. It was often difficult to read between the lines, especially as all the important battles were hidden from view. The arrogant governmental belief that people did not know what was best for them, knowing that the proxy wars they were instigating and funding would never be tolerated by post-Vietnam voters (especially if they knew the repulsive details), brought real democracy to its knees. When learning in 1987 of CIA Director William Casey's proposed development of an independent self-sustaining political/military entity with the power and ability to carry out covert operations without knowledge or approval from Congress, Senator Warren Rudman commented that this idea carried to its logical extreme would not be democracy. Interesting.

CHAPTER 17

Rebalancing the Planet

It appears that the dangerous social and political situation that now exists in the world among and between adherents of the three basic monotheistic religions of Judaism, Christianity, and Islam can be traced back almost three thousand years to that moment in the Sinai Desert when Moses, reputedly under the command of Yahweh, gave orders to his tribe of Semitic nomads to kill all those who believed in and worshipped other gods and goddesses than Him (sparing the virgin females, sexual booty who could be used to propagate God's chosen people).

When Hitler, Mao, and Pol Pot (to name just a few "gods" from recent times) went on their killing sprees—always in the name of progress and betterment for their chosen tribes—most of us had no problem condemning their actions as sociopathic. The vast majority of people everywhere agree that the behavior of these world leaders was extremely antisocial, to say the least. Archeological research has shown us that a time existed long ago, before Moses's dedication to the words of an invisible god, when the mass execution of Canaanites would also have been considered an egregious assault on humanity, not an act of religious faith.

Before Yahweh's time, when Earth Goddesses were the Primary Deities, humanity appears to have been much less barbaric, not more so as has been implied throughout *written* history. The average person conjures up an image of a caveman dragging his woman around by the hair when thinking about prehistoric (prewritten) times, or believes early humans ruthlessly slaughtered each other until God came along and taught them how to be good—after He ordered them to kill all those folk who disagreed with Him, that is.

The introduction of and forced compliance with monotheism that took ahold of humanity at just the time the alphabet became a permanent fixture on the landscape has changed the way people view not only the world but everyone in it, starting with themselves. The New Religion was based almost exclusively on the individual's relationship with the Words of the new God rather than on the ritualistic, community-based, multi-deity (gods and goddesses), shamanistic-type "worship" replete with the sound, color, light, and movement that had been an integral part of the human experience for tens of thousands of years. These new monotheistic religions transformed the face of humanity and have led us to this moment of terror, where we seem to be witnessing a standoff between what we perceive as the good and evil forces of humanity. The problem, as usual, concerns itself with definitions, as each side has determined it is they who are the Good and the other who is the Evil, and no one shows any signs of backing down. The bad behavior of some members of all three of the world's monotheistic religions has become increasingly sociopathic, with little remorse for the suffering of fellow human beings who happen to be on the other side of imaginary boundaries.

While studying sociopathic behavior in graduate school, I began thinking once again about the similarities between my life and the outside world; both spaces were experiencing excruciating turmoil and disruption. My husband's self-centered and risk-taking behavior was threatening to destroy everything decent and sane in our family at the same time I was watching various politicians in the world—elected and unelected—treat the citizens of the planet as though they were paper figures in a shadow play, that is, not real, therefore incapable of real suffering. Everywhere I looked, sociopathic behavior seemed to rule the day, with reasonable people and ideas pushed to the background and ignored.

If Dr. Shlain's theory was correct, the unrelenting turmoil and chaos that was disrupting both my home and the world at large was to be expected, as various new forms of communication have undoubtedly played havoc with our brains in terms of hemispheric lateralization. The tumultuous landscape that has resulted from this onslaught of new age communications has enabled sociopaths to have a field day as individuals and whole societies become disoriented and a little mad. In response to the madness, many new age Dionysian figures have emerged, and some of them are not just crazy but mean. These remorseless sociopaths are able to do their damage with few interruptions as they are less vulnerable than those on whom they prey, and are not as subject to the post-traumatic stress brought on by difficult challenges facing ordinary citizens of the world today.

The core characteristic of sociopathic behavior (also known as antisocial personality disorder) is the absence of a conscience; sociopaths can and do commit acts ranging from insensitive to barbaric without feeling remorse or guilt. Exuding a superficial but often intense charm, sociopaths usually have a grandiose sense of self-worth and entitlement, which better allows them to seduce the world around them. Sociopaths are not only charming but are also often risk takers, and they delight in persuading others to go along with their schemes, whether they be political, financial, social, or otherwise. People who study human nature have tried to determine the origin of sociopathology, as this difficult behavior is becoming increasingly prevalent and affects us on an individual and societal basis, causing everything from nervous breakdowns to genocides. According to *The Sociopath Next Door* by Dr. Martha Stout, research shows that 4 percent of the people in this country are sociopaths—that's one out of every twenty-five people! Unfortunately, antisocial personality disorder is a growing phenomenon as studies also show a continuous increase in the number of sociopaths living among us, at least in Western society.

Scientific investigation shows there are actual differences in the functioning of the cerebral cortex in the brain of a sociopath as compared to a so-called normal person. For most people, measured electrical activity in the brain becomes more intense when it comes across emotional words such as "love" and "kisses" than when the brain processes neutral words such as "window" or "book." The cerebral cortex of the person with antisocial personality disorder does not respond any differently to words that have emotional content than it does to neutral words, appearing unable to discern the difference. This indicates that emotional stimuli at the level of the cerebral cortex are processed differently in sociopaths than in others. Researchers believe this altered processing is likely inherited to some degree and appears to be reinforced or not, depending on the environment of the hapless carrier of these "defective" and potentially toxic genes.

We know child abuse can have many tragic outcomes for its victims, including depression, suicide, anxiety, eating disorders, substance abuse, and delinquency. Studies show, however, that child abuse or neglect alone does not necessarily lead to sociopathic behavior, and conversely, a sociopath does not need to be neglected or abused as a child to develop his or her disorder. Recent studies indicate that to become truly sociopathic (i.e., having undifferentiated emotional responses or lacking in conscience relating to the pain and difficulty he or she has inflicted on others), a person most likely needs to have the genetic cerebral cortex defect as well as to come under the influence of a broader cultural message encouraging the promotion of self over others. Studies of incarcerated sociopaths show they actually appear to have been less influenced by their early familial surroundings as compared to other inmates who were not considered sociopathic. The sociopaths who made it to prison seem to have been more responsive than other inmates to a broader societal-cultural message they perceived as giving them tacit permission for behavior according to their own dictates, without conscience and without concern for the impact they have on others.

According to research, some people will be genetically programmed to respond to and imitate an aggressive and indifferent culture that has little regard for those it chews up and spits out; some of these individuals (one out of twenty-five!) will likely develop into full-fledged sociopaths. Because of their charm and self-assurance, these sociopaths will attract followers who do not have a genetic tendency toward sociopathy but who do have a tendency to follow the leader, even when it's off a cliff. According to my encyclopedia, lemmings don't really follow each other off cliffs en masse, so I guess it is just us humans stampeding each other to jump off the precipice.

Dr. Stout believes that preventing the rise of antisocial behavior in society cannot involve merely altering the behavior of individuals and families, which is extremely difficult but possible. She believes the values and belief systems of entire cultures must be altered over a long period of time if we hope to stem the rising tide of persons with antisocial personality disorder. A sociologist early in the twentieth century said that the time to influence the character of a child is one hundred years before he or she is born. A 1991 epidemiological study sponsored by the National Institute of Mental Health showed that in the fifteen-year-period that preceded the study, antisocial personality disorder nearly doubled among America's youth. Yet according to the research of Dr. Stout, east Asian countries such as China and Japan are experiencing a much lower incidence of antisocial personality disorder, ranging from .03 percent to .14 percent compared to the Western world's average of 4 percent. In other words, in the average Western culture the incidence of antipersonality disorder can be found in one out of every twenty-five individuals whereas in Eastern cultures this malady is found in only three to fourteen people out of ten thousand—a substantial difference!

From its very beginnings, our North American culture has placed a premium value on individuality and the domination of others, starting with the almost complete destruction of the indigenous people "discovered" here with their Stone Age reverence for nature and the interconnectedness of life. Dr. Stout believes the overriding social-political-religious-economic systems of various cultures influence whether or not sociopathic behavior is encouraged or discouraged. She deems the Western culture's emphasis on the rights of the individual, in contrast with the Asian belief in the inter-responsibility of all people, can be seen in the different rates of sociopathology found in the two cultures. Asian cultures promote a sense of connectedness and interrelatedness, setting the stage for the development of a true and deep concern for others, which is the basis of conscience. Western cultures often reward people who act solely in their own best interests, showering the "winners" with money, property, and even sexual privileges.

Dr. Stout laments that a Western family cannot by itself redeem a member born with genes that encourage sociopathology, as the influences of our me-first culture are too pervasive for such a person to resist responding in negative self-serving ways. It is clear work must be done to change the entire value system of our Western culture if we hope to stem the tide of our own multiplying sociopaths, who together with their loyal followers exert too much influence in the current political, economic, and social arena. Other cultures will have to look carefully at their own situation to determine the role sociopaths play in their societies, as it is the extremists in each culture who are largely determining the course of world events today.

Social scientists Lawrence Kohlberg and Carol Gilligan both contributed to groundbreaking research on moral development by studying how boys (Kohlberg) and girls (Gilligan) arrive at moral decisions. In Kohlberg's study, boys responded more to the idea of justice and the rules of society when making moral decisions; the girls in Gilligan's study were more influenced by the importance of relationships and the need to care for people when faced with the moral complexities of life. More recent research has revealed that the development of morals is much more complex than simply a division between male and female approaches to difficult issues, and both sexes use variations on the "ethics of justice" and the "ethics of care" dichotomies to guide them in their decision-making process.

Culture plays a significant role in determining moral responses, not just for sociopaths but for everyone. Research sponsored by Yale University compared the Hindu culture in India with American culture and found that while Hindus emphasize interdependence and subordination of individual ambitions to the goals of the group, American culture celebrates the cult of the individual and personal achievement. Hindus regard responsibilities to family and society as irrevocable and socially enforceable, whereas in America these kinds of decisions are often based on the individual's "moral" right to steer his or her life in whatever direction he or she pleases; sometimes this involves a caring conscience, sometimes not.

American culture does not absolutely require that certain moral responsibilities be met; a parent housed in a nursing home and rarely visited or a child left alone at home too often with the television will not sufficiently alter impressions about a person's character in the United States, especially if that person has money and/or power. People in India tend to believe that the moral thing to do is usually what a person is inclined to do anyway, whereas Americans tend to think accepting moral responsibility is often an unpleasant burden that requires sacrifices—of time, money, whatever.

The Western emphasis on the rights of the individual over the group also encourages a climate ripe for the promotion of warriors who can win individual awards for bravery and collect booty simply for having the courage and conviction to kill others who the government wishes to eliminate and/or dominate. Wartime studies have shown us that the average man does not wish or choose to kill, and in fact will often not shoot a gun or will shoot it less frequently if there is no senior officer around who expects or demands it from him. Post-traumatic stress disorder in soldiers often results when normal men find themselves in a position where they are forced to kill or be killed. Sociopaths are superior warriors who feel no guilt when they take the lives of others, and are often so cocksure of themselves they can't imagine it will be they who will die in battle. They add considerable strength to armies wishing to conquer and subdue other nations and peoples. At the rate of one out of twenty-five, it is a wonder there are not more wartime atrocities committed by soldiers who happen to be sociopaths. We hear and read too often of inexplicable attacks against innocent civilians during wartime, which are always much to the detriment of honorable soldiers, especially when they have the misfortune to be fighting dishonorable wars.

Additional sociopathic traits such as impulsivity and lack of responsibility—characteristics that have become more common among the general population and more tolerated in recent times—also help produce cultures where people are encouraged and rewarded for manipulating not only their neighbors but the rest of the world. There can be no doubt from reading world history that many of the builders and rulers of glorious empires achieved their positions in society because of unchecked sociopathic behavior, with the most brutal of them becoming the biggest winners of all. We as a world population have become inured to systems that hand out trophies such as land and slaves (women, blacks, Mexicans, or whoever) to the most vicious among us; we even vote for them in elections because we believe they will protect us with their very ruthlessness, if need be. In the areas of the world that have been subjected to and injected with the most Western thought, the 4 percent of sociopaths (and growing) that exist in society will often not feel they are different, nor will they be treated differently because at this point in time they represent the ideal rather than a perversion of the ideal.

What happens to the remaining 96 percent of the population who are not sociopaths? How do they behave when confronted with powerful leaders, at least some of whom will be afflicted with antisocial personality disorder? Yale University Professor Stanley Milgram left little to the imagination regarding this issue with his famous 1962 experiment that pitted conscience and care against obedience and authority. The study required that volunteer subjects give electric shocks (that were really fake) to people who were actually accomplices in the experiment and who complained loudly and even screamed in an effort to get the "shocks" to stop. This obedience study has been replicated many times and has always shown that the majority of people are willing to shock a person to the point of lethal danger if they are told to do so by an authority figure. Some of the instructions to raise shock levels were even given over the phone by never-seen instructors (with "credentials"), and yet still people complied and did what they were told. Men's and women's responses in these studies are similar; both sexes are generally troubled by having to go against the dictates of their moral conscience, but most will ultimately obey commands given by an authority figure to shock innocent people. The only difference in the behavior of the two sexes was that women suffered more stress than men as they increased the levels of shocks while listening to the desperate protests and even shrieks of the fake subjects.

Clearly, many of us are not prepared and do not wish to be political or even social leaders, which makes the job of acquiring a position of leadership much easier for a sociopath who desperately wants power and prestige. The very definition of sociopath—charming and ruthless without a conscience—is synonymous with the view that many people have of politicians from political parties throughout the world today.

While Western-style psychological health places a great deal of emphasis on strong interpersonal boundaries and individual assertiveness, Eastern cultures tend to value emotional connectedness and the experience of oneness and unity. Many Westerners can be seen rushing after a hard day's work to unwind at centers offering Eastern relaxation techniques such as yoga, meditation, and tai chi; these practices allow people who spend their days trying to rise above the herd pretend at least for a few minutes they are one with nature and the world.

Backlash

The overtly masculine civilizations that are threatening to destroy the planet with their emphasis on aggression and domination (and on One Male God) encourage not only wars and corporate greed but the epidemic of domestic violence we are now experiencing, and which I could now identify with on a very personal basis. Women and children are being subjected to domestic abuse, rape, and murder in record numbers. In addition, pornography has infiltrated every aspect of our society and has created a tolerance for behavior heretofore considered unacceptable; it is impossible to imagine who next might be capable of committing the most lewd and lascivious acts in the most inappropriate of circumstances. Does it just seem that more mothers are killing their children and more fathers are killing their wives and babies, born or unborn? Something is terribly twisted, yet the majority of media possibilities that might help to air grievances and unite the concerned are devoted to the most banal entertainment, with few exceptions, and news sound bites repeated over and over and over again.

Most media messages actually serve to strip females of their individual identities, making them vulnerable as targets for violence. A growing number of men seem to believe their lives are so important they should be allowed to eliminate any woman or child who irritates them or takes up too much of their space or time. Children viewing the exaggerated stereotypes of women and men in the media are apt to accept them as real and ideal, and are likely to incorporate these models into their own psychological schemas. Over a very short time, my own son had changed in his attitude toward women, and this change had been encouraged not only by his father but by our society at large. Everywhere I looked I saw evidence of a huge masculine counterforce pitting itself against everything women had struggled to achieve over the years. I was experiencing this backlash in my own family, and I knew I would have to work hard not only to undo the damage that had already been done but to prevent more from occurring.

Dr. Shlain's theory that the original power imbalance between the sexes was an inadvertent byproduct of the invention of the alphabet appealed to me not only because it actually makes sense and covers all the bases but also because it takes a lot of pressure off of men for being the original bad guys and even alters the stigma of victimhood for women. According to the doctor's theory, the brains and sensitivities of both men and women were altered by the onslaught of the orderly, linear brainwork necessary to survive in the newly literate world, thus changing both sexes in terms of how they viewed and valued feminine (right brain) and masculine (left brain) characteristics and ideals.

It is encouraging that because of scientific investigation we are now beginning to better understand the powerful influence music and dance have on the human brain. Researchers have discovered that specifically chosen rhythmic patterns of sound and movement and even well-timed silences can assist in rebalancing the hemispheres of human brains that have been inundated with words. The sensual activities of music and dance are primitive and right brain, and through the use of "sonic driving" (using sound in specific ways to alter brainwaves), people's brains can be rebalanced and the left and right sides can be brought into harmony to better achieve mental and spiritual health.

Populations not overly steeped in literacy generally promote a passionate involvement with music and dance. Because of their ability to lose themselves in the moment and to feel ecstatically attuned to the music, these people are often called "primitive." We are now able to recognize how incredibly intuitive and sophisticated the ancients' knowledge of the human brain and body was, and we are able to grasp why shamans and healers everywhere have used drums and cymbals and all sorts of other rhythmic devices in their treatment of the spiritually ill. It's certainly a far cry from popping antidepressants. New age therapists increasingly use sound therapy in their practices, often combining sonic driving and other rhythmic sounds and movements with healing modalities such as behavioral modification or ego-oriented interventions.

Barbara Tedlock explores the female roots of religion and medicine in her book *The Woman in the Shaman's Body*, explaining how and why women's role in our earliest spiritual and healing practice (or religion) has been misinterpreted and suppressed. It is easy to be ignorant and arrogant while viewing primitive people dressed up in feathers, and dancing and chanting in garbled tongue. They appear as exotic remnants from a past to which most of us would not choose to return. In reality, the ancients were truly wise people, whose expertise at balancing the brain and body served humanity well for tens of thousands of years.

Perhaps the reason pre-Biblical women were considered such powerful healers was that their brains were especially responsive to sounds and sights, enabling them to help others to heal. Science has now taught us that the number and density of neurons in the female brain is significantly greater than in males, the connective passageway between right and left hemispheres (the corpus callosum) is larger in women than in men, and the anterior commissure (another neural passage linking the two hemispheres) is also notably larger and denser in women than in men. Also, a third passageway—the massa intermedia—is a band of fibers more often found in the brains of females than in males.

For whatever reason women are born with these extra capabilities, in ancient times they put them to good use by figuring out how to use music, dance, chanting, and so forth, to help cure the ill or unbalanced members of their tribes. It is curious that at the beginning of all patriarchal monotheistic religions, the male powers-that-be outlawed music, dance, and color to gain control of the masses (bright colors often appear during shamanic trances as a result of the energy experienced). It would be interesting to know to what extent the patriarchal monotheists were aware of what they were doing by forbidding these sensual aspects of life associated with the right brain and feminine influences.

The spiritual journeys of shamans everywhere, even today, have used sensory overstimulation and deprivation to electrically trigger reactions in the brain to help rebalance the body. Medical research in the 1930s established that the brain is continuously generating electrical currents, which pulse through the cells of both of its hemispheres. Neurophysiologists have since discovered that rhythmic sounds such as those used by shamans can alter brain wave patterns and induce trances; what the ancients thought of as supernatural, today we consider science. Percussive/rhythmic sounds such as those that come from drums, rattles, or gongs can change asynchronous brainwave patterns into synchronous ones through a process called "sonic driving" or "entrainment." The intense sensory ("mystical") experiences resulting from these rhythmic sounds cause the image-based right hemisphere of the brain to dominate the left hemisphere; prolonged exposure to this rhythmic state will serve to slowly rebalance a brain that has been overly exposed to left-brain stimuli such as reading and writing and the continuous bombardment of patriarchal left-brain messages.

Mystical states are like dreams in that they are essentially nonlinear and nonlinguistic, which is why it is often difficult for people to accurately describe their dreams or mystical experiences using words. It is often easier to reveal information about a dream or mystical state using visual imagery such as painting. Music that encourages dancing is an especially powerful way to bring on a trance, as both music and dance are right-brain experiences that can alter the structure of our consciousness and change how we experience space and time. The physiological responses that result from strenuous dancing stimulate the brain to release endorphins that create painkilling compounds resembling opiates. Shamans have found that the vital electrical energy released by the brain through music, song, and dance enable the brain to heal (or rebalance), and now neuroscientists are able to measure and verify what these healers have known for many thousands of years.

Because we know and understand so much more about the brain, presumably we should be able to rebalance people's brains just by engaging in more activities that involve music, dance, and visual stimulation. In addition, we could practice allowing more fluidity and less rigidity to enter our lives, more right brain and less left brain. It is interesting that the generation of hippies and love-ins was criticized for its music, dance, and colorful garb, and its rejection of war. It's also interesting to note that with the advent of radio, television, movies, and computers, a resistance to reading has developed, especially among the young. Trying to teach kids to love books and not watch so much television or play so many video games has become a real job for many parents and educators. There seems to be a strong (mostly unconscious) countermovement to rebalance the brain and move back into harmony with nature, to rebalance words with images, to synchronize left brain with right brain. It is strange that it took such complicated technological advances to push us back toward the right, more primitive part of our brains. If we could once again achieve a proper balance between masculine left-brain and feminine right-brain influences and values, we could perhaps all work together to fix what's wrong with the world—One Team instead of One God.

Now that humanity is in the (largely inadvertent) crazy-making process of resynchronizing the brain utilizing a variety of new age technologies, we must pay careful attention to all of the oppositional-backlash forces that are being created so they do not destroy us in our time of madness. It was not too long ago that the Hebrew people were considered an oppositional force to the Christian majority in the Western world; robust Jew-hating pogroms carried out the "work of God" throughout Christendom. Today the Jew has formed an alliance with the Christian in opposition to the Arab, and vice versa, and this unbalanced triad is responsible for much of the ill wind blowing in the world today.

It is always popular for politicians and others to declare that the qualities of the oppositional culture(s) are primitive and even evil. "Our" side claims it is evil to strap a bomb around your waist but okay to irradiate the planet with depleted uranium bombs. "Their" side adheres to the idea that we are infidels with tainted morals and as such must be conquered and/or destroyed. Neither side is willing to take ownership of any wrongdoing or ideology-run-amok.

It is no longer possible to remove ourselves from most of what is happening to people in the rest of the world; they are coming to us, and we to them, whether we or they like it or not. I believe we are all connected, and the pain and sorrow endured by my small family is only part and parcel of a misery that is much larger and more inclusive, and which at this point is threatening to end life as we know it. I must continue to help my son in his fight against addiction by supporting the natural healing processes that lead to psychosocial integration, just as I must do my share to help us all return to a gentler, more harmonious way of living so we will not destroy the chance to revive our wonderful and still mysterious planet.

AFTERWORD

I want to bring my saga to a close with a story about the power of love, a mother's love for her children and vice versa—the basis of most everything held dear to humans everywhere. Palestinian poet Mourid Barghout speaks in his memoir *I Saw Ramallah* of the events that took place immediately upon hearing about the death in Paris of one of his brothers, who had been residing far from his home and family since his displacement after the 1967 War when Israel defeated the Arabs; many Palestinians who happened to be outside of the country when the war broke out found it impossible to return. Overcome with grief and believing his mother would not survive the news of her son's death without him beside her, Mourid, himself displaced in Egypt, told her over the phone his brother had been hurt in an accident in France but was alive. He believed his only duty at that moment was to protect his mother and if she could be kept alive for two days, the time required for him to arrive in Ramallah from Egypt, she would survive the devastating blow that the news would certainly deliver without him there to comfort her. When he finally arrived and found her surrounded by people dressed in mourning, she asked Mourid why everyone was dressed in black if her son was not dead. Holding her, the poet asked his mother to promise him she would stay alive; he then gently told her to go and put on her black clothes.

I cannot read this passage about a mother's grief without tears coming to my eyes; for me it symbolizes what we are losing, what we all have lost—a connection to our connections, whether that be family or homeland or just the plain sense of normalcy and security that makes life enjoyable and endurable. We must all try harder to empathize with others and the burdens they must carry; we humans were born innocent and we all deserve to exist in a world that offers hope and understanding and the chance, no the probability, of living well.

Peace.

ABOUT THE AUTHOR

Ann Meyer is a pseudonym for a very real mother, artist, and social worker who felt the need to protect the privacy of her children while writing this memoir of a very tragic time in their lives. Meyer's love of research and longtime interest in history combined to inspire this story of her family in relation to the troubled world surrounding them. The author lives in the country with her children and their dogs, outside of a major city.

BIBLIOGRAPHY

Ackerman, N. W., MD. *The Psychodynamics of Family Life: Diagnosis and Treatment of Family Relationships.* New York: Basic Books, 1958.

Alexander, B. *Peaceful Measures: Canada's Way Out of the "War on Drugs."* Toronto: University of Toronto Press, 1990.

Bancroft, L. *Why Does He Do That? Inside the Minds of Angry and Controlling Men.* New York: Penguin, 2003.

Barghouti, M. *I Saw Ramallah.* New York: Anchor Books, 2003.

Booth, M. *Cannabis: A History.* New York: Thomas Dunne Books, St. Martin's Press, 2003.

Boyd, S. "Feminist Research on Mothers and Illegal Drugs." *Resources for Feminist Research,* Vol. 28. Spring-Summer 2001: 113–132.

Boyd, S. *Mothers and Illicit Drugs: Transcending the Myths.* Toronto: University of Toronto Press, 1999.

Brownmiller, S. *In Our Time: Memoir of a Revolution.* New York: Random House Press, 1999.

Conrad, C. *Hemp for Health: The Medicinal and Nutritional Uses of Cannabis Sativa.* Rochester, Vermont: Healing Arts Press, 1997.

Davis, A. *Let's Get Well.* New York: Signette, Mentor & Plume Books, 1965.

Doweiko, H. E. *Concepts of Chemical Dependency.* Pacific Grove, California: Brooks/Cole, 2002.

Eisler, R. *The Chalice and the Blade: Our History, Our Future.* San Francisco: Harper Collins, 1988.

Epstein, B. "The Successes and Failures of Feminism." *Journal of Women's History,* Vol. 14, No. 2. June 2002: 1–8.

Erikson, E. *Identity, Youth and Crisis.* New York: W.W. Norton and Co., 1968.

Faludi, S. *Backlash: The Undeclared War Against American Women.* New York: Crown Publishers, 1991.

Finnegan, J., and D. Gray. *Recovery From Addiction.* Berkeley, California: Celestial Arts, 1990.

Goldstein, E. *Ego Psychology and Social Work Practice.* New York: The Free Press, 1995.

Hitti, P. 1937, Khalidi, W. *History of the Arabs.* Revised Tenth Edition. New York: Palgrave MacMillan, St. Martin's Press, 1937, 2002.

Karoll, B., and J. Poertner. "Indicators for Safe Family Reunification: How Professionals Differ." *Journal of Sociology and Social Welfare,* Vol. 30, No. 39. September 2003: 39–62.

Keller, T., K. Catalano, and K. Haggerty. "Parent Figure Transitions and Delinquency and Drug Use Among Early Adolescent Children of Substance Abusers." *American Journal of Drug and Alcohol Abuse,* Vol. 28, No. 3. August 2002: 399–428.

Lefkowitz, M. *Women in Greek Myth.* Baltimore: John Hopkins University Press, 1986.

Lovern, J. D., PhD. *Pathways to Reality: Erickson Inspired Treatment Approaches to Chemical Dependency.* New York: Brunner/Mazel, 1991.

Mamdami, M. *Good Muslim, Bad Muslim: America, the Cold War and the Roots of Terror.* New York: Three Leaves Press, Doubleday, 2005.

Manchester, W. *A World Lit by Fire: The Medieval Mind and the Renaissance, Portrait of an Age.* New York: Back Bay Books, Little, Brown and Co., 1992.

Noble, V. *Shakti Woman: Feeling Our Fire, Healing Our World, The New Female Shamanism.* San Francisco: Harper Collins, 1991.

Nurco, D., R. Blatchley, and T. Hanlon. "The Family Experiences of Narcotic Addicts and Their Subsequent Parenting Practices." *American Journal of Drug and Alcohol Abuse,* Vol. 24. February 1998: 37–60.

Page, L. *Healthy Healing Guide to Menopause and Osteoporosis.* Carmel Valley, California: Healthy Healing Publications, 1997.

Patai, R. *The Arab Mind.* New York: Hatherleigh Press, 2002.

Pendery, M. L., I. M. Maltzman, and L. J. West. "Controlled Drinking by Alcoholics? New Findings and Reevaluation of a Major Affirmative Study." *Science,* Vol. 217. July 9, 1982: 169–175.

Schlosser, E. *Reefer Madness: Sex, Drugs and Cheap Labor in the American Black Market.* New York: Houghton Mifflin Company, 2003.

Schuckit, M. A., MD. *Drug and Alcohol Abuse: A Clinical Guide to Diagnosis and Treatment.* New York: Plenum Medical Book Company, 1989.

Shlain, L. *The Alphabet Versus the Goddess: The Conflict Between Word and Image.* New York: Penguin Putnam, 1998.

Sobell, M. B., and L. C. Sobell. "Individualized Behavior Therapy for Alcoholics." *Behavior Therapy,* Vol. 4. November 1973: 49–72.

Stout, M., PhD. *The Sociopath Next Door.* New York: Broadway Books, 2005.

Tedlock, B. *The Woman in the Shaman's Body: Reclaiming the Feminine in Religion and Medicine.* New York: Bantam Dell, Random House, 2005.

Zimmer, L., and J. Morgan. *Marijuana Myths, Marijuana Facts: A Review of the Scientific Evidence.* New York and San Francisco: The Lindesmith Center, 1997.

INDEX

A Problem from Hell, 179
A World Lit Only by Fire, 156
ABCNews.com, 118
abuse:
  child, consequences of, 184–185
  domestic, 103
Adderall, 121
addiction, 107–111
  and incarceration as a result of, 90
  and legal perspective on, 88–91
  and predisposition to, 87
  as a failure of psychosocial integration, 87
alcohol:
  and taxation of, 92–96
  chronic abuse of, 66
  legalization of (*see* Prohibition)
  physical harm caused by, 65–66
Alcoholics Anonymous, 109
Alexander, Bruce, 86, 108
Allah (*see also* God, Yahweh), 142, 148, 162, 163, 166, 171, 175
The Alphabet Versus the Goddess: The Conflict Between Word and Image, 126, 127, 133, 152
Alzheimer's disease, 114
American Bar Association (ABA), 79
American Medical Association (AMA), the, 74, 75, 79
Anslinger, Harry, 72–85
antidepressants, 9, 60, 63–64, 98, 191
Aphrodite (*see also* Earth/ Mother Goddess), 128
Apsu, 136
The Arab Mind, 164
archeology, 135–148
Ark of the Covenant, 143
Armstrong, Louis, 77
Asherah (*see also* Earth/ Mother Goddess), 128
aspirin, 119–120
  and death as a result of use of, 120
Astarte (*see also* Earth/ Mother Goddess), 128
Attention Deficit Hyperactivity Disorder (ADHD), 120–121

The Bacchae, 147
Bacon, Francis, 154
Bancroft, Lundy, 102
Bayer Company, the, 119
Beatles era, the, 84
Bernstein Brothers, the, 95, 96
bhanga (*see* ganga)
black cohosh, 117
Bob Dylan, 80
Booth, Martin, 67
brain, the:
  and domination of right and left, 133–134
  evolution of the human, 130–133
Bureau of Alcohol, Tobacco and Firearms, 96

Calvin, John, 160
cannabis *(see also* marijuana), 5, 7, 8, 9, 17, 29, 31, 37, 38, 40, 41, 56, 62, 66–76, 78, 81, 83–85, 91, 93, 97–100
  addictive qualities of, 70
  use of in history, 68–71

Cannabis, 67
Capone, Al, 96
Carter, Jimmy, 81, 82, 88, 179
Casey, William, 181
Central Intelligence Agency (CIA), 176, 177, 178, 179, 180, 181
chicken pox virus, 112–113
cholesterol, 113, 115–116
chlorine, in drinking water, 114
cigarettes, 6, 8, 17, 24, 38, 57, 62, 63, 78, 86, 89, 106, 108
circumcision, female, 167
Civil War, the, 71
Clark Amendment of 1976, the, 178
Clinton, Bill, 9
coca plant (*see also* cocaine), 91
Coca-Cola, 86, 120
  and cocaine in, 86
cocaine, 31, 37, 38, 57, 60, 62, 70, 78, 83, 85, 86, 90, 91, 110
  use of in Europe, 91
Codex Alimentarius, 118, 121
color, red, as symbol of female sexuality, 151–152
Columbus, Christopher, 170
Comitatus Act of 1878, the, 82, 83
Crusades, the, 173, 174
culture, Arab, and Western exposure on, 170–172

Dark Ages, the, 151
Davis, Adelle, 116
Demeter (*see also* Earth/ Mother Goddess), 128
Dionysus, 146, 147, 148
ditch weed (*see also* hemp), 75
Dow, Neil, 93, 94
drug abuse, impact of, 60–63
Drug Policy Alliance, 79
drug use:
  patterns of, 89
  use of historically, 65–85
DuPont, Lammont, 74, 75
DuPont Company, the, 75

Earth/Mother Goddess, 127, 128, 129, 133, 135, 136, 138, 140, 145–148, 150, 151, 153, 164, 182
Eighteenth Amendment, the, 73, 94
Equal Rights Amendment (ERA), 104
Euripedes, 147

family, patriarchal emphasis on, 100–103
Federal Bureau of Narcotics (FBN), 72, 77, 78, 79, 80
fluoridation, 114–116
  impact of on health, 114–116
Food and Drug Administration (FDA), 121
food, genetically altered, 117–118
Ford Motor Company, the, 74
Ford, Gerald, 81
Freud, Sigmund, 91

Gabriel, 142, 162, 163, 172
Galen, 68
ganga (*see also* cannabis), 69, 71
Garden of Eden, 140, 158
Gates, Robert, 179
Gilligan, Carol, 186
God (*see also* Yahweh, Allah), 67, 128, 129, 136, 138, 139, 140, 141, 142, 143, 144, 145, 146, 147, 148, 149, 150, 151, 157, 158, 159, 160, 161, 163, 173, 175, 176, 182, 183, 189, 193
Goddess, the,
  end of the worship of the, 145–148
  worship of, 135–145
Golden Age of Greece, downfall of the, 147
Golden Age of Islam, the, 165
Good Muslim, Bad Muslim, 173, 176
Grand Goddess (*see also* Earth/ Mother Goddess), 128
Great Depression, the, 72
Gutenberg, Johann, 68

Hamilton, Alexander, 93
Hammer of Witches, the, 154
Hammurabi's Code of Laws, 137
Hancock, John, 92, 98
Harvey, William, 154
Hearst, William Randolph, 72, 74, 75

hemp (*see also* marijuana), 67–69, 74–76
growth of in history, 69
Henry VIII, King, 68
Herodotus, 68, 142
heroin, addiction to, 60–61
Hestia, 146
hieroglyphics, 137, 139
High Times magazine, 29, 34
Hindus, 153, 187
Hitler, Adolph, 182
Hoffman, Abbie, 80
Holy Trinity, the, 148, 151
homosexuality, 147
honor, concept of in the Arab world, 167–168
Hoover, J. Edgar, 72
hormone replacement therapy (HRT), 116
and manufacture of synthetic estrogen, 117
Horus, 128–129
Hughes, Howard, 120
Humanist Renaissance, the, 154
Hussein, Saddam, 179

Immaculate Conception, the, 158
Inanna (*see also* Earth/ Mother Goddess), 128, 136
Indians, South American, and use of coca plant, 91
Isis (*see also* Earth/ Mother Goddess), 128, 138

James I, King, 68
Jefferson, Thomas, 69
Jesus, 67, 128, 129, 141, 142, 149, 150, 151, 157, 158, 162, 163, 164, 171
jihad, concept of, 173–176
Johnson, Junior, 96

King Pentheus, 148
King Tut, 138
Kohlberg, Lawrence, 186
Koran, the, 142, 145, 161–168, 172
Korea, 79
Krupa, Gene, 77

"La Cucaracha," 70
La Guardia, Fiorello, 76
Let's Get Well, 116
Levi-Strauss, Claude, 129
Lindesmith, Alfred, 79
Link TV, 125
Long Day's Journey into Night, 86
Los Angeles Times, the, 180
Lumumba, Patrice, 178

Maat, 138
Machiavelli, 157
Madison, James, 69
Magna Carta, the, 143
Mamdani, Mahmood, 173, 175, 176, 178, 180
Manchester, William, 156
Mao, 182
Marduk, 136, 137
Marijuana Tax Act of 1937, the, 74, 75, 76
marijuana:
and acceptance of use of in modern society, 97–100
legalization of for medical use, 38
legalization of, 38, 55–56, 63
legalization of, and impact on pharmaceutical companies, 63
Martin Luther, 157–159, 161
martyrdom, in early Christianity, 149
medicine, ancient Chinese, 66
Medusa, 152
methadone, 110–111
methadone maintenance programs, 110–111
MGM, 80
Milgram, Stanley, 188
Mitchum, Robert, 77
Mohammed, 142, 162–165, 171, 172, 173
Mom's Marijuana, 83
Monk, Thelonius, 77
moonshine, 93, 94, 96
Moors (*see also* Muslims), 161, 170
morality, impact of culture on, 187–188
More, Thomas, 154
Moses, 141, 143, 144, 163, 182
Mother Jones magazine, 63

Muslims (*see also* Moors), 153, 162, 163, 164, 165, 170, 171, 173, 174, 175–176

Narcotics Act of 1914, the, 38, 70
NASCAR, 96
National Commission on Marijuana and Drug Abuse, 81
National Institute of Mental Health, 84, 185
Nefertiti, 138
Netherlands, the, and drug laws, 84–85
New York Academy of Medicine, the, 76
New York State Rockefeller laws, 90
New York Times, 90, 120
Nixon Doctrine, the, 177
Nixon, Richard M., 81

O'Keeffe, Georgia, 152
O'Neil, Eugene, 86, 87, 93, 108, 109, 111, 120,
Old Testament, 126, 141, 145, 152, 153, 157, 172, 173
Olympian Golden Circle of Twelve Deities, the, 146
opiates, 38, 72, 84, 86, 110, 192
    addiction to, 86–87
OxyContin, 50

Page, Linda, 117
painkillers, addiction to, 60
Paracelsus, 154
Patai, Raphael, 164, 166
Paxil, 64
Paul, 149, 150, 158
Peaceful Measures: Canada's Way Out of the War on Drugs, 86
Pfizer
Pharaoh Amenhotep IV, 138
PINS, 36
poly-drug abuse, definition of, 109–110
Pope Alexander VI, 156
Pope Leo, 155
pornography:
    and recent popularity of, 125
    early, 145
Portland Rum Riot, the, 94
post-traumatic stress disorder, 187
Pot, Pol, 182
Powers, Samantha, 179
Predestination, 158
Premarin, 117
prison, population in United States, 65
Prohibition, 66, 72, 73, 82, 94, 95, 96, 99, 107
projective identification, 101
Purgatory, 155
Purple Gang, the, 95

Qutb, Sayyid, 175–176

Reagan, Nancy, 82
Reagan, Ronald, 82, 96, 179, 180, 181
red clover, 117
Reefer Madness, 79
Reformation, Protestant, 157, 159
Renaissance, 68, 154, 155, 160, 165
Revolutionary War, the, 93
Roosevelt, Franklin D., 96
Rudman, Warren, 181
Rum Row, 95
rum-runners, 95, 96

Saladin, 173
School of the Americas (SOA), 178
Scripps, Edward, 74
Seven Tablets of Creation, the, 136
Shafer Commission, 81
Shlain, Leonard, 126–127, 128, 129, 131, 132, 133, 137, 138, 140–141, 143, 152, 154, 155, 183, 190
Siddhartha, Prince, 68
slavery, end of in United States, 69
Smith, Bessie, 94
society, overtly masculine and impact of on, 189–193
Society of Muslim Brothers, the, 175–176
The Sociopath Next Door, 184
sociopathic behavior, core characteristic of, 184–189
Songs of the Doomed, 44
Spanish American War, 71
Spanish Armada, defeat of, 68
St. Peter's Basilica, 155

St. Saint Augustine, 150, 157–159
Stout, Martha, 184, 185, 186
Student Non-Violent Coordinating Committee (SNCC), 104
Students for a Democratic Society (SDS), 104
suicide bombing, 149

Tedlock, Barbara, 191
Temperance Movement, the, 93
Ten Commandments of Yahweh, 141, 143, 161
THC, 5, 44, 48, 51, 69, 75
Thompson, Hunter, 44, 80
Tiamat, 136, 137
trans fats, 113
Tylenol, 119

U.S. Army Medical Corps, 70
U.S. Coast Guard, the, 95
U.S. Constitution, the, 143
U.S. Department of Agriculture, 75
U.S. National Institute of Mental Health, the, 84
U.S. Treasury Department, the, 77, 93
United Nations Single Convention Treaty, the, 85
USA Today, 121
Utopia, 154

vaccinations, 112–113
Vatican, the, 155–157
Vedas, the, 67
Vietnam, 79, 103, 104, 116, 177, 178, 179, 181
Vietnam War, 177–181
Villa, Pancho, 70
Virgin Mary, the, 128, 129, 150, 151, 153, 160, 163
  worship of, 150–151
vitamin industry, and regulation of by government, 118–119
vitex, 117

War Powers Act of 1973, the, 178
Washington, George, 69, 93, 176, 178
water, chlorinated, 115
Why Does He Do That? Inside the Minds of Angry and Controlling Men, 102
Wilson, Woodrow, 94
witch hunts, 153–160
witches, in history, 26, 153–155, 159, 160
The Woman in the Shaman's Body, 191
women:
  and changing societal view of, 124–127
  role of in ancient times, 128–133
Wootton Report, the, 84
World Trade Organization, 118
World War II, 75, 79, 111

Yahweh (*see also* God, Allah), 126, 143, 144, 148, 152, 153, 157, 182
Yale University, 187, 188

Zeus, 152
Zoloft, 64